Preserving Sandcastles

The Educational Paradox

By Jiles Smith II and Dr. Sheila Mallett-Smith

Published by Isham Media Group LLC

The Smith & Smith Collaborative

This book is for educational purposes. It is not legal, medical, or clinical advice. Readers should consult qualified professionals for guidance specific to their situation.

ISBN: 978-1-967055-19-7

1st Edition

Table of Contents

Foreword

By Earl Smith, M.Ed.

When I first heard the phrase "preserving sandcastles," I paused.

If you have ever worked in an alternative high school, you know exactly what that image feels like. You spend months building something steady; attendance improves, conflicts decrease, credits accumulate, hope returns, and then life happens. A student's housing falls apart. A family crisis erupts. A court date intervenes. A relapse. A suspension. The tide comes in.

And sometimes it feels like you are starting over again.

When I stepped into the leadership of an alternative high school day program, the graduation rate was painfully low. Many of our students had already been labeled—"at risk," "disengaged," "behavior problems." But what I saw were young people carrying more than most adults ever have to carry. They were not short on intelligence. They were short on stability, safety, and consistent belief.

Turning that school around was not about discovering a new curriculum or implementing a flashy initiative. It was about restoring fundamentals. We focused on relationships first. We paid attention to how adults spoke to students—and to one another. We created structures that allowed students to recover from mistakes without being permanently defined by them. We insisted on accountability, but we paired it with dignity. Over time, graduation rates rose dramatically.

But what changed most was not the number on a report. It was the climate. Students began to see themselves as capable. Staff began to see behavior as communication rather than defiance.

Families began to trust that their children would be treated as whole human beings.

I did not invent the idea that learning requires regulation, or that resilience can be cultivated. Those truths have been present in education for generations. What this book does, and what I appreciate about it, is articulate those truths in a way that connects research, neuroscience, and lived experience. It gives language to what many educators know intuitively: no meaningful learning happens in chaos, and no young person thrives without both structure and compassion.

The work of education is fragile. It is deeply human. It requires adults to remain steady when circumstances are not. It asks us to hold high expectations while understanding the storms our students are navigating. It asks us to build sandcastles, knowing the tide will come, and to rebuild them, stronger each time.

If this book helps educators see their work not as a series of daily crises, but as the long arc of developing accountability, respect, conflict resolution, emotional intelligence, and resilience, then it will have served its purpose.

The educators who show up every day in difficult conditions are doing work that is both demanding and meaningful. My hope is that this book strengthens their resolve and affirms their calling.

The tide will come.

The question is whether we are building in ways that help our students stand when it does.

— Earl Smith, M.Ed.

Acknowledgments

We are deeply grateful to the generations of educators in our family whose lives and stories made this book possible. From my grandfather Isham Tate who opened a Negro school in 1902, to the 23 relatives who have stood in classrooms, cafeterias, offices, and playgrounds across decades, this work is a continuation of their courage and commitment. Their experiences, both joyful and painful, gave us the raw material for honest reflection.

We also want to thank the students and families who trusted us enough to show up as their full selves. The children who challenged us, resisted us, made us laugh, and forced us to grow have been some of our greatest teachers. Many of the insights in these pages came from trying, failing, learning, and trying again with them in mind.

To our colleagues in education – teachers, paraeducators, school psychologists, counselors, administrators, office staff, classroom aides, bus drivers, custodians, security workers, and cafeteria workers – we see you. Your daily work often goes uncelebrated, even as you absorb the emotional weight of school life. Your informal conversations, shared classroom strategies, and hallway wisdom helped shape the practical tools in this book.

We extend appreciation to the school and district leaders who supported reflective practice and allowed room for experimentation. In systems that are often overregulated and under-resourced, your willingness to protect spaces for learning, collaboration, and professional honesty made this work more than theory.

Finally, we thank our families and loved ones, who have lived with late nights, early mornings, and long conversations about students, lessons, and difficult days. Your patience, encouragement, and reminders to rest made it possible to finish this project. This book is dedicated not only to those who stand in front of the classroom, but also to those who quietly hold them up behind the scenes.

Introduction

Preserving Sandcastles: The Educational Paradox

In our family, education is not an abstract value; it is a lived tradition. Across four generations, at least twenty-three relatives have served as teachers, principals, counselors, professors, coaches, or system leaders. That story begins, in a formal sense, in 1902, when our grandfather opened a school for Negro children in an era when laws and customs were designed to deny Black students' meaningful access to education. The school was modest in size, but historically it represented an act of resistance and faith: a declaration that Black children deserved not only literacy, but dignity, structure, and adults who believed their minds mattered.

From that first schoolhouse to today's classrooms, districts, and community programs, our family has watched the same tension play out in different forms. On one hand, schooling holds a powerful promise: that education can expand opportunity, interrupt cycles of poverty and oppression, and help young people develop the skills needed to flourish in work, family, and civic life (Darling-Hammond, 2010; Noguera, 2003). On the other hand, educators and families know the uneasy feeling that too much of what is built during the school year is washed away by forces outside the classroom: economic instability, trauma, racism, family stress, policy shifts, and the sheer pace of change (Bronfenbrenner, 1979; Osher, Cantor, Berg, Steyer, & Rose, 2020).

My brother, Earl Smith, a long-serving principal, captured this reality in a single image. He described most school days as "building sandcastles." Staff work all year to shape routines, skills, and relationships. Children show growth in reading, math, and behavior. Then a long weekend, a summer break, or a family crisis arrives. The tide rolls in. When students return, it can feel as if half of the sandcastle has been swept away and the adults are back at the shoreline, bucket and shovel in hand, starting again.

This image gives the book both its title and its central question:

What does it mean to preserve sandcastles in education – to design schooling so that more of what children, families, and educators build together can endure between tides?

Purpose and Central Argument

This book argues that from transitional kindergarten (TK) through adulthood, education should be organized around a small set of transferable human capacities that undergird both academic learning and long-term development:

1. Accountability
2. Respect for self and others
3. Emotional intelligence
4. Conflict resolution
5. Resilience

These are not "extras" or soft skills. They are the conditions that allow students to stay engaged with challenging content, recover from mistakes, and participate in families, workplaces, and communities in healthy ways (Brackett, 2019; Masten, 2014). When these capacities are fragile, even the strongest curriculum sits on sand.

A central premise of this book is straightforward: no significant, lasting learning occurs until students are regulated emotionally, physiologically, and relationally. This premise is consistent with the

Prevention, De-escalation, and Resilience (PDR) framework articulated by Smith and Smith (2026), which situates escalation not in isolated behavior but in nervous system activation shaped by perception, stress, and environmental cues. When a child's nervous system is overwhelmed by fear, shame, hunger, or chronic stress, the brain systems that support attention, memory, and problem-solving are compromised (Immordino-Yang, 2016; Perry & Szalavitz, 2017). Social and emotional learning (SEL) is therefore not a side program; it is the foundation for academic learning. When students learn to name and manage emotions, read social cues, take others' perspectives, and repair harm, they are not just "behaving better"; they are building internal infrastructure that supports literacy, numeracy, and higher-order thinking (Durlak, Weissberg, Dymnicki, Taylor, & Schellinger, 2011; Osher et al., 2020).

The Relational Paradox

At the center of schooling sits a relational paradox. Many educators see themselves as allies, advocates, and even "extended family" for their students. They show up early, stay late, and carry students' stories home in their minds and hearts. Yet many parents—particularly those managing multiple jobs, single parenting, limited formal education, or painful past experiences with schools—experience educators as temporary custodians: professionals hired to fulfill a function, similar to a sports coach contracted for a season (Hoover-Dempsey & Sandler, 1997; Ishimaru, 2019). When schools ask for additional support at home, some parents understandably respond, "That's your job" (Mapp & Kuttner, 2013).

This disconnect is not just about communication style or "parent involvement." It is shaped by history, structural inequities, generational trauma, and the ways in which schools have at times harmed or excluded the very communities they now ask to trust them (Darling-Hammond, 2010; Tatum, 2017). For a parent who has lived through biased discipline, tracked coursework, or subtle disrespect, a teacher's statement—"I love your son"—may sound like a script rather than a promise. The words and the wound occupy the same sentence.

Against this backdrop, *Preserving Sandcastles: The Educational Paradox* advances three core claims:

1. **Academic learning is inseparable from social, emotional, and relational development.** Efforts to raise test scores without addressing regulation, belonging, and relational safety will at best produce short-term gains and at worst deepen inequities (Durlak et al., 2011; Osher et al., 2020).
2. **Parents and educators must be repositioned as co-builders, not separate contractors.** Trust, shared language, and joint problem-solving are necessary for sustainable change (Hoover-Dempsey & Sandler, 1997; Ishimaru, 2019; Mapp & Kuttner, 2013).
3. **Systems either protect or erode sandcastles.** Policies, schedules, staffing models, and funding decisions can strengthen SEL, mental health, and family partnership, or quietly undermine them (Adelman & Taylor, 2006; Maier, Daniel, Oakes, & Lam, 2017; Mallett-Smith & Smith, 2026).

The Educational Paradox

The "paradox" in the subtitle has several layers.

First, schools are asked to produce outcomes they do not fully control. Students arrive shaped by housing instability, racism, neighborhood violence, media saturation, and economic pressures that lie far beyond the school's direct influence (Bronfenbrenner, 1979; Noguera, 2003). Yet public discourse often evaluates schools as if they were the sole determinant of academic and behavioral outcomes.

Second, educators are expected to be content experts, behavior specialists, mental-health responders, cultural interpreters, and risk managers, all within schedules and staffing patterns designed for a very different era. Under these conditions, demoralization and burnout are not surprising; they are predictable (Jennings & Greenberg, 2009; Santoro, 2018).

Third, policy frameworks send mixed messages. Systems call for higher test scores and more inclusive practices, more "rigor" and more attention to SEL, tighter accountability and deeper family partnership, often without the structural changes needed to reconcile these demands (Darling-Hammond, 2010; Fullan, 2016). The paradox is not that individual educators or parents lack commitment; it is that the system's expectations and its conditions are fundamentally misaligned.

A 30,000-Foot View with Ground-Level Stories

This book takes a "30,000-foot view" of education while staying grounded in real lives. The vantage point is deliberately broad. It stretches:

- From a 1902 Black school founded in defiance of segregation to contemporary classrooms shaped by standardized testing and digital devices.

- From early childhood settings to secondary schools, community colleges, and first jobs.
- From individual student–teacher interactions to district policies, city partnerships, and risk-management frameworks that shape safety, staffing, and cost.

At the same time, the book stays close to the ground: the child whose reading gains seem to evaporate each summer; the single parent who feels accused rather than supported; the teacher who feels invisible to leadership; the principal caught between policy mandates and what she knows her students need.

How This Book Is Organized

The book is organized into four major parts, preceded by this introduction and followed by an epilogue and practical appendices:

1. **Foundations: Sandcastles, SEL, and the Four Pillars**
   These early chapters define the sandcastle metaphor, review research on SEL, regulation, and learning, and introduce the four pillars of accountability, respect, emotional intelligence, and conflict resolution, with resilience woven throughout (Brackett, 2019; Durlak et al., 2011; Immordino-Yang, 2016; Masten, 2014).

2. **Relationships in Context: Families, Educators, and Communities**
   The middle chapters examine the dynamics between parents and educators, the role of race and class in trust, and how city and community partners influence what happens in schools. The social-ecological model is used to show how individual behavior is embedded in family, school, and community contexts (Bronfenbrenner, 1979;

Ishimaru, 2019; Mallett-Smith & Smith, 2026; Noguera, 2003).

3. **Systems and Risk: Policy, Safety, and Cost**
   A third set of chapters draws on risk management and public administration to explore how discipline policies, staffing decisions, training investments, and inter-agency collaborations affect both safety and learning. SEL and relational safety are framed as central to risk reduction and fiscal stewardship, not as optional add-ons (Adelman & Taylor, 2006; Maier et al., 2017; Mallett-Smith & Smith, 2026).

4. **Practice: Tools, Cases, and Implementation**
   The final part translates theory into practice, offering case studies, scripts, protocols, and implementation roadmaps for classrooms, schools, districts, and city partnerships. It closes with a focus on adult well-being, arguing that preserving sandcastles requires preserving the builders themselves (Jennings & Greenberg, 2009; Souers & Hall, 2016).

An epilogue returns to the shoreline, synthesizes key insights, and extends a cautious but genuine invitation: to stand together at the water's edge, fully aware of the tide, and choose to build anyway.

How to Use This Book: Actions, Not Just Ideas

Although the book is grounded in research and written for academic and professional audiences, it is designed to be **used**, not just read. Each chapter will include:

- **Short stories or vignettes** from classrooms, homes, and communities.

- **Reflection questions** for educators, parents, and leaders.
- **"Practice in Action" steps** – concrete moves that readers can try in their own setting (for example, a co-regulation routine to start the school day, a script for a difficult parent–teacher conversation, or a way to frame discipline in terms of accountability rather than punishment).

These action steps are intentionally modest. They are built for real schools, real families, and real constraints. The goal is not perfection. The goal is movement: one more student regulated, one conversation handled with more dignity, one policy revised so it better supports the five lifelong competencies.

Intended Audiences

This book is written for several overlapping groups (Adelman & Taylor, 2006; Ishimaru, 2019):

- **Educators** at all levels who feel the gap between what they know students need and what existing structures make possible.
- **Parents and caregivers** who want genuine partnership with schools but carry understandable skepticism or exhaustion.
- **School and district leaders** responsible for aligning policy, staffing, and resources with both academic and social-emotional goals.
- **City officials, risk managers, and community partners** who recognize that youth outcomes are inseparable from public safety, health, and economic development.

- **Scholars and practitioners** in education, psychology, social work, and public policy who are working at the intersection of SEL, equity, and systems change.

The writing aims to be rigorous enough for academic use and accessible enough for professional development in schools, districts, and municipal settings.

A Hopeful Beginning

Our grandfather's 1902 school reminds us that education has always been both fragile and resilient. The sandcastles of that era—Black children learning to read in defiance of segregation—were threatened daily by law, violence, and scarcity. Yet the learning that took root there traveled across generations.

The chapters that follow are an attempt to honor that legacy. They ask how we might design schools, partnerships, and policies so that more of what we build with children endures—not only through the weekend or the summer, but across their lives. The tide will always come. Our task is to learn, together, how to build and rebuild in ways that preserve what matters most.

References

Adelman, H. S., & Taylor, L. (2006). *The school leader's guide to student learning supports: New directions for addressing barriers to learning*. Corwin Press.

Brackett, M. A. (2019). *Permission to feel: Unlocking the power of emotions to help our kids, ourselves, and our society thrive*. Celadon Books.

Bronfenbrenner, U. (1979). *The ecology of human development: Experiments by nature and design*. Harvard University Press.

Darling-Hammond, L. (2010). *The flat world and education: How America's commitment to equity will determine our future*. Teachers College Press.

Durlak, J. A., Weissberg, R. P., Dymnicki, A. B., Taylor, R. D., & Schellinger, K. B. (2011). The impact of enhancing students' social and emotional learning: A meta-analysis of school-based universal interventions. *Child Development, 82*(1), 405–432.

Fullan, M. (2016). *The new meaning of educational change* (5th ed.). Teachers College Press.

Hoover-Dempsey, K. V., & Sandler, H. M. (1997). Why do parents become involved in their children's education? *Review of Educational Research, 67*(1), 3–42.

Immordino-Yang, M. H. (2016). *Emotions, learning, and the brain: Exploring the educational implications of affective neuroscience*. W. W. Norton.

Ishimaru, A. M. (2019). *Just schools: Building equitable collaborations with families and communities*. Teachers College Press.

Jennings, P. A., & Greenberg, M. T. (2009). The prosocial classroom: Teacher social and emotional competence in relation to student and classroom outcomes. *Review of Educational Research, 79*(1), 491–525.

Maier, A., Daniel, J., Oakes, J., & Lam, L. (2017). *Community schools as an effective school improvement strategy: A review of the evidence*. Learning Policy Institute.

Mallett Smith, S., & Smith II, J. (2026). *Prevention, De-escalation, and Resilience (PDR): Strategies for Navigating Adversity.* Isham Media Group LLC.

Mapp, K. L., & Kuttner, P. J. (2013). *Partners in education: A dual capacity-building framework for family–school partnerships*. SEDL.

Masten, A. S. (2014). *Ordinary magic: Resilience in development.* Guilford Press.

Noguera, P. A. (2003). The trouble with Black boys: The role and influence of environmental and cultural factors on the academic performance of African American males. *Urban Education, 38*(4), 431–459.

Osher, D., Cantor, P., Berg, J., Steyer, L., & Rose, T. (2020). Drivers of human development: How relationships and context shape learning and development. *Applied Developmental Science, 24*(1), 6–36.

Perry, B. D., & Szalavitz, M. (2017). *The boy who was raised as a dog: And other stories from a child psychiatrist's notebook* (Rev. ed.). Basic Books.

Santoro, D. A. (2018). *Demoralized: Why teachers leave the profession they love and how they can stay*. Harvard Education Press.

Souers, K., & Hall, P. (2016). *Fostering resilient learners: Strategies for creating a trauma-sensitive classroom.* ASCD.

Tatum, B. D. (2017). *"Why are all the Black kids sitting together in the cafeteria?" And other conversations about race* (20th anniversary ed.). Basic Books.

Chapter 1

Building Sandcastles

Why School Feels Fragile

The Sandcastle on the Shore

Earl Smith, a longtime principal, once described his work this way:

"Most days feel like carefully building sandcastles with staff and students. We shape routines, lessons, and relationships. We start to see children grow. Then a long weekend, a break, or a crisis comes. The tide rolls in, and when they return it feels like starting again with the bucket and shovel."

For many educators, this is not just a poetic image; it is a daily emotional reality. They are not only teaching content. They are repeatedly rebuilding basic skills, norms, and trust in the presence of forces over which they have little influence: unstable housing, community violence, food insecurity, shifts in caregiving, unresolved trauma, and unaddressed emotional needs (Bronfenbrenner, 1979; Osher, Cantor, Berg, Steyer, & Rose, 2020).

Families often stand on a very different part of the same shoreline. For some caregivers, school represents continuity and opportunity. For others, it recalls earlier experiences of exclusion, judgment, or confusion. A parent who feels intimidated during a conference, worried about being evaluated for their parenting, or unsure how to help with homework after a night shift may experience school more as a test of adequacy than as a partner in a child's growth (López, 2001; Tatum, 2017).

Between those two realities stands the child, trying to learn. This book is written at that intersection. It refuses the impulse to blame any single group and instead asks a structural question: if the tide is predictable, why are we surprised when sandcastles alone are not enough?

What We Think School Is For

When adults are asked what school is for, the answers are familiar:

- To learn reading, writing, and mathematics.
- To prepare for college or career.
- To get a "good job" and become a productive citizen.

Students often offer a more immediate list: to pass, to see friends, to avoid trouble, to make it through the day.

These answers are not wrong, but they are incomplete. Long after students forget the details of the water cycle or a specific historical date, they remember something more basic: how school made them feel about themselves and their place in the world. Many remember whether adults took their questions seriously, whether they were allowed to make mistakes and repair them, and whether a single incident became a permanent label.

Decades of research in child development and learning science show that academic learning does not occur on top of a neutral emotional state. It is intertwined with students' sense of safety, belonging, and emotional regulation (Brackett, 2019; Immordino-Yang, 2016; Osher et al., 2020). Children learn and retain more when they feel seen, supported, and challenged within secure relationships; they learn less when they feel threatened, shamed, or invisible. Yet public conversation about schooling still centers largely on test scores, graduation rates, and rankings. We measure the sandcastles in precise detail and rarely name the tides.

The Tide: Life Outside the Classroom

For educators, "the tide" refers to what happens outside the school day that either reinforces or erodes learning.

For some students, home life strengthens the castle. A caregiver checks in about the day, assists with homework, attends events, and communicates regularly with teachers. School and home feel connected.

For many others, the story is more complicated. Home may be loving but stretched thin. A single caregiver may work multiple jobs. Grandparents may care for several children while managing their own health. Some adults did not have positive school experiences and feel embarrassed trying to help with assignments they do not understand. Their commitment to the child is not in doubt; their time, energy, and confidence are simply rationed across many demands (López, 2001).

These realities appear at school as missing homework, chronic lateness, fatigue, or challenging behavior. They also appear as fierce protection. When an educator says, "I am concerned about your child's behavior," some parents hear, "You are failing," especially if they are already carrying guilt or worry about what they cannot provide. When an educator says, "I care deeply about your child," a parent whose trust in institutions has been bruised may think, "You are with them for one year; I have been with them since birth" (Tatum, 2017).

From the educator's vantage point, the same conversation may feel very different. The teacher may believe they are asking for partnership and offering insight into patterns and triggers that require joint attention. When they hear, "That is your job," it can feel dismissive or painful, particularly in systems that already demand emotional labor with limited structural support (Ingersoll, Merrill, & Stuckey, 2014; Santoro, 2018).

Two groups of adults who care about the same child can quickly find themselves on opposite sides of a conversation, each feeling misunderstood. The tide, in those moments, is not just time away from school; it is the accumulation of history, stress, and expectation that both parties bring to the shoreline.

No Significant Learning Without Regulation

No significant academic learning occurs until a child is regulated. Social and emotional learning (SEL), in this view, is not an optional subject or a "nice to have" program; it is the foundation that allows academic learning to occur in a sustainable way. This position is consistent with the Prevention, De-escalation, and Resilience (PDR) framework articulated by Smith and Smith (2026), which situates escalation not in isolated behavior but in nervous system activation shaped by perception, stress, and environmental cues.

Evidence supports this claim. Large-scale meta-analyses of school-based SEL programs show that when students receive explicit instruction in self-awareness, self-management, social awareness, relationship skills, and responsible decision-making, they demonstrate improved behavior, more positive attitudes toward school, and meaningful gains in academic performance (Durlak, Weissberg, Dymnicki, Taylor, & Schellinger, 2011; Taylor, Oberle, Durlak, & Weissberg, 2017). In one meta-analysis, participation in SEL programs was associated with an average 11-percentile-point increase in academic achievement compared with control groups (Durlak et al., 2011).

Neuroscience explains why these patterns are not accidental. Emotions are not separate from cognition; they organize attention, memory, and decision-making (Immordino-Yang, 2016). When children are anxious, ashamed, fearful, or chronically stressed, neural systems associated with protection and threat detection dominate. In that state, the capacity to focus, hold information in working memory, and integrate feedback is reduced (Perry &

Szalavitz, 2017). What appears externally as "defiance" or "disengagement" may, internally, be a defensive response to perceived danger.

High-quality SEL, therefore, cannot be reduced to posters on classroom walls or occasional assemblies. At its best, it is a set of daily practices that help children and adults notice physiological and emotional cues, name what they are experiencing, and choose responses aligned with values rather than impulses (Brackett, 2019; Goleman, 2006). When schools bypass this foundation, they effectively ask dysregulated students to engage in highly regulated tasks:

- "Sit still."
- "Pay attention."
- "Use your words."

without ensuring students have the internal tools and external supports necessary to do so.

The 30,000-Foot View: What Are We Really Building?

If we rise above the minute-by-minute demands of classrooms and look from a 30,000-foot view, the central challenges that concern adults across the lifespan become clearer. Most of the difficulties that surface in schools, workplaces, and relationships are not fundamentally about algebra, grammar, or test-taking strategies. They are about:

- Taking responsibility for one's actions even when it is uncomfortable.
- Treating oneself and others with dignity.

- Navigating conflict without destroying relationships or self-respect.
- Understanding, expressing, and managing emotions in healthy ways.
- Recovering from setbacks rather than remaining stuck or retaliating.

In this book, these recurring challenges are organized as five lifelong competencies: accountability, respect, conflict resolution, emotional intelligence, and resilience. They appear in different forms at different ages—a preschooler waiting for a turn, an adolescent responding to peer pressure, an employee receiving critical feedback, a caregiver managing anger after a long day—but the underlying capacities are strikingly consistent (Masten, 2014; Osher et al., 2020).

When schools and families ignore these competencies or treat them as secondary to academic content, they risk preparing students for tests rather than for life. Conversely, when systems deliberately cultivate these capacities, academic learning has a stronger, more enduring base.

The Educational Paradox

This brings us to the paradox at the center of contemporary schooling.

On paper, mission statements regularly affirm commitment to "the whole child." In practice, many accountability systems still prioritize short-term academic outputs and easily measured indicators. Schools are evaluated by test scores, graduation rates, and incident counts far more often than by evidence of students' growth in accountability, respect, conflict resolution, emotional intelligence, or resilience (Darling-Hammond, 2010; Fullan, 2016).

At the same time, adults in schools are asked to do more with less. Educators are expected to function as content specialists, behavior managers, mental health first responders, cultural interpreters, and risk managers, often in systems designed for a very different era. Under such conditions, burnout and demoralization are not anomalies; they are predictable outcomes (Jennings & Greenberg, 2009; Santoro, 2018).

The paradox deepens when we consider discipline and accountability. In many settings, accountability is enacted **on** students rather than with them. Zero-tolerance policies, exclusionary discipline, and public shaming practices can give an illusion of order and consequence but often erode trust and disproportionately harm students of color, students with disabilities, and other marginalized groups (Skiba, Arredondo, & Williams, 2014). In those environments, the sandcastle of learning and belonging is quietly undercut by the very policies intended to protect it.

The system, in other words, asks schools to produce emotionally mature, academically successful graduates while organizing much of its daily work around short-term outputs and inconsistent adult partnerships. Children live at the center of that contradiction.

Parents, Educators, and the "Temporary Custodian" Mindset

Many of the tensions between home and school are shaped by implicit metaphors.

Some caregivers view educators as partners, almost like extended family, walking with them through a child's development. Others view educators more as temporary custodians or specialized coaches: professionals employed to manage a specific phase of life. In the latter frame, when school staff call with concerns, families may experience those calls as evidence that educators are not fulfilling the role they were paid to assume.

Educators have their own metaphors. Some see families as allies, carrying deep contextual knowledge about children's histories, cultures, and strengths. Others, often worn down by repeated conflict or limited contact, may begin to see families as critics, obstacles, or unknown quantities. Those perceptions shape communication patterns: who calls, when they call, and what tone they adopt (Hoover-Dempsey & Sandler, 1997; Ishimaru, 2019).

These metaphors do not develop in isolation. Race, language, class, immigration status, and historical inequities all influence how families and educators interpret each other's actions (López, 2001; Tatum, 2017). Communities that have experienced disproportionate discipline, tracking, or exclusion often carry a protective posture into new interactions. Educators who feel chronically overworked and under-supported may have limited emotional bandwidth for difficult conversations. Both sides can feel tired. Both can feel judged.

Without explicit work to surface and shift these metaphors, the child's sandcastle becomes collateral damage in a conflict that neither side fully intends.

Why Saying "I Love Your Son" Is Not Always Heard as Love

Consider a brief but revealing moment.

An educator sits across from a parent and says sincerely, "I really care about your son. I want him to succeed." From the educator's perspective, this is honest. They have spent many hours with the child and have seen both strengths and struggles. The statement is meant to communicate commitment before raising concerns.

The same words can land very differently for the parent. If the caregiver's own schooling involved bias or harm, if they have heard similar phrases just before decisions that negatively affected their family, or if they carry shame about what they cannot provide, "I care about your son" may register as a scripted line rather than a genuine bond (López, 2001; Tatum, 2017). The caregiver might think, "You know him for one year; I have known him his entire life."

In that moment, two truths coexist. The educator's care is real. The parent's doubt is real. The disconnect is not about the child's worth; it is about the long arc of institutional trust, power, and lived experience. Healthy systems do not demand that either party ignore this history. Instead, they name it, acknowledge it, and create structures in which trust has time to grow rather than being assumed.

From Blame to Shared Conditions

Conversations about preserving sandcastles often drift toward blame:

- If only families supported learning more consistently at home.
- If only teachers differentiated better and showed more empathy.
- If only administrators prioritized relationships over paperwork.
- If only policymakers funded mental health supports and reduced testing pressures.

There is partial truth in each statement, yet taken alone, each easily becomes a weapon rather than a tool.

A more useful approach is to ask not "Who is at fault?" but "What conditions are we all reacting to?" The single caregiver working two jobs is not missing a meeting because they do not care; they may be choosing between attending and losing essential income. The teacher who appears distant may be protecting their own mental health after repeated experiences of loss or conflict. The principal who focuses on numbers may be responding to district or board pressures that make data feel like the only defensible language (Darling-Hammond, 2010; Ingersoll et al., 2014).

Recognizing shared conditions does not excuse harmful behavior. It situates that behavior in context and opens the door to broader solutions: changes in policy, scheduling, staffing, and community partnership that align expectations with reality.

How This Book Will Work

The chapters that follow are organized around the five lifelong competencies introduced here:

1. Accountability
2. Respect for self and others
3. Conflict resolution
4. Emotional intelligence
5. Resilience

Later chapters examine how these competencies develop across the lifespan, how they show up in homes and schools, and how structural inequities and daily constraints can distort or support them. Stories from classrooms, families, and community settings are used not to single out individuals but to illuminate patterns that many readers will recognize.

Rather than offering prescriptive formulas, this book invites reflection. Each chapter weaves together research, lived experience, and systems-level analysis to explore how regulation, relationship, and environment interact over time. Readers will encounter conceptual framing grounded in developmental science, illustrative examples drawn from practice, and questions designed to prompt deeper consideration of their own contexts.

The aim is not to provide quick fixes, but to widen perspective. Change in education rarely comes from a single strategy; it emerges from sustained attention to culture, language, expectations, and design.

Throughout, the central assumption remains: social-emotional learning is not separate from academic learning. It is the soil in which all other learning must take root if we hope to preserve sandcastles over time.

A Hopeful Beginning

For educators, this chapter may evoke both relief and frustration. Relief that the emotional realities of the work are being named; frustration that daily efforts are still often reduced to test scores and classroom management.

For parents and caregivers, it may surface a different mix of feelings: recognition of exhaustion, pride in what they have managed to hold together, and perhaps anger about moments when systems made them feel small.

The intention of this book is not to minimize those emotions or to offer simple solutions. It is to widen the frame. When we step back to a 30,000-foot view, the shoreline looks different. We see that no single group can preserve sandcastles alone, and that the tide is powerful but not random. With shared language, clearer structures, and attention to the five lifelong competencies, it becomes possible to build in ways that honor both the fragility and the resilience of what children, families, and educators create together.

References

Bronfenbrenner, U. (1979). *The ecology of human development: Experiments by nature and design*. Harvard University Press.

Darling-Hammond, L. (2010). *The flat world and education: How America's commitment to equity will determine our future*. Teachers College Press.

Durlak, J. A., Weissberg, R. P., Dymnicki, A. B., Taylor, R. D., & Schellinger, K. B. (2011). The impact of enhancing students' social and emotional learning: A meta-analysis of school-based universal interventions. *Child Development, 82*(1), 405–432.

Fullan, M. (2016). *The new meaning of educational change* (5th ed.). Teachers College Press.

Hoover-Dempsey, K. V., & Sandler, H. M. (1997). Why do parents become involved in their children's education? *Review of Educational Research, 67*(1), 3–42.

Immordino-Yang, M. H. (2016). *Emotions, learning, and the brain: Exploring the educational implications of affective neuroscience*. W. W. Norton.

Ingersoll, R. M., Merrill, L., & Stuckey, D. (2014). *Seven trends: The transformation of the teaching force* (Updated April 2014). Consortium for Policy Research in Education.

Jensen, E. (2009). *Teaching with poverty in mind: What being poor does to kids' brains and what schools can do about it*. ASCD.

Jennings, P. A., & Greenberg, M. T. (2009). The prosocial classroom: Teacher social and emotional competence in relation to student and classroom outcomes. *Review of Educational Research, 79*(1), 491–525.

Ladson-Billings, G. (2009). *The dreamkeepers: Successful teachers of African American children* (2nd ed.). Jossey-Bass.

López, G. R. (2001). The value of hard work: Lessons on parent involvement from an (im)migrant household. *Harvard Educational Review, 71*(3), 416–437.

Maier, A., Daniel, J., Oakes, J., & Lam, L. (2017). *Community schools as an effective school improvement strategy: A review of the evidence.* Learning Policy Institute.

Masten, A. S. (2014). *Ordinary magic: Resilience in development.* Guilford Press.

Noguera, P. A. (2003). The trouble with Black boys: The role and influence of environmental and cultural factors on the academic performance of African American males. *Urban Education, 38*(4), 431–459.

Osher, D., Cantor, P., Berg, J., Steyer, L., & Rose, T. (2020). Drivers of human development: How relationships and context shape learning and development. *Applied Developmental Science, 24*(1), 6–36.

Santoro, D. A. (2018). *Demoralized: Why teachers leave the profession they love and how they can stay.* Harvard Education Press.

Mallett Smith, S. & Smith II, J. (2026). *Prevention, De-escalation, and Resilience (PDR): Strategies for Navigating Adversity.* Isham Media Group LLC.

Tatum, B. D. (2017). *"Why are all the Black kids sitting together in the cafeteria?" And other conversations about race* (20th anniversary ed.). Basic Books.

Zins, J. E., Weissberg, R. P., Wang, M. C., & Walberg, H. J. (Eds.). (2004). *Building academic success on social and emotional learning: What does the research say?* Teachers College Press.

Chapter 2

The Educational Paradox

High Expectations, Shaky Foundations

Naming the Paradox

In Chapter 1, the sandcastle metaphor helped name a feeling: educators build routines and skills, the tide of life rolls in, and part of the castle washes away.

Chapter 2 asks a harder question:

If we know the sand is unstable, why do we keep pretending we are building on concrete and then blame people when the structure does not hold?

This is the educational paradox. On paper, we expect schools to produce graduates who are:

- Academically skilled
- Emotionally mature
- Socially responsible
- Ready for college, careers, and democratic life

In practice, we organize schools in ways that routinely undermine the conditions required to reach these outcomes (Darling-Hammond, 2010; Fullan, 2016). We place students in classrooms while they are hungry, anxious, or carrying trauma; we ask teachers to teach without adequate planning time, mental-health support, or collaboration; and we measure success mainly with test scores and graduation rates rather than the deeper qualities we say we care about.

The paradox is **not** simply that some schools "fail." It is that we treat shaky foundations as if they were solid and then locate failure in individual students, teachers, or parents instead of in the design of the system (Noguera, 2003).

What We Ask of Schools

Consider just a partial list of responsibilities that contemporary schools are expected to fulfill:

- Teach core academic content to increasingly rigorous standards.
- Prepare students for college, careers, and citizenship in a complex, technology-rich world.
- Identify and respond to learning differences and disabilities.
- Support mental health and respond to trauma.
- Prevent and address bullying, harassment, and violence.
- Teach digital citizenship and manage the impact of social media.
- Provide meals, health screenings, and sometimes clothing or hygiene supplies.
- Conduct safety drills and comply with extensive documentation and accountability mandates.

In many communities, schools also function as de facto community centers, food distribution hubs, and informal counseling services (Maier, Daniel, Oakes, & Lam, 2017). When everything else in a child's life is unstable, the school is often the only institution that opens its doors at the same time every morning.

None of these roles are wrong. Many are morally compelling. The problem is that we layer these expectations on top of one another without proportionally changing time, staffing, training, or emotional support for the people responsible for the work

(Jennings & Greenberg, 2009; Santoro, 2018). Teachers and school leaders are asked to do "whatever it takes," but the structure around them still reflects a model built for a different era.

Shaky Foundations: Poverty, Stress, and Unequal Conditions

The educational paradox becomes clearer when we zoom out from the school building itself.

Children do not arrive at the classroom door as blank slates. They arrive shaped by:

- Housing stability or instability
- Food security or insecurity
- Access to healthcare or chronic untreated conditions
- Exposure to violence, racism, or community stress
- Relationships with caregivers who may be rested and available, or exhausted and stretched thin

Bronfenbrenner's ecological theory reminds us that development is nested: individual behavior is shaped by family, neighborhood, institutions, and broader social forces (Bronfenbrenner, 1979). Neighborhood violence, local labor markets, discriminatory housing policies, and immigration enforcement patterns all show up in classrooms as attention problems, "defiance," withdrawal, or perfectionism (Noguera, 2003; Jensen, 2009).

Yet accountability systems often act as if schools alone control outcomes. We ask:

- "Why did reading scores drop by three points?"
- "Why is there a gap between Group A and Group B?"

Those are important questions, but they can be misleading when they ignore the context in which learning happens. When a child's family loses housing, when a parent is deported, or when a community experiences a traumatic event, it is not realistic to expect their academic trajectory to remain unaffected. A test score without context is a number, not a story.

The paradox is that we know these contextual factors matter – educators see them every day – but our dominant measures and public narratives often leave them out.

SEL and the Accountability Mismatch

At the same time that schools are asked to close achievement gaps, they are rarely given coherent guidance on how to address the emotional and relational gaps that sit underneath them.

Research on social and emotional learning shows that explicit SEL instruction, when well designed and implemented, leads to improvements in student behavior, attitudes, and academic performance (Durlak, Weissberg, Dymnicki, Taylor, & Schellinger, 2011; Zins, Weissberg, Wang, & Walberg, 2004). SEL programs that build skills in self-awareness, self-management, social awareness, relationship skills, and responsible decision-making are associated with an average 11-percentile-point gain in academic achievement compared with control groups (Durlak et al., 2011).

Despite this evidence, SEL is often treated as:

- An optional "extra" to be squeezed in after testing season.
- A short-term initiative rather than a core part of the instructional day.
- A set of posters, slogans, or assemblies rather than daily practice.

This creates a mismatch. Systems demand higher scores and better behavior, but they underinvest in the relational and emotional infrastructure that would make those outcomes sustainable (Immordino-Yang, 2016; Osher, Cantor, Berg, Steyer, & Rose, 2020).

The result is predictable:

- Teachers are told to "hold students accountable" without the time or tools to teach the underlying skills.
- Students are told to "self-regulate" without consistent modeling or co-regulation from adults.
- Schools are faulted for not closing gaps quickly enough while remaining under-resourced to address the drivers of those gaps.

That, in essence, is the paradox: **we hold schools responsible for outcomes that require capacities we have not systematically taught or supported.**

Educators in the Squeeze

In this context, it is not surprising that many educators describe feeling "squeezed." They stand between:

- Policy makers who emphasize measurable outcomes
- Families who want safety, opportunity, and respect
- Students who bring complex needs, strengths, and histories to the classroom

Teachers and principals are asked to be content experts, mental-health first responders, conflict mediators, translators between cultures, and risk managers, often within rigid schedules and limited planning time (Ingersoll, Merrill, & Stuckey, 2014; Jennings & Greenberg, 2009).

Over time, this role overload can lead to:

- **Burnout**, when emotional resources are depleted faster than they are replenished
- **Demoralization**, when educators feel unable to do the work in ways that align with their values (Santoro, 2018)
- **Cynicism or emotional withdrawal**, as self-protection

The paradox is that systems rely on educators' deep care for students while often providing structures that make it hard for that care to be expressed in sustainable ways. When test scores dominate the conversation, the careful, relational work of SEL and family partnership can feel invisible, even when it is what keeps students connected to school at all.

Later in the book, we will return to this tension through the lens of role and identity, including the idea of educators viewing themselves as "on stage" – not as inauthentic performers, but as professionals who can hold a healthy boundary between their personal self and the role they inhabit in front of students. That reframing can help protect educators from taking every student behavior as a personal attack and can make it easier to stay regulated and effective in the face of daily stressors.

Parents Under Pressure

Parents and caregivers live in their own version of the paradox.

They are told, explicitly and implicitly, that:

- Their children's academic performance reflects their quality as parents.

- They must "support learning at home" through reading, homework help, and attendance at events.
- They should be "partners" with schools.

Many do all of this and more. Others desperately want to, but are constrained by work schedules, transportation, health, literacy, or immigration status (Hoover-Dempsey & Sandler, 1997; López, 2001). Some carry painful memories of their own schooling – memories of tracking, humiliation, or being misunderstood – and walk into school buildings already braced for judgment (Ladson-Billings, 2009; Tatum, 2017).

When a teacher calls to report a behavior concern, a caregiver who is already stretched thin and scared of "failing" may hear:

- "You are not a good parent."
- "Your child is a problem."

Their defensive reaction – arguing, minimizing, or avoiding – may be less about disagreement with the teacher's concern and more about self-protection in the face of shame and powerlessness (López, 2001).

This, too, is part of the paradox. We ask families to act as full partners in education, but we rarely address the structural barriers and historical mistrust that make partnership difficult. We invite them into spaces that may feel foreign or hostile and then interpret discomfort as disinterest.

High Expectations on Shaky Ground

Taken together, these patterns create a system in which expectations are high, but the ground under everyone's feet is uneven.

- We expect academic excellence, but accept persistent inequality in funding, staffing, and access to experienced teachers (Darling-Hammond, 2010).
- We expect orderly behavior, but provide inconsistent access to mental-health services, SEL, and safe spaces for students to process stress.
- We expect family engagement, but schedule events at times that are incompatible with low-wage work and provide limited childcare or translation.
- We expect teachers to stay, but normalize workloads and emotional demands that make long-term sustainability difficult.

The paradox is not in wanting high expectations; ambitious hopes for children are appropriate and necessary. The paradox lies in pretending those expectations can be met **without** aligning resources, structures, and adult learning with the realities children and families face.

The Five Lifelong Competencies as a Different Measure of Success

Against this backdrop, we offer a different way to define what it means for education to "work well." From TK through adulthood, the real test of schooling is not only whether students recall content, but whether they are developing five interrelated competencies:

1. **Accountability** – taking responsibility for one's actions, making amends, and learning from mistakes without collapsing into shame.

2. **Respect for self and others** – recognizing one's own dignity and extending that same dignity across lines of difference.
3. **Conflict resolution** – staying at the table, listening, and working through disagreement rather than avoiding or escalating.
4. **Emotional intelligence** – noticing, naming, and managing emotions in ways that support rather than sabotage relationships and goals.
5. **Resilience** – recovering from setbacks, disruptions, and losses in ways that preserve core values and connections.

These competencies show up in different forms across the lifespan:

- A five-year-old learning to wait for a turn or say "I'm sorry" with support.
- A thirteen-year-old handling peer conflict without resorting to physical or online aggression.
- A high school student receiving critical feedback without shutting down.
- A young adult navigating a workplace disagreement without quitting or exploding.

When we center these competencies as the long-term outcomes of schooling, the paradox looks different. The question is no longer simply, "Did the student meet the standard on this test?" but, "Are we building the internal capacities that will allow this young person to keep learning, working, and relating in healthy ways long after the test is forgotten?" (Masten, 2014; Osher et al., 2020).

This reframing does not dismiss academic content. Instead, it treats academics as one of the main contexts in which accountability, respect, conflict resolution, emotional intelligence, and resilience are learned and practiced.

Looking Ahead: From Paradox to Purpose

This chapter has tried to name the educational paradox clearly:

- We pile high expectations on schools, educators, and families.
- We underinvest in the emotional, relational, and structural foundations that make those expectations realistic.
- We then blame individuals for predictable system-level outcomes.

The rest of the book is about moving from paradox to purpose. Chapter 3 will zoom out further to ask a simple but transformative question:

From transitional kindergarten to adulthood, what are we really trying to build in the lives of young people, and how do the five lifelong competencies give us a more honest blueprint?

In that chapter, we will trace how accountability, respect, conflict resolution, emotional intelligence, and resilience evolve across developmental stages and what it means to design schooling around those outcomes instead of around test scores alone. We will also begin to connect these competencies to adult roles – for example, how seeing teaching as a role or "character" on a professional stage can protect educators' mental health and help them embody these competencies in front of students.

For now, it is enough to acknowledge the tension without minimizing it. The sand is real. The tide is real. So is our capacity, together, to build differently.

References

Brackett, M. A. (2019). *Permission to feel: Unlocking the power of emotions to help our kids, ourselves, and our society thrive.* Celadon Books.

Bronfenbrenner, U. (1979). *The ecology of human development: Experiments by nature and design.* Harvard University Press.

Darling-Hammond, L. (2010). *The flat world and education: How America's commitment to equity will determine our future.* Teachers College Press.

Durlak, J. A., Weissberg, R. P., Dymnicki, A. B., Taylor, R. D., & Schellinger, K. B. (2011). The impact of enhancing students' social and emotional learning: A meta-analysis of school-based universal interventions. *Child Development, 82*(1), 405–432.

Fullan, M. (2016). *The new meaning of educational change* (5th ed.). Teachers College Press.

Goleman, D. (2006). *Social intelligence: The new science of human relationships.* Bantam Books.

Hoover-Dempsey, K. V., & Sandler, H. M. (1997). Why do parents become involved in their children's education? *Review of Educational Research, 67*(1), 3–42.

Immordino-Yang, M. H. (2016). *Emotions, learning, and the brain: Exploring the educational implications of affective neuroscience.* W. W. Norton.

Ingersoll, R. M., Merrill, L., & Stuckey, D. (2014). *Seven trends: The transformation of the teaching force* (Updated April 2014). Consortium for Policy Research in Education.

Ishimaru, A. M. (2019). *Just schools: Building equitable collaborations with families and communities.* Teachers College Press.

Jennings, P. A., & Greenberg, M. T. (2009). The prosocial classroom: Teacher social and emotional competence in relation to student and classroom outcomes. *Review of Educational Research, 79*(1), 491–525.

López, G. R. (2001). The value of hard work: Lessons on parent involvement from an (im)migrant household. *Harvard Educational Review, 71*(3), 416–437.

Masten, A. S. (2014). *Ordinary magic: Resilience in development.* Guilford Press.

Osher, D., Cantor, P., Berg, J., Steyer, L., & Rose, T. (2020). Drivers of human development: How relationships and context shape learning and development. *Applied Developmental Science, 24*(1), 6–36.

Perry, B. D., & Szalavitz, M. (2017). *The boy who was raised as a dog: And other stories from a child psychiatrist's notebook* (Rev. ed.). Basic Books.

Santoro, D. A. (2018). *Demoralized: Why teachers leave the profession they love and how they can stay.* Harvard Education Press.

Skiba, R. J., Arredondo, M. I., & Williams, N. T. (2014). More than a metaphor: The contribution of exclusionary discipline to a school-to-prison pipeline. *Equity & Excellence in Education, 47*(4), 546–564.

Tatum, B. D. (2017). *"Why are all the Black kids sitting together in the cafeteria?" And other conversations about race* (20th anniversary ed.). Basic Books.

Taylor, R. D., Oberle, E., Durlak, J. A., & Weissberg, R. P. (2017). Promoting positive youth development through school-based social and emotional learning interventions: A meta-analysis of follow-up effects. *Child Development, 88*(4), 1156–1171.

Chapter 3

From TK to Adulthood

What Are We Really Trying To Build?

Beyond Grades and Diplomas

If you ask most adults what they want for the children in their lives, they rarely talk about test scores. They say things like:

- "I want them to be happy."
- "I want them to be decent human beings."
- "I want them to be able to take care of themselves and others."

When you push a little deeper, people talk about character, confidence, values, relationships, and purpose, not about a particular benchmark in third grade reading. They want young people who can stand on their own feet, treat others well, and navigate a world that is complicated and often unfair.

Yet we still behave as if "education" is mostly what happens from roughly age five to eighteen, inside a school building, measured by grades, credits, and diplomas. Once a student walks across the stage, we talk as if the work is finished.

Developmental psychology tells a different story. Human beings keep learning, stumbling, and relearning across the entire lifespan. Different stages bring different tasks, but the raw materials are very familiar: responsibility, respect, conflict, emotion, and the ability to bounce back (Erikson, 1968; Masten, 2014).

A toddler who grabs a toy, a middle school student dealing with group chats, a high school student facing a failing grade, and an adult trying not to snap at a co-worker after a long day are all working with the same basic ingredients. What changes is the context, the stakes, and the supports around them.

This chapter pulls the camera back and asks a simple question:

Across a lifetime, what are we really trying to build?

A Lifespan Lens on Learning

A lifespan lens helps us stop treating graduation as a finish line and start seeing it as one milestone in a much longer story. Researchers describe development as a set of tasks and transitions that unfold over time. Each stage builds on the previous one and sets the stage for what comes next (Baltes, Lindenberger, & Staudinger, 2006; Lerner, 2018).

Seen through that lens, the five lifelong competencies in this book are not just school goals. They are human goals that keep reappearing in new clothes.

- **Accountability** looks like learning to say "I did it" in kindergarten, taking responsibility for online posts in middle school, and owning mistakes at work as an adult.
- **Respect** begins as basic kindness and manners, grows into respect for different identities and viewpoints in adolescence, and becomes a practiced commitment to dignity in personal and professional relationships.
- **Conflict resolution** starts with "use your words" and "take turns," becomes negotiation with friends and teachers, and later becomes the ability to disagree, set boundaries, and still preserve relationships.
- **Emotional intelligence** moves from naming basic feelings to understanding complex mixed emotions and reading social cues in high stakes situations.
- **Resilience** begins when a young child tries again after a fall and continues through job loss, grief, illness, and other adult storms.

When we see behavior through this developmental frame, the sandcastle metaphor shifts. The goal is not to build one perfect structure that never erodes. The goal is to help children learn how to build and rebuild with increasing skill and confidence, supported by adults and systems that understand what they are practicing at each stage.

Early Childhood and TK: Sand, Buckets, and First Foundations

In the early years, most of the work happens in the body and in relationships. Young children are learning to:

- Wait a few moments for something they want.
- Share, even when they do not feel like it.
- Calm down after disappointment.
- Follow simple directions and routines.

This is accountability in its earliest form. A child who throws blocks after being told to clean up is not a "bad kid." They are a child who is still learning how to manage frustration and accept limits. Respect is visible in how they touch other children, how they respond when a peer says "stop," and how they begin to use words instead of hands.

In this stage, adults often want to "fix" behavior quickly. It helps to remember that every conflict over toys, line order, or turn taking is a small lab for conflict resolution, emotional intelligence, and resilience. When an adult co-regulates, names feelings, and guides repair rather than simply punishing, the child practices the skills that later allow them to handle peer conflict, feedback, and stress in more complex settings (Denham et al., 2014; Perry & Szalavitz, 2017).

Middle Childhood: Rules, Fairness, and Friendship

In elementary school, the social world widens. Peers matter more. Rules become a big focus. Children at this stage often say things like, "That's not fair," or "But he did it too." That is not just complaining. It is an early attempt to work through accountability and justice.

Respect now includes understanding different family structures, languages, and cultures. Children notice who is praised and who is always in trouble. They notice whether adults keep their word. When rules feel consistent and fair, students are more willing to accept consequences. When rules feel arbitrary, they may either resist or withdraw (Wentzel, 2014).

Conflict resolution in this stage means coaching children to:

- Tell their side of the story without attacking.
- Listen to another perspective.
- Move toward a solution that repairs harm.

Emotional intelligence grows as students learn that emotions can show up in the body, can coexist, and can be expressed in more than one way. A child might say "I don't care" while their posture and behavior say the opposite. Guiding them to notice those contradictions is part of the work.

Resilience shows up when a student receives a poor grade, loses a game, or has a falling out with friends. Adults have a choice. They can send the message, "This one moment defines you," or "This is hard, and we can learn from it and try again." That framing shapes how students respond to future setbacks.

Adolescence: Identity, Risk, and Belonging

Adolescence is a time of rapid change. Brain development, identity questions, peer relationships, social media, and expanded academic demands collide. It is also the period when many adults begin to talk as if "kids should know better by now."

From a developmental point of view, adolescence is a second chance to refine all five competencies.

- **Accountability** now involves choices with real consequences, including driving, digital footprints, substance use, and academic pathways. Owning those choices without collapsing into shame is not automatic; it often depends on how adults respond when mistakes happen (Steinberg, 2014).
- **Respect** includes identity, culture, and power. Teens are learning what it means to respect themselves in relationships and to stand against disrespect based on race, gender, orientation, or ability.
- **Conflict resolution** becomes more complex as romantic relationships, group dynamics, and online conflicts enter the picture. Ghosting, subtweeting, and group chat drama are all modern arenas for this old human skill.
- **Emotional intelligence** is essential for managing stress, social comparison, and shifting moods. Many adolescents experiment with numbing or distraction instead of regulation, especially when they do not see healthy models.
- **Resilience** is tested by academic failure, friendship changes, family stress, and sometimes serious trauma. Whether students experience these events as proof that

they are "broken" or as painful but survivable chapters is shaped by the messages and supports around them (Masten, 2014; Osher et al., 2020).

Schools often respond to adolescent behavior mainly through grades and discipline. A developmental lens does not excuse harmful choices. It does ask us to recognize that many "attitude problems" are the visible part of a larger struggle with identity, belonging, and emotional pain.

College, Work, and Adulthood: When the Grades Are Gone

Once young people leave K–12 systems, something interesting happens. The formal language of "student" and "teacher" fades. The five competencies do not.

In college or training programs, accountability means managing deadlines without a parent or teacher constantly reminding you. Respect shows up in how students relate to roommates, professors, and staff. Conflict resolution appears in group projects and relationships. Emotional intelligence becomes crucial for navigating stress, freedom, and new experiences.

In the workplace, the sandcastle metaphor is still visible. A new employee may learn skills and routines, then experience a life crisis that wipes out focus or motivation for a time. Supervisors who only see output may assume laziness. Leaders who understand human development ask better questions:

- "What support do you need?"
- "What can we adjust while you get back on your feet?"

Accountability for adults means owning errors, giving and receiving feedback, and following through on commitments even when no one is watching. Respect includes recognizing power differences, avoiding harassment, and honoring colleagues' boundaries. Conflict resolution often determines whether teams grow stronger through disagreement or fracture. Emotional intelligence is tied to leadership, customer service, and collaboration. Resilience is tested by job loss, illness, caregiving, and loss.

In other words, the competencies that we hope children start practicing in TK are the same ones that make or break careers, marriages, and community leadership.

The Five Competencies as a Lifelong Curriculum

When schools and families adopt a lifelong view, the five competencies stop looking like "extras" and start looking like the real curriculum that sits underneath reading, math, and science.

- A TK lesson on sharing is not just about getting through circle time. It is early practice in conflict resolution and respect.
- A fifth grade project on group work is not just about the content; it is a lab for accountability and communication.
- A high school restorative circle after a fight is not just about avoiding suspension; it is an intensive class in emotional intelligence, responsibility, and repair.
- A first job at a grocery store or fast food restaurant becomes a practicum in punctuality, customer respect, handling stress, and bouncing back after mistakes.

If we treat these moments as random incidents, we miss their teaching power. If we see them as part of a coherent, lifelong curriculum, we can be more intentional about how we respond, coach, and reflect.

This is where educator role and identity matter. When teachers see themselves as professionals playing a role on a public stage, rather than as their entire private self, it becomes easier to coach these competencies instead of taking every behavior personally. That idea will return in a later chapter that looks closely at the "on stage" mindset as a tool for educator well-being and effectiveness.

Implications for Schools and Systems

A TK-to-adulthood perspective has practical consequences. It suggests that systems should:

- Define success in terms of the five competencies as well as academic outcomes.
- Align curriculum, SEL programs, and discipline practices with what we know about development.
- Train adults not only in content, but in coaching accountability, respect, conflict resolution, emotional intelligence, and resilience at different ages.
- Track growth over time, not just through one-year snapshots.
- Partner with families and community organizations that shape these competencies outside school hours.

It also invites humility. No single teacher, parent, or program "builds" these capacities alone. Each of us contributes pieces of the sandcastle over time. Some seasons involve rebuilding after erosion. Others involve adding new layers. The question is not whether the tide will come. It will. The question is whether children leave each stage of life with stronger tools for rebuilding, and with adults around them who understand that process.

Looking Ahead

This chapter has argued that education is a lifespan project and that the five competencies give us a more honest blueprint for what we are trying to build.

In the next part of the book, we turn to regulation and emotional safety as the foundation that allows this lifelong curriculum to take hold. We will look more closely at what it means to say "no significant learning without regulation" and how brain science, classroom practice, and family life all point in the same direction.

The sandcastles our grandfather's students built in 1902 did not last physically. The chalk boards, benches, and books are gone. The competencies they practiced – responsibility, respect, courage, and persistence – traveled forward into the lives of their children and grandchildren. That is the kind of preservation this book is aiming for.

References

Baltes, P. B., Lindenberger, U., & Staudinger, U. M. (2006). Lifespan theory in developmental psychology. In W. Damon & R. M. Lerner (Eds.), *Handbook of child psychology* (6th ed., Vol. 1, pp. 569–664). Wiley.

Denham, S. A., Bassett, H. H., Mincic, M., Kalb, S., Way, E., Wyatt, T., & Segal, Y. (2014). Social–emotional learning profiles of preschoolers' early school success: A person-centered approach. *Learning and Individual Differences, 30*, 38–52.

Erikson, E. H. (1968). *Identity: Youth and crisis.* W. W. Norton.

Immordino-Yang, M. H. (2016). *Emotions, learning, and the brain: Exploring the educational implications of affective neuroscience.* W. W. Norton.

Lerner, R. M. (2018). *Concepts and theories of human development* (4th ed.). Routledge.

Masten, A. S. (2014). *Ordinary magic: Resilience in development.* Guilford Press.

Osher, D., Cantor, P., Berg, J., Steyer, L., & Rose, T. (2020). Drivers of human development: How relationships and context shape learning and development. *Applied Developmental Science, 24*(1), 6–36.

Perry, B. D., & Szalavitz, M. (2017). *The boy who was raised as a dog: And other stories from a child psychiatrist's notebook* (Rev. ed.). Basic Books.

Steinberg, L. (2014). *Age of opportunity: Lessons from the new science of adolescence.* Houghton Mifflin Harcourt.

Wentzel, K. R. (2014). Prosocial behavior and schooling. In L. M. Padilla-Walker & G. Carlo (Eds.), *Prosocial development: A multidimensional approach* (pp. 241–268). Oxford University Press.

Chapter 4

No Significant Learning Without Regulation

Stress, Neurobiology, and the Conditions for Academic Success

This chapter deepens a core proposition advanced throughout this book, that meaningful academic learning depends on emotional and physiological regulation, and aligns it with a systems-based understanding of escalation and prevention consistent with the PDR framework (Smith & Smith, 2026).

"Sit Still and Pay Attention" Meets Brain Science

For generations, classroom expectations in the United States have been built around a simple formula: students are asked to sit still, listen quietly, and focus on the task at hand. When those behaviors do not appear, adults often interpret the problem as a lack of motivation, respect, or discipline.

Neuroscience tells a different story. Emotions and cognition are not separate systems that occasionally bump into each other; they are tightly braided together in the brain (Immordino-Yang, 2016). When a student's nervous system is activated by fear, shame, hunger, or chronic stress, the brain prioritizes survival over reflection. In that state, the prefrontal cortex areas responsible for impulse control, planning, and working memory have less capacity to engage (Jensen, 2009; Perry & Szalavitz, 2017).

From the outside, a dysregulated student might look restless, oppositional, checked out, or "dramatic." From the inside, the student is often doing exactly what their nervous system has learned to do: scan for threat, protect against embarrassment, and conserve emotional energy. Asking such a student to "just focus" is similar to asking a sprinting athlete to solve a complex math problem mid-race. The request misunderstands their physiological state.

Understanding regulation reframes many common classroom moments. A student who blurts out answers is not always seeking attention; they may be trying to manage anxiety by controlling the pace of interaction. A student who puts their head down may be attempting to avoid an emotional flood, not simply refusing to participate. When educators see these behaviors through a regulatory lens, the question shifts from "How do I make them comply?" to "What state are they in, and how can I help them return to a learning state?" (Immordino-Yang, 2016; Osher, Cantor, Berg, Steyer, & Rose, 2020).

What Regulation Actually Is (and Is Not)

In everyday conversation, "regulation" is sometimes reduced to "calm" or "self-control." In this book, regulation is more precise. It refers to the capacity to notice internal states (emotions, bodily sensations, thoughts), label them, and select responses that are aligned with one's values and goals rather than with momentary impulses.

Regulation includes at least three intertwined dimensions:

1. **Physiological regulation.** Heart rate, breathing, and muscle tension that signal whether the body is in fight, flight, freeze, or rest states.
2. **Emotional regulation.** Awareness and management of feelings such as anger, frustration, shame, or excitement.
3. **Relational regulations.** The ability to use connection with others—trusted adults, peers, and communities to restore safety and perspective.

Importantly, regulation is not the same as suppression. A quiet classroom can be full of dysregulated students who have simply learned to shut down. Likewise, a classroom that includes movement, discussion, and visible emotion can be deeply regulated if students and adults are able to recognize, name, and work with those states safely (Brackett, 2019; Souers & Hall, 2016).

When regulation is misunderstood as compliance or silence, schools may unintentionally reward surface-level control while ignoring the internal chaos that later emerges as anxiety, depression, or explosive behavior. When regulation is understood as a developmental skill to be taught, modeled, and practiced, schools can treat emotional upswings and downswings as opportunities for learning rather than solely as disruptions.

The Neurobiology of Learning and Stress

Two broad brain systems are especially relevant to this discussion:

- The **threat detection and survival system**, sometimes summarized as "fight, flight, or freeze."
- The **executive function system**, which supports attention, planning, working memory, and inhibitory control.

Under stable, supportive conditions, students can move in and out of mild stress and challenge without losing access to executive functions. A difficult math problem or a classroom debate may elevate heart rate slightly, but students who feel emotionally safe can remain curious and engaged. Researchers call this zone "optimal arousal" (Immordino-Yang, 2016).

Under chronic stress, however, the balance shifts. Children exposed to community violence, persistent economic hardship, family conflict, or discrimination are more likely to experience what researchers term "toxic stress," especially when protective adult relationships are limited (Jensen, 2009). Over time, this state can sensitize the threat system, making it easier to trigger and harder to deactivate.

In such a context, relatively minor classroom events, a raised voice, a public correction, a peer's joke, can push students into survival mode. Once there, the brain prioritizes rapid responses: arguing, shutting down, leaving the room, or lashing out verbally or physically. These are not "bad choices" in a simple moral sense; they are strategies the nervous system has rehearsed to handle perceived threat (Perry & Szalavitz, 2017).

If schools ignore this neurobiological reality, they risk building academic expectations on a foundation that cannot hold. If, instead, they design routines, relationships, and instructional practices that intentionally support regulation, they create the conditions under which higher-order learning becomes both possible and sustainable (Durlak, Weissberg, Dymnicki, Taylor, & Schellinger, 2011; Osher et al., 2020).

Layers of Dysregulation: Individual, Family, Community

Regulation is often discussed as an individual trait: some children are "good at self-control," others are "impulsive." While there are temperament differences, focusing solely on the individual misses the broader social-ecological context (Bronfenbrenner, 1979).

- At the **family level**, caregivers may be juggling multiple jobs, health issues, or their own unaddressed trauma. A child may move between different caregiving arrangements, each with different rules, routines, and expectations.
- At the **community level**, neighborhood safety, housing stability, and access to resources such as healthcare and child care profoundly shape stress levels.

- At the **school level**, class sizes, disciplinary climates, and staff turnover influence whether students experience classrooms as predictable and caring or unpredictable and threatening.

Students arrive at school with nervous systems shaped by these overlapping conditions. A child who lives in a noisy apartment with frequent conflict may already be in a heightened state before the first bell rings. A teenager who worries about immigration enforcement or family finances may carry a constant background hum of anxiety into every interaction.

An equity-focused view of regulation recognizes that dysregulation does not distribute itself randomly. Communities historically exposed to racism, economic disinvestment, and systemic neglect are more likely to bear the cumulative burdens of toxic stress (Noguera, 2003; Tatum, 2017). To focus on regulation without acknowledging these structural realities is to risk pathologizing children for what are, in part, predictable responses to chronic adversity.

SEL as Daily Practice, Not a Poster

If regulation is foundational, then social and emotional learning cannot be confined to a weekly lesson or a one-time assembly. The most robust SEL outcomes occur when skills such as self-awareness, emotional vocabulary, problem-solving, and perspective-taking are woven into daily instruction and routines (Durlak et al., 2011; Zins, Weissberg, Wang, & Walberg, 2004).

In regulated classrooms, the following practices are common:

- **Predictable routines.** Clear openings and closings to lessons, consistent signals for transitions, and transparent expectations reduce uncertainty.

- **Emotional check-ins.** Brief opportunities at the start of class for students to name how they are arriving—through mood meters, quick writes, or hand signals—normalize emotional awareness.
- **Language for states and strategies.** Teachers and students share a common vocabulary for internal states ("escalating," "shut down," "overwhelmed") and for strategies ("take a breath," "ask for a pause," "use the reflection chair").
- **Repair processes.** When conflict or misbehavior occurs, adults guide students through reflection and repair rather than relying solely on exclusionary discipline.

These practices signal that emotions are neither ignored nor allowed to dominate; they are acknowledged, explored, and channeled toward growth. Such classrooms may not always be quiet, but they tend to be emotionally coherent.

Importantly, SEL is not a substitute for academic rigor. Research consistently finds that well-implemented SEL is associated with gains in standardized test scores and other academic indicators (Durlak et al., 2011). In other words, regulation and relationships do not "take time away" from learning; they create the conditions under which learning can occur more efficiently and deeply.

Regulation as an Equity Strategy

Because stress exposure and access to protective relationships are unevenly distributed, regulation work has direct implications for educational equity. Students from historically marginalized communities are more likely to experience both heightened stress and harsher disciplinary responses when they show signs of dysregulation (Skiba, Arredondo, & Williams, 2014).

For example, research has documented that Black students, particularly Black boys, are disproportionately suspended or expelled for subjective offenses such as "disrespect" or "defiance" even when behavior is similar to that of their peers (Ladson-Billings, 2009; Skiba et al., 2014). When educators interpret stress-driven behaviors through a deficit lens—seeing them as evidence of poor character or parenting rather than as signals of dysregulation—they may escalate punishment rather than support.

An equity-oriented approach to regulation includes:

- Training adults to recognize how bias influences their interpretation of student behavior.
- Designing de-escalation and restorative practices that respond to behavior while preserving dignity.
- Ensuring that counseling, mental-health services, and SEL supports are available in the schools and neighborhoods that experience the greatest cumulative stress.

In this sense, regulation is not just about helping individual students "behave better." It is a commitment to creating learning environments in which all students, especially those furthest from opportunity, can access the cognitive and emotional resources required to succeed.

Adult Regulation and Co-Regulation

Students rarely become more regulated than the adults around them. Teachers, administrators, and parents who are themselves exhausted, anxious, or unsupported may struggle to provide the calm, consistent presence that children need (Jennings & Greenberg, 2009).

Co-regulation describes the process by which one person's regulated nervous system helps another person move from a state of distress back toward balance. A teacher who maintains a steady tone, grounded posture, and predictable responses during a student outburst is not simply "keeping control"; they are lending their nervous system as a stabilizing resource.

However, asking adults to do this without attending to their own working conditions is unrealistic. High student–teacher ratios, constant schedule changes, inadequate planning time, and limited emotional support can lead educators to experience chronic stress or demoralization (Santoro, 2018). Under such conditions, even skilled teachers may find themselves reacting from frustration rather than from intentional practice.

Intentional adult-focused strategies might include:

- Professional learning communities that explicitly address emotional labor and regulation.
- Access to coaching or supervision that integrates SEL principles for adults.
- Schoolwide rituals that allow staff to pause, reflect, and reconnect with purpose.

Later chapters will explore in more depth how educators can adopt an "on-stage" professional persona in the classroom—similar to an actor inhabiting a role—which can create healthy psychological distance between their personal identity and students' moment-to-moment behaviors. Framed thoughtfully, this stance can protect adults from taking student dysregulation as a personal attack and free them to respond with curiosity and support rather than defensiveness (Brackett, 2019; Souers & Hall, 2016).

From Crisis Response to Regulation Systems

Many schools invest significant energy in crisis response: behavior plans, safety protocols, suspension processes, and threat assessments. These tools are necessary. Yet if they are not paired with proactive regulation systems, staff can feel like they are constantly reacting to the tide rather than building structures that shape it.

A regulation-centered system includes:

- **Universal supports**, such as schoolwide SEL routines, explicit teaching of emotional vocabulary, and environments designed for sensory comfort where possible.
- **Targeted supports**, such as small groups for students experiencing grief or anxiety, check-in/check-out systems with trusted adults, and skill-building groups that teach coping strategies.
- **Intensive supports**, including trauma-informed counseling, coordinated services with community mental-health providers, and individualized safety and regulation plans for students with complex needs (Adelman & Taylor, 2006; Maier, Daniel, Oakes, & Lam, 2017).

In this framework, crisis events are treated as data about where regulation systems are breaking down, not just as isolated incidents to be managed. Over time, schools can examine patterns: Which times of day are most dysregulated? Which spaces? Which transitions? This data can inform changes to schedules, staffing, and routines that reduce the overall load on students' and adults' nervous systems.

Conclusion: Regulation as Bedrock, Not Decoration

The sandcastle metaphor that frames this book is not only about skills washing away over summer; it is about the ground beneath those sandcastles. Regulation is that ground. Without it, the most carefully designed curriculum, the most passionate teaching, and the most detailed behavior plans will continue to feel fragile.

Recognizing that "no significant learning without regulation" is not an excuse for low expectations. On the contrary, it is a call to align expectations with what we know about the human brain and the realities of children's lives. It invites educators, families, and systems leaders to ask, before every initiative and every policy:

Are we strengthening or weakening the conditions for regulation?

If the answer is unclear, the work of preservation remains incomplete. In the chapters that follow, we will explore how emotional intelligence, resilience, and other lifelong competencies build on this regulatory foundation and how adults, across roles, can cultivate these capacities in themselves and the children they serve.

References

Adelman, H. S., & Taylor, L. (2006). *The school leader's guide to student learning supports: New directions for addressing barriers to learning.* Corwin Press.

Brackett, M. A. (2019). *Permission to feel: Unlocking the power of emotions to help our kids, ourselves, and our society thrive.* Celadon Books.

Bronfenbrenner, U. (1979). *The ecology of human development: Experiments by nature and design.* Harvard University Press.

Durlak, J. A., Weissberg, R. P., Dymnicki, A. B., Taylor, R. D., & Schellinger, K. B. (2011). The impact of enhancing students' social and emotional learning: A meta-analysis of school-based universal interventions. *Child Development, 82*(1), 405–432.

Immordino-Yang, M. H. (2016). *Emotions, learning, and the brain: Exploring the educational implications of affective neuroscience.* W. W. Norton.

Jensen, E. (2009). *Teaching with poverty in mind: What being poor does to kids' brains and what schools can do about it.* ASCD.

Jennings, P. A., & Greenberg, M. T. (2009). The prosocial classroom: Teacher social and emotional competence in relation to student and classroom outcomes. *Review of Educational Research, 79*(1), 491–525.

Ladson-Billings, G. (2009). *The dreamkeepers: Successful teachers of African American children* (2nd ed.). Jossey-Bass.

Maier, A., Daniel, J., Oakes, J., & Lam, L. (2017). *Community schools as an effective school improvement strategy: A review of the evidence.* Learning Policy Institute.

Mallett Smith, S., & Smith II, J. (2026). *Prevention, De-escalation, and Resilience (PDR): Strategies for Navigating Adversity.* Isham Media Group LLC.

Noguera, P. A. (2003). The trouble with Black boys: The role and influence of environmental and cultural factors on the academic performance of African American males. *Urban Education, 38*(4), 431–459.

Osher, D., Cantor, P., Berg, J., Steyer, L., & Rose, T. (2020). Drivers of human development: How relationships and context shape learning and development. *Applied Developmental Science, 24*(1), 6–36.

Perry, B. D., & Szalavitz, M. (2017). *The boy who was raised as a dog: And other stories from a child psychiatrist's notebook* (Rev. ed.). Basic Books.

Santoro, D. A. (2018). *Demoralized: Why teachers leave the profession they love and how they can stay.* Harvard Education Press.

Skiba, R. J., Arredondo, M. I., & Williams, N. T. (2014). More than a metaphor: The contribution of exclusionary discipline to a school-to-prison pipeline. *Equity & Excellence in Education, 47*(4), 546–564.

Souers, K., & Hall, P. (2016). *Fostering resilient learners: Strategies for creating a trauma-sensitive classroom.* ASCD.

Zins, J. E., Weissberg, R. P., Wang, M. C., & Walberg, H. J. (Eds.). (2004). *Building academic success on social and emotional learning: What does the research say?* Teachers College Press.

Chapter 5

Emotional Intelligence

The Core Skill Under Every Skill

Why Emotional Intelligence Sits at the Center

In earlier chapters, we focused on regulation: the ability to move from a dysregulated state back to a place where learning is possible. Emotional intelligence is the set of tools that makes that journey repeatable and intentional.

At its core, emotional intelligence (EI) involves four capacities (Mayer, Salovey, & Caruso, 2004):

1. Recognizing emotions in yourself and others.
2. Using emotions to support thinking and decision making.
3. Understanding how emotions develop and change.
4. Managing emotions in ways that align with your values and goals.

For students in classrooms, that might look like:

- Noticing a rising feeling of embarrassment and choosing to ask for help anyway.
- Realizing that anger in a friend is really hurt and disappointment.
- Understanding that anxiety will spike before a test, then drop afterwards.
- Choosing to walk away from a conflict and talk later, instead of throwing a punch or posting something online.

When these skills are weak, students tend to be pulled around by feelings. When they are stronger, students can still feel intense emotions but have more ways to respond. That difference often separates a hallway argument that fizzles from one that ends in a suspension. It also separates a student who gives up at the first sign of struggle from one who can say, "This is hard, and I can keep going."

Research links higher emotional intelligence in students with better social relationships, less bullying, fewer behavior problems, and stronger academic outcomes (Brackett, Rivers, & Salovey, 2011; Durlak, Weissberg, Dymnicki, Taylor, & Schellinger, 2011). In adults, higher EI is associated with more effective leadership, better teamwork, and healthier coping under stress (Goleman, 1995; Mayer et al., 2004). In other words, this is not an extra. It is the operating system beneath almost everything else we say we want from education.

Naming Feelings: Vocabulary as a Tool

Many students arrive at school with a very limited emotional vocabulary. They can say they feel "mad," "sad," or "fine," but not much more. Some have learned that certain feelings are not allowed. A boy may hear that sadness makes him "weak." A girl may be told that anger makes her "dramatic." In some cultures and families, talking about emotion at all is seen as risky or unnecessary (Zembylas, 2007).

Without words, experiences get stuck. A student who only knows "mad" may use anger for everything: fear, shame, disappointment, jealousy, hurt. Teachers see "attitude" or "defiance," but underneath there is a pile of unnamed states.

Building emotional intelligence starts with expanding language. Tools such as mood meters, emotion charts, or simple sentence stems help (Brackett, 2019):

- "Right now I feel … because …"
- "Underneath my anger I might also feel …"

- "My body tells me I am getting upset when …"

As students learn more precise words for their internal states, they gain a little space between stimulus and response. They can say, "I am frustrated because I do not understand this," instead of throwing a pencil. They can say, "I feel embarrassed," instead of storming out of the room.

For multilingual students, it can be powerful to invite emotional vocabulary in home languages as well. Some feelings do not translate neatly into English. Allowing students to bring those words into the classroom honors identity and expands everyone's emotional toolkit.

From Reacting to Responding

Emotional intelligence is not about feeling less. It is about responding rather than reacting.

A reaction is fast and automatic. A student is teased, and the fist comes up before thought. A teacher feels disrespected and raises their voice immediately. A parent receives a call from school and goes on the defensive before hearing the full story.

A response still acknowledges the feeling, but pauses long enough to choose a next step. That small pause is where emotional intelligence lives (Brackett, 2019; Gross, 2015).

Students can be taught simple processes, such as:

1. Notice: "What am I feeling right now?"
2. Name: "Can I find a word or phrase for it?"
3. Normalize: "Is it understandable to feel this way?"
4. Choose: "What can I do that fits who I want to be?"

This is not magic. It is practice. At first, the pause comes only after the explosion, in reflection: "What happened there?" Over time, with coaching, the pause can move closer to the moment: "I can feel myself getting heated. I need a break."

Adults need the same moves. When a student rolls their eyes or refuses to work, a teacher's first internal reaction might be anger or shame: "They are disrespecting me," or "I am failing at classroom management." Emotional intelligence lets the teacher notice that story, breathe, and respond differently: "Something is happening here. Let me get curious instead of escalating." (Jennings & Greenberg, 2009).

Reading Others: Empathy and Perspective Taking

Emotional intelligence is not only about self-awareness. It is also about reading others accurately. In classrooms, this shows up in many ways:

- A student learns to notice when a classmate is overwhelmed and offers help instead of teasing.
- A teacher senses when a class is tired or anxious and adjusts the lesson.
- A principal hears a parent's anger as fear and love for their child, not just as hostility.

Empathy involves recognizing another person's emotional state and responding with care. Perspective taking goes a step further and tries to understand how the situation looks from their point of view (Eisenberg, Spinrad, & Morris, 2014).

These skills are not automatic. They are shaped by culture, modeling, and opportunity. Classrooms can either reinforce narrow views of empathy ("Be nice") or help students learn to ask deeper questions:

- "What might be going on for them right now?"
- "How would I feel if this were happening to me?"
- "What am I missing about their experience?"

Teaching perspective taking does not mean that every viewpoint is equally healthy or that harmful behavior is excused. It means that before deciding how to respond, students have practiced imagining more than one story. This is essential for conflict resolution, anti-bullying work, and any serious talk about justice or equity (Zins, Weissberg, Wang, & Walberg, 2004).

How Emotional Intelligence Supports the Other Four Competencies

Emotional intelligence is not just one more item on a list. It is the skill that helps the other four competencies in this book work in real time.

- **Accountability.** To take responsibility for your actions, you have to tolerate shame, guilt, or disappointment without collapsing. Emotional intelligence helps students face those feelings, make amends, and move forward instead of denying or blaming.
- **Respect for self and others.** Respect requires recognizing both your own dignity and that of others. Emotional awareness helps students notice when they are shrinking themselves or inflating themselves, and adjust back toward mutual respect.

- **Conflict resolution.** Disagreements are easier to navigate when people can name what they feel, listen to others' feelings, and work to de-escalate instead of inflame.
- **Resilience.** Bouncing back from setbacks requires the ability to feel pain, fear, or grief without getting stuck permanently. Emotional intelligence provides tools to process those feelings and find meaning on the other side (Masten, 2014; Osher, Cantor, Berg, Steyer, & Rose, 2020).

In this sense, emotional intelligence is the "core skill under every skill." Without it, accountability looks like punishment, respect looks like manners training, conflict resolution looks like forced apologies, and resilience looks like "toughen up." With it, each competency becomes a living, human practice rather than a slogan.

Barriers and Misconceptions

Despite strong research support, emotional intelligence still faces resistance in some schools and communities. Common misconceptions include:

- "Emotions are private. School should focus on academics."
- "Talking about feelings will make students weak or overly sensitive."
- "We do not have time for this with all our standards and testing."

These beliefs often rest on an old split between mind and body, or between reason and emotion. Neuroscience has repeatedly shown that this split is inaccurate. Reason and emotion constantly interact; you cannot strengthen one by ignoring the other (Immordino-Yang, 2016).

There are also cultural nuances. Some communities, for good historical reasons, teach children to be cautious about vulnerability in public, especially in systems that have harmed them. Emotional intelligence work that ignores these realities can feel invasive or unsafe (Ladson-Billings, 2009; Tatum, 2017).

The response is not to abandon emotional intelligence, but to approach it with cultural humility. That includes:

- Inviting families' perspectives on how emotions are handled at home.
- Using examples, stories, and language that reflect students' cultures and experiences.
- Making clear that emotional intelligence is not about spilling every feeling, but about being able to work with feelings wisely.

When positioned as a strength, not a confession, EI becomes a tool for protection and agency, rather than something done to students.

Building Emotional Intelligence in Classrooms

Emotional intelligence can be taught, but it does not happen only through lectures. It is built through repeated experiences, modeling, and guided practice (Brackett, 2019; Durlak et al., 2011). Some practical classroom moves include:

- **Feelings in the routine.** Start or end the day with brief check ins. Use emotion charts or short prompts, not long therapy sessions.
- **Modeling by adults.** When teachers name their own states appropriately, they normalize the process: "I am feeling

frustrated with the noise level right now. I am going to take a breath and try again."

- **Language for conflict.** Teach and practice sentence stems such as "When you did X, I felt Y, and I need Z." Practice them in low-stakes role plays before real conflicts.
- **Reflection after incidents.** When something goes wrong, guide students to reflect on what they felt, what they needed, and what they might do next time. This turns mistakes into lessons instead of labels.
- **Integrating EI into content.** Literature, history, science, and art all offer natural windows into emotion and decision making. Asking "What might this character have felt, and why?" is emotional intelligence work.

These practices do not require a new program, although high-quality SEL curricula can help. They require a stance: teaching content and emotional skills at the same time, instead of treating them as separate tracks.

Home and Community as Emotional Classrooms

Families and communities are the first and often most powerful teachers of emotional intelligence. Children watch how adults respond when frustrated, afraid, or sad. They notice whether feelings are named or ignored, punished or supported.

Schools that honor this reality treat caregivers as partners in EI development, not as obstacles. That might include:

- Sharing simple strategies for emotional labeling and problem solving that families can adapt at home.

- Offering workshops that connect EI to goals families already care about, such as staying out of trouble, keeping friendships, or handling stress.
- Listening to families' wisdom about what calms or escalates their children.

Community organizations, sports teams, faith communities, and after-school programs can also reinforce or erode emotional skills. A coach who humiliates players for mistakes teaches one set of lessons; a coach who uses mistakes as teachable moments teaches another.

When schools, families, and community partners share even a basic common language about emotions, students experience more consistency and safety across settings (Osher et al., 2020).

Emotional Intelligence and Adult Role

For educators, emotional intelligence is not an abstract concept. It is part of the role they play every day in front of students. Some teachers have found it helpful to think of themselves as professionals on a stage. That does not mean being fake. It means recognizing that the "teacher self" is a role that can be guided by purpose rather than by moment-to-moment emotion.

An emotionally intelligent educator can:

- Notice their own fatigue or irritation and choose to respond to students with steadiness.
- Separate a student's behavior from their own worth as a teacher.
- Use tone, body language, and pacing deliberately to regulate the room.

Seeing teaching as a role can create healthy distance. Students' outbursts or silence are less likely to be experienced as personal attacks and more as signals about needs and states. That mental shift can protect educators from burnout and make it easier to model the very skills they are trying to teach (Jennings & Greenberg, 2009; Souers & Hall, 2016).

A later chapter will go deeper into this "on stage" idea, exploring how an acting mindset can support both adult well-being and student regulation. For now, it is enough to note that emotional intelligence is not just for students. It is the hidden backbone of adult practice.

Conclusion: The Skill Beneath the Sand

If the sandcastle is the visible structure of lessons, grades, and classroom routines, emotional intelligence is the pattern in the sand underneath. It shapes how students experience success and failure, how they relate to peers and adults, and how they carry school lessons into the rest of their lives.

When EI is ignored, schools may produce students who can pass tests but struggle in relationships, workplaces, and crises. When EI is taken seriously, schools are more likely to graduate young people who can handle feedback, face stress without collapsing, and stay connected to others even in conflict.

Emotional intelligence does not remove the tide. Life will still bring loss, injustice, and change. But it gives children and adults a better set of tools for rebuilding when the water recedes. In the next chapter, we will turn to resilience and perseverance, the muscles that allow students and adults to start again when sandcastles are damaged or swept away.

References

Brackett, M. A. (2019). *Permission to feel: Unlocking the power of emotions to help our kids, ourselves, and our society thrive*. Celadon Books.

Brackett, M. A., Rivers, S. E., & Salovey, P. (2011). Emotional intelligence: Implications for personal, social, academic, and workplace success. *Social and Personality Psychology Compass, 5*(1), 88–103.

Durlak, J. A., Weissberg, R. P., Dymnicki, A. B., Taylor, R. D., & Schellinger, K. B. (2011). The impact of enhancing students' social and emotional learning: A meta-analysis of school-based universal interventions. *Child Development, 82*(1), 405–432.

Eisenberg, N., Spinrad, T. L., & Morris, A. S. (2014). Empathy-related responding in children. In M. Killen & J. G. Smetana (Eds.), *Handbook of moral development* (2nd ed., pp. 184–207). Psychology Press.

Goleman, D. (1995). *Emotional intelligence: Why it can matter more than IQ*. Bantam Books.

Gross, J. J. (2015). Emotion regulation: Current status and future prospects. *Psychological Inquiry, 26*(1), 1–26.

Immordino-Yang, M. H. (2016). *Emotions, learning, and the brain: Exploring the educational implications of affective neuroscience*. W. W. Norton.

Jennings, P. A., & Greenberg, M. T. (2009). The prosocial classroom: Teacher social and emotional competence in relation to student and classroom outcomes. *Review of Educational Research, 79*(1), 491–525.

Ladson-Billings, G. (2009). *The dreamkeepers: Successful teachers of African American children* (2nd ed.). Jossey-Bass.

Masten, A. S. (2014). *Ordinary magic: Resilience in development.* Guilford Press.

Mayer, J. D., Salovey, P., & Caruso, D. (2004). Emotional intelligence: Theory, findings, and implications. *Psychological Inquiry, 15*(3), 197–215.

Osher, D., Cantor, P., Berg, J., Steyer, L., & Rose, T. (2020). Drivers of human development: How relationships and context shape learning and development. *Applied Developmental Science, 24*(1), 6–36.

Souers, K., & Hall, P. (2016). *Fostering resilient learners: Strategies for creating a trauma-sensitive classroom.* ASCD.

Tatum, B. D. (2017). *"Why are all the Black kids sitting together in the cafeteria?" And other conversations about race* (20th anniversary ed.). Basic Books.

Zembylas, M. (2007). Emotional capital and education: Theoretical insights from Bourdieu. *British Journal of Educational Studies, 55*(4), 443–463.

Zins, J. E., Weissberg, R. P., Wang, M. C., & Walberg, H. J. (Eds.). (2004). *Building academic success on social and emotional learning: What does the research say?* Teachers College Press.

Chapter 6

Resilience and Perseverance

Rebuilding After Every Tide

Why Resilience Matters More Than Ever

Across TK–12 and higher education, adults often describe students as "fragile," "checked out," or "quicker to give up" than in prior generations. At the same time, data show rising indicators of youth anxiety, depression, and suicidality (Twenge, Cooper, Joiner, Duffy, & Binau, 2019). The world has not become gentler. In many ways, the waves hitting young people are stronger: social media exposure, economic uncertainty, community violence, racism, and high-stakes testing all compound to create a more turbulent shoreline.

In that context, resilience and perseverance are not inspirational slogans. They are survival tools. Resilience, in the research literature, refers to patterns of positive adaptation in the face of adversity (Masten, 2014). It is "ordinary magic," built from everyday protective factors like caring relationships, clear expectations, and opportunities to contribute, not from heroic moments alone.

When we look at school through the sandcastle metaphor, resilience is the difference between a child who sees the tide as proof that "there's no point in trying" and a child who learns, over time, "I can rebuild, and I am not rebuilding alone." That shift does not happen by accident. It is taught, modeled, and reinforced by adults and systems (Fergus & Zimmerman, 2005; Jones & Kahn, 2017).

What Resilience Is (and Is Not)

In popular culture, resilience is sometimes portrayed as toughness: the ability to endure hardship without complaint. In schools, it can get reduced to "grit" or "growth mindset" posters on the wall. Students are told to "push through," "try harder," or "never give up," even when the conditions around them are unreasonable or harmful.

This version of resilience is dangerous for at least three reasons:

1. **It can disguise injustice.** Asking a student to "be resilient" in the face of chronic bullying, racism, or hunger risks shifting responsibility from systems to individuals (Ladson-Billings, 2009; Noguera, 2003).

2. **It can glorify suffering.** When adults praise students only for enduring hardship, they may unintentionally send the message that pain is a necessary proof of worth.

3. **It can shame those who struggle.** Students who cannot "bounce back" quickly may feel defective, rather than appropriately overwhelmed.

A more accurate definition of resilience includes:

- **Realistic appraisal of difficulty.** Naming that something is genuinely hard or unfair.

- **Access to internal and external resources.** Skills, relationships, and supports that make coping possible.

- **Movement toward adaptation.** Over time, finding ways to function, grow, or change conditions, not just endure them (Fergus & Zimmerman, 2005; Masten, 2014).

Perseverance sits inside this broader process. It is the willingness to stay engaged with a task or goal over time, adjusting strategies as needed. Perseverance without reflection can become stubbornness. Resilience without perseverance can become retreat. Schools need both.

Rebuilding After Every Tide

The sandcastle image has always been about more than loss. It is also about return. Every time adults and students come back to the beach after a weekend, a break, or a crisis, they are engaging in small acts of resilience.

Consider three levels of rebuilding:

1. **Moment-to-moment resilience.**
    - A child makes an error while reading aloud, blushes, and wants to stop. With coaching, they take a breath and try again.
    - A teenager gets a low quiz score, feels discouraged, but decides to ask for help instead of disengaging.
2. **Event-level resilience.**
    - A family moves in the middle of the school year. The student must adjust to a new curriculum, peers, and expectations.
    - A teacher has a lesson that fails badly. Instead of withdrawing, they reflect, adjust, and reteach.
3. **Life-course resilience.**
    - A young person grows up in persistent economic hardship but finds pathways through school, mentors, and community programs into stable work and healthy relationships (Eccles & Roeser, 2011; Fergus & Zimmerman, 2005).

In each of these scenarios, the outcome depends less on "toughness" and more on:

- Whether adults frame setbacks as normal parts of learning or as permanent verdicts.
- Whether students have tools for managing the emotions that accompany failure.
- Whether the environment offers second chances, scaffolds, and feedback.

Resilience becomes visible in the pattern: not "never knocked down," but "knocked down and able, over time, to get up differently."

Developmental Pathways: TK Through Adulthood

Resilience does not look the same at every age. A TK student's "bounce back" capacity is not a college student's, but the roots are connected (Erikson, 1993; Lerner, 2018).

- **Early childhood (TK–Grade 2).**

  Young children build resilience through predictable routines, secure attachment to caregivers and teachers, and manageable challenges. Learning to try a puzzle again, to apologize after hitting, or to return to a group after a meltdown are foundational acts of perseverance.

- **Upper elementary (Grades 3–5).**

  Students begin to internalize narratives about their abilities: "I'm good at math," "I'm bad at reading," "I always get in trouble." Resilience work here involves gently challenging fixed labels, using feedback to refine effort, and showing students that mistakes are data, not identity (Dweck, 2006; Denham, 2006).

- **Middle school.**

  Identity, belonging, and peer dynamics intensify. Resilience often centers on social experiences: friendship conflicts, exclusion, online drama, and early romantic relationships. Adults can support students in seeing social pain as survivable and in developing healthy coping (Eccles & Roeser, 2011).

- **High school.**

  Academic pressures, family responsibilities, work, and future planning converge. Resilience involves longer-term goal setting, navigating disappointment (college admissions, sports cuts, job loss), and making meaning out of setbacks.

- **College and adulthood.**

  The stakes shift from grades to employment, housing, relationships, and parenting. The same core processes remain: feeling knocked off balance, drawing on internal and external resources, and re-engaging with life tasks.

Viewing resilience developmentally helps educators avoid unrealistic expectations ("Why can't this seven-year-old self-motivate like a senior?") and highlights how small experiences of repair in early years build toward greater adaptability later (Masten, 2014).

The Role of Mindset – Used Carefully

"Growth mindset" research suggests that when students believe abilities can develop through effort, strategies, and support, they are more likely to persist in the face of difficulty (Dweck, 2006). Well-implemented mindset interventions have been associated with small but meaningful gains in academic achievement, especially for students facing stereotype threat or prior underperformance.

However, growth mindset has sometimes been implemented as a slogan rather than as a practice. Telling a student to "have a growth mindset" while leaving grading policies, tracking systems, or disciplinary practices unchanged can feel hollow or even hypocritical.

Used carefully, growth mindset becomes part of resilience work when:

- Effort is paired with explicit strategy: "Let's try a different approach," not just "Try harder."
- Feedback is specific and focused on process: "You stuck with this even when it was confusing, and you tried two new methods."
- Adults demonstrate their own learning: "I taught this lesson in a way that didn't work. I'm going to adjust and try again tomorrow."

In this framing, mindset is less about "positive thinking" and more about a shared understanding that skills – academic and social – are plastic, not fixed.

School Practices That Cultivate Resilience

Resilience flourishes in environments that offer both high expectations and high support (Masten, 2014; Jones & Kahn, 2017). Some concrete school practices include:

1. **Normalizing struggle.**
    - Teachers regularly say things like, "If you're stuck, that means your brain is growing," and share stories of their own learning challenges.
    - Classrooms use protocols like "My Favorite Mistake" where students analyze and celebrate errors as learning opportunities.
2. **Building routines for repair.**
    - When conflicts occur, students are guided through structured reflection and restitution, not simply punished.
    - Restorative conversations help students understand impact and make amends, reinforcing the idea that relationships can be repaired after harm.
3. **Providing structured second chances.**
    - Policies allow for reassessment or revision, paired with reflection on what changed.
    - Students learn that perseverance sometimes means "go back, learn more, and try again," not "do the same thing harder."

4. **Highlighting multiple sources of worth.**
    - Adults emphasize not only academic success but kindness, creativity, persistence, and contribution.
    - Students who struggle in one domain see themselves reflected positively in others, which buffers against all-or-nothing thinking.
5. **Embedding coping skills into the day.**
    - Short practices such as breathing exercises, movement breaks, or journaling are used not as emergency tools alone, but as regular maintenance for the nervous system.

These practices do not remove adversity. They change how students and adults experience and interpret it.

Equity, Context, and "Who Gets to Be Resilient?"

Resilience research has sometimes been criticized for focusing attention on individual adaptation while sidestepping structural inequities (Ladson-Billings, 2009; Noguera, 2003). A student who "overcomes the odds" can become a heart-warming story that leaves the odds themselves unchallenged.

An equity-minded resilience approach acknowledges that:

- Some communities are asked to be resilient in the face of hardships that others never face: chronic underfunding, racial profiling, environmental hazards, or language oppression.
- Systems often celebrate exceptional individuals while ignoring the many who are harmed by the same conditions.

- Asking marginalized students to simply "bounce back" without changing those conditions can deepen harm.

In schools, this means pairing resilience-building with:

- Honest conversations about race, class, and power.
- Advocacy for structural changes (e.g., smaller class sizes, culturally responsive curricula, fair discipline practices).
- Recognition that resistance and boundary-setting can also be forms of resilience, not just compliance.

When framed this way, resilience is not about teaching students to accept anything that happens to them. It is about developing the internal and collective capacities to survive, adapt, and, when possible, transform their environments.

Adult Resilience and the "On-Stage" Educator

Students are watching how adults respond to their own tides: budget cuts, leadership changes, family stress, and vicarious trauma. When a teacher models healthy coping – asking for help, setting boundaries, apologizing after missteps, and returning after discouragement – they are giving students a living curriculum in resilience (Jennings & Greenberg, 2009; Souers & Hall, 2016).

For many educators, one helpful frame is to see teaching as a professional "on-stage" role. This does not mean being fake. It means recognizing that the "teacher self" is a character shaped deliberately for the work: calm when possible, predictable, and able to separate personal worth from students' moment-to-moment reactions.

Seen through this lens:

- A student's angry comment is less likely to be interpreted as a personal attack and more as a sign of dysregulation or pain.
- A difficult class period becomes a "scene" that can be reflected on, revised, and replayed differently, rather than evidence that the educator is failing as a human being.
- Colleagues become part of the cast and crew, not competitors or judges.

This professional distance can protect educators' own nervous systems, making it more possible for them to stay regulated and to model the steady perseverance they ask of students. A later chapter will develop this acting-and-stage metaphor more fully, connecting it to teacher well-being, classroom management, and the blending of personal and professional identities in U.S. culture.

Resilience as a Shared Project

Resilience and perseverance are often framed as individual virtues: qualities that reside inside a child's mind or character. This chapter has argued that they are also relational and systemic projects. Children learn to rebuild after tides when:

- They experience adults who return, again and again, even after conflict.
- They see schools adjust practices that are not working, rather than doubling down on harmful routines.
- They feel part of communities that value their presence, not just their performance.

In a risk-management sense, resilience is a wise investment. Students who can navigate setbacks without collapsing or lashing out are less likely to disengage, drop out, or become involved in serious behavioral incidents (Jones & Kahn, 2017; Osher, Cantor, Berg, Steyer, & Rose, 2020). In a human sense, resilience is what allows a person to carry their sandcastle story forward: not as a tale of repeated loss, but as a record of how, with others, they learned to build again.

In the next chapters, we will look closely at the five lifelong competencies that interact with resilience – accountability, respect, conflict resolution, and emotional intelligence – and consider how each one can either support or erode a child's ability to persevere across the lifespan.

References

Denham, S. A. (2006). Social–emotional competence as support for school readiness: What is it and how do we assess it? *Early Education and Development, 17*(1), 57–89.

Dweck, C. S. (2006). *Mindset: The new psychology of success.* Random House.

Eccles, J. S., & Roeser, R. W. (2011). Schools as developmental contexts during adolescence. *Journal of Research on Adolescence, 21*(1), 225–241.

Erikson, E. H. (1993). *Childhood and society* (2nd ed.). W. W. Norton.

Fergus, S., & Zimmerman, M. A. (2005). Adolescent resilience: A framework for understanding healthy development in the face of risk. *Annual Review of Public Health, 26*, 399–419.

Jones, S. M., & Kahn, J. (2017). The evidence base for how we learn: Supporting students' social, emotional, and academic development. *The Aspen Institute National Commission on Social, Emotional, and Academic Development.*

Jennings, P. A., & Greenberg, M. T. (2009). The prosocial classroom: Teacher social and emotional competence in relation to student and classroom outcomes. *Review of Educational Research, 79*(1), 491–525.

Ladson-Billings, G. (2009). *The dreamkeepers: Successful teachers of African American children* (2nd ed.). Jossey-Bass.

Lerner, R. M. (2018). *Concepts and theories of human development* (4th ed.). Routledge.

Masten, A. S. (2014). *Ordinary magic: Resilience in development.* Guilford Press.

Noguera, P. A. (2003). The trouble with Black boys: The role and influence of environmental and cultural factors on the academic performance of African American males. *Urban Education, 38*(4), 431–459.

Osher, D., Cantor, P., Berg, J., Steyer, L., & Rose, T. (2020). Drivers of human development: How relationships and context shape learning and development. *Applied Developmental Science, 24*(1), 6–36.

Souers, K., & Hall, P. (2016). *Fostering resilient learners: Strategies for creating a trauma-sensitive classroom*. ASCD.

Twenge, J. M., Cooper, A. B., Joiner, T. E., Duffy, M. E., & Binau, S. G. (2019). Age, period, and cohort trends in mood disorder indicators and suicide-related outcomes in a nationally representative dataset, 2005–2017. *Journal of Abnormal Psychology, 128*(3), 185–199.

Chapter 7

Teaching on a Stage

Role, Identity, and Not Taking It Personally

"If They Misbehave, I Must Be Failing"

In U.S. culture, the question "What do you do?" is often treated as a proxy for "Who are you?" Professional role and personal identity are tightly fused. For teachers, this fusion can be especially strong. Many enter the profession with a deep sense of mission: they want to change lives, give back to their communities, or "be the teacher they did or did not have" growing up (Hargreaves, 1998; Santoro, 2018).

That sense of calling is a strength. It fuels persistence in hard conditions. It is also a vulnerability. When identity and work are fully blended, every classroom challenge can feel like a verdict on the self:

- A student rolls their eyes → "They do not respect me."
- A class is off-task → "I am a bad teacher."
- A parent complains → "I am failing these children."

In this frame, student behavior is not just data about regulation, trauma, or peer dynamics; it is interpreted as a comment on the adult's worth. Over time, that pattern can lead to shame, defensiveness, or emotional withdrawal (Jennings & Greenberg, 2009; Maslach & Leiter, 2016).

A subtle but powerful shift is possible. Rather than collapsing identity into role, educators can develop a professional stance—a deliberately crafted "teacher self" that stands between the private person and the daily tides of classroom life. This distinction does not require emotional detachment or inauthenticity. Instead, it reflects a form of regulated professionalism in which adults maintain self-awareness and emotional differentiation under stress. Adult self-regulation, in turn, shapes the climate in which students attempt to regulate (Smith & Smith, 2026). By differentiating identity from role, teachers preserve both their humanity and their effectiveness.

Front Stage, Backstage: A Dramaturgical Lens

Sociologist Erving Goffman (1959) used a theatre metaphor to describe social life:

- **Front stage** is where we perform roles for an audience (students, parents, colleagues).
- **Backstage** is where we step out of those roles, process feelings, and prepare for the next performance.

Teaching is one of the clearest front-stage professions. Every gesture, facial expression, tone of voice, and pause carries meaning for students. Even in a small classroom, a teacher is constantly "on," reading the room and being read in return (Hargreaves, 1998; Sutton, Mudrey-Camino, & Knight, 2009).

Trouble arises when there is no real backstage. Many educators report feeling that they must be "on" from the parking lot to the drive home:

- Staff rooms are not safe spaces to decompress.
- Planning periods are swallowed by supervision, email, or meetings.
- Cultural expectations frame emotional struggle as weakness.

Without backstage time and identity, the front-stage role can swallow the person. The "teacher self" becomes the only self. That is emotionally expensive, especially in high-need settings where dysregulation, trauma, and conflict are daily realities (Jennings & Greenberg, 2009; Maslach & Leiter, 2016).

Reclaiming the idea of teaching as a role is one way to re-create that boundary. It allows educators to say, in effect, "When I am in this classroom, I am stepping into a professional character with specific tools, limits, and responsibilities. When I leave, I step out of that character and return to my full self."

Emotional Labor and the Cost of "Always On"

Arlie Hochschild (1983) coined the term emotional labor to describe the work of managing one's own feelings to produce a desired emotional state in others—for example, a flight attendant creating a sense of calm and welcome. Teaching involves intense emotional labor:

- Maintaining patience when students are defiant or disengaged.
- Conveying enthusiasm for content when personally exhausted.
- Offering empathy during student disclosures while holding boundaries.

Studies show that chronic, unacknowledged emotional labor contributes to teacher burnout, characterized by emotional exhaustion, depersonalization, and a reduced sense of accomplishment (Jennings & Greenberg, 2009; Maslach & Leiter, 2016).

When teachers lack tools to manage this burden, two common coping patterns emerge:

1. **Over-identification.** The teacher merges fully with the role, taking every outcome personally. This can lead to

workaholism, boundary violations ("I am available to students 24/7"), and eventual collapse.

2. **Defensive detachment.** The teacher emotionally withdraws to avoid pain: "I am just here for the paycheck." Students experience this as coldness or inconsistency.

Neither extreme is sustainable. A role-based, "on-stage" mindset offers a middle path: engaged but not engulfed, compassionate but not consumed.

The Educator as Professional Actor

Thinking of teachers as actors can feel uncomfortable at first, especially in a profession that values authenticity. The point is not to promote dishonesty. It is to recognize that **every** professional role involves some level of performance: choosing which parts of the self to foreground, how to express emotion, and what boundaries to maintain.

A professional acting lens invites educators to:

- **Define the character.**
  - What values do I want my "teacher self" to embody (e.g., calm, curiosity, fairness, humor)?
  - What does that look like in my voice, body language, and routines?
- **Use scripts strategically.**
  - Having phrases ready for common situations ("I can see you're upset; let's figure this out," "We're going to pause and reset") reduces reactivity and supports regulation.

- **Practice role distance.**
    - Recognizing that "the way this period went" is feedback about the role and conditions, not a full verdict on the person.

From this perspective, a student's outburst is not primarily an attack on the teacher's personal worth. It is a cue for the professional self: "Right now, my role is to regulate myself, protect safety, and understand what need is underneath this behavior" (Souers & Hall, 2016).

This shift aligns directly with earlier chapters: a regulated adult, operating from a well-defined professional role, is better able to co-regulate students, model emotional intelligence, and foster resilience (Brackett, 2019; Osher, Cantor, Berg, Steyer, & Rose, 2020).

Benefits of an "On-Stage" Mindset

1. Less personalization of student behavior

When educators see themselves as characters on a stage, student reactions are interpreted through a developmental and contextual lens rather than a purely personal one. A sixth grader's sarcasm becomes data about peer culture and regulation, not proof that "they hate me." This reduces defensiveness and creates space for curiosity: "What is this behavior communicating?" (Jennings & Greenberg, 2009).

2. Stronger boundaries and work–life separation

Role-based thinking helps teachers leave work at work. End-of-day rituals—closing the classroom door, brief journaling, changing clothes, or listening to specific music—signal the shift from "teacher self" to personal self. This separation is protective in a culture where jobs easily colonize evenings, weekends, and identity (Maslach & Leiter, 2016).

3. More consistent regulation in the classroom

Actors learn to use breath, posture, and voice to hold a room. Teachers can do the same. When educators consciously step into their professional role, they can draw on practiced regulation strategies even when personally stressed. Students experience this as steadiness and safety, which supports their own regulation and learning (Immordino-Yang, 2016; Souers & Hall, 2016).

4. Clearer alignment with values

A professional persona is not a mask hiding values; it is a container that expresses them intentionally. If a teacher values dignity, equity, and accountability, their "on-stage" choices—how they correct, praise, and respond—can be designed to reflect those commitments, even on hard days.

Risks and Misunderstandings

Like any metaphor, the acting/stage frame can be misused. There are at least three risks to avoid:

1. **Performance without authenticity.** If teachers treat the role as pure show, students quickly sense inauthenticity. Research on teacher–student relationships consistently finds that authenticity and care are central to engagement (Roorda, Koomen, Spilt, & Oort, 2011). The goal is guided authenticity, not pretending to be someone you are not.

2. **Emotional suppression.** Acting is not the same as numbing. Students benefit from seeing real, appropriately expressed emotion: "I am disappointed by what happened today, and I care about us doing better tomorrow."

Suppressing all feeling can increase stress and reduce connection (Gross, 2015; Sutton et al., 2009).

3. **Individualizing systemic problems.** A stage metaphor cannot fix oversized classes, inadequate prep time, or structural inequities. If systems use the language of "professional persona" to avoid addressing working conditions, the burden of resilience falls unfairly on individual teachers (Santoro, 2018).

A healthy use of the metaphor acknowledges these limits and keeps it grounded in purpose: protecting the educator's humanity so they can better support students.

Practical Strategies for Stepping On and Off Stage

Clarify your teacher persona

Educators can start by asking:

- "If students described me at my best in three words, what would I hope they say?"
- "What do those words look like in practice when a student is dysregulated, when a lesson fails, or when a parent is angry?"

Writing a brief "teacher role statement" can help:

"When I am in front of students, I am calm, firm, and curious. I protect dignity, hold clear boundaries, and assume behavior has a story."

This statement becomes a touchstone during stressful moments.

Use micro-rituals for transitions

- Before class: a few deep breaths, a phrase ("Step into the role"), or a small physical gesture (touching the door frame) can mark the entrance to the stage.
- After class: a quick note about what worked and what did not, then a conscious release ("This period is over; I can revisit it later if needed").

These rituals help the nervous system differentiate between roles and reduce lingering emotional residue.

Build backstage spaces and relationships

Schools can support teachers by:

- Protecting at least one space (physical or virtual) where staff can speak honestly about emotions without fear of judgment.
- Encouraging peer debriefing: brief check-ins after hard incidents to share what happened, how it felt, and what might happen next time.
- Providing access to coaching or supervision that includes attention to emotional labor, not just classroom management techniques (Adelman & Taylor, 2006; Jennings & Greenberg, 2009).

Backstage is where the person can catch up with the role—processing anger, grief, or discouragement so that it does not leak unexamined into future performances.

How the Stage Mindset Helps Children

This chapter is not just about adult comfort. When educators adopt a healthy role-based stance, children benefit in concrete ways:

- **Less retaliatory discipline.** Teachers are less likely to escalate or punish from hurt ego when they do not interpret misbehavior as a personal insult.
- **Clearer modeling of SEL skills.** Adults who can say, "I felt disrespected in that moment, so I paused and chose a different response," are demonstrating emotional intelligence, accountability, and conflict resolution in real time (Brackett, 2019).
- **More stable attachment figures.** For many students—especially those experiencing instability at home—teachers are key attachment figures. A regulated, consistent professional persona provides a reliable base from which students can explore and learn (Osher et al., 2020; Souers & Hall, 2016).

Seeing teaching as a role can also help students reflect on their own roles. Adolescents in particular may respond to being invited to consider who they want to be "on their own stage": in school, online, with friends, and at home. This aligns with the book's broader goal of building accountability, respect, conflict resolution, emotional intelligence, and resilience across the lifespan.

Implications for Preparation and Policy

If we take the "on-stage" metaphor seriously, it has implications beyond individual teachers:

- **Teacher preparation programs** should explicitly address emotional labor, identity, and role, not just curriculum and methods.
- **Induction and mentoring** should include time to talk about how novice teachers construct their professional persona and how that evolves.
- **Policy makers and leaders** should recognize that each new initiative adds to the emotional load of front-stage work and should design schedules, staffing, and evaluation systems that allow for backstage recovery.

These shifts do not replace the need for structural justice, mental health services, or improved working conditions. They complement those changes by giving educators tools to navigate the reality they inhabit right now.

Conclusion: Protecting the Builder to Preserve the Sandcastle

Throughout this book, the sandcastle has served as a metaphor for the fragile yet meaningful work of education. Earlier chapters focused on the child—how tides of life, regulation, emotion, and resilience shape learning. This chapter has focused on the adults who stand at the shoreline.

When teachers believe they **are** the sandcastle, every wave feels like a personal failure. When they understand themselves as builders **on** a stage, working with imperfect tools in shifting conditions, they can hold their role with both seriousness and compassion. They can care deeply without being destroyed by every setback.

That stance—professional, purposeful, and bounded—does not distance teachers from children. It allows them to be more fully present. It creates the stability students need to practice the five lifelong competencies, even when their own lives feel chaotic. And it offers educators a way to stay in this work long enough to see the sandcastles they help build outlast a single tide.

References

Adelman, H. S., & Taylor, L. (2006). *The school leader's guide to student learning supports: New directions for addressing barriers to learning.* Corwin Press.

Brackett, M. A. (2019). *Permission to feel: Unlocking the power of emotions to help our kids, ourselves, and our society thrive.* Celadon Books.

Goffman, E. (1959). *The presentation of self in everyday life.* Doubleday.

Gross, J. J. (2015). Emotion regulation: Current status and future prospects. *Psychological Inquiry, 26*(1), 1–26.

Hargreaves, A. (1998). The emotional practice of teaching. *Teaching and Teacher Education, 14*(8), 835–854.

Hochschild, A. R. (1983). *The managed heart: Commercialization of human feeling.* University of California Press.

Immordino-Yang, M. H. (2016). *Emotions, learning, and the brain: Exploring the educational implications of affective neuroscience.* W. W. Norton.

Jennings, P. A., & Greenberg, M. T. (2009). The prosocial classroom: Teacher social and emotional competence in relation to student and classroom outcomes. *Review of Educational Research, 79*(1), 491–525.

Mallett Smith, S., & Smith II, J. (2026). *Prevention, De-escalation, and Resilience (PDR): Strategies for Navigating Adversity.* Isham Media Group LLC.

Maslach, C., & Leiter, M. P. (2016). Understanding the burnout experience: Recent research and its implications for psychiatry. *World Psychiatry, 15*(2), 103–111.

Osher, D., Cantor, P., Berg, J., Steyer, L., & Rose, T. (2020). Drivers of human development: How relationships and context shape learning and development. *Applied Developmental Science, 24*(1), 6–36.

Roorda, D. L., Koomen, H. M. Y., Spilt, J. L., & Oort, F. J. (2011). The influence of affective teacher–student relationships on students' school engagement and achievement: A meta-analytic approach. *Review of Educational Research, 81*(4), 493–529.

Santoro, D. A. (2018). *Demoralized: Why teachers leave the profession they love and how they can stay*. Harvard Education Press.

Mallett Smith, S., & Smith II, J. (2026). *Prevention, De-escalation, and Resilience (PDR): Strategies for Navigating Adversity.* Isham Media Group LLC.

Souers, K., & Hall, P. (2016). *Fostering resilient learners: Strategies for creating a trauma-sensitive classroom.* ASCD.

Sutton, R. E., Mudrey-Camino, R., & Knight, C. C. (2009). Teachers' emotion regulation and classroom management. *Theory Into Practice, 48*(2), 130–137.

Chapter 8

Accountability

Owning Choices Without Shame

What We Talk About When We Say "Accountability"

In everyday school language, "accountability" often sounds like something adults do *to* students:

- "We have to hold them accountable."
- "There need to be consequences."
- "He has to learn there are real-world results."

Underneath those phrases is a real concern. Educators and families want young people to understand that choices matter. They want children to learn that actions have impact on themselves and others, and that part of becoming an adult is taking responsibility even when it is uncomfortable (Dweck, 2006; Lerner, 2018).

But in practice, accountability is frequently conflated with blame and shame. A child makes a mistake, and the response focuses on:

- **Who did it?**
- **Who is at fault?**
- **What rule was broken?**

There may be little attention to **why** the behavior happened, what skills were missing, or how repair will occur. In those moments, students learn powerful lessons that may have little to do with accountability and much to do with fear:

- "If I admit what I did, I will be humiliated or rejected."
- "The safest move is to lie, minimize, or blame someone else."
- "Adults are mainly interested in punishment, not understanding."

Research on school discipline shows that exclusionary practices like suspensions and expulsions are associated with higher dropout rates, lower academic achievement, and disproportionate harm to Black, Latino, Indigenous, and disabled students (Skiba, Arredondo, & Williams, 2014; Tatum, 2017). These practices often operate under the banner of "accountability," but they rarely build the skills that true accountability requires.

In this chapter, we reframe accountability as a lifelong competency that can be intentionally developed from transitional kindergarten through adulthood. We treat it not as a tool for sorting "good kids" from "bad kids," but as a shared capacity that allows people to live and work together with integrity.

Accountability vs. Shame

Psychologist Brené Brown (2012) distinguishes between guilt ("I did something bad") and shame ("I *am* bad"). Guilt, when handled well, can motivate repair. Shame tends to produce hiding, aggression, or disconnection.

Many traditional discipline systems lean heavily on shame:

- Public call-outs or sarcasm in front of peers.
- Repetitive reminders of past mistakes ("You always do this").
- Labels that become identities ("problem student," "bully," "lazy").

When children internalize these messages, it becomes harder—not easier—for them to take responsibility. Admitting a mistake feels like confirming a negative identity, not like a courageous step toward growth.

Accountability, by contrast, involves three elements:

1. **Owning behavior.**
    - "This is what I did or failed to do."
2. **Recognizing impact.**
    - "This is how it affected others and me."
3. **Taking action to repair and learn.**
    - "This is what I will do to make it better and to prevent it next time."

In an accountable culture, adults send a consistent message:

"Your behavior is your responsibility, and you *always* remain a person worthy of respect and support."

This distinction is not soft on harm. In fact, it asks more of the person who caused harm: not just to accept a one-time punishment, but to stay in relationship long enough to listen, repair, and change (Gregory & Evans, 2020).

Accountability Across the Lifespan

Because this book takes a TK-to-adulthood view, accountability must be understood developmentally (Eccles & Roeser, 2011; Lerner, 2018).

Early Childhood (TK–Grade 2)

Young children are still learning cause and effect, impulse control, and perspective taking. At this stage, accountability looks like:

- Naming the behavior in concrete terms ("You pushed your friend").

- Connecting to impact in simple language ("He got hurt and felt scared").
- Guiding toward repair ("What can we do to help him feel better?").

Adults often need to scaffold the process: offering choices ("Would you like to bring an ice pack or say you're sorry?") and praising genuine efforts to make amends. The goal is not to induce shame, but to link actions and consequences in ways a young brain can process.

Upper Elementary (Grades 3–5)

Children develop a stronger sense of fairness and reputation. They are more sensitive to embarrassment and more able to understand others' perspectives. Accountability here involves:

- Helping students reflect on patterns ("When you rush through your work, what tends to happen?").
- Encouraging them to anticipate consequences ("If you keep interrupting, how will that affect your group?").
- Introducing structured restitution (clean-up tasks, written apologies, or redoing work).

At this stage, group norms and peer dynamics matter. Classrooms that foster collective accountability ("We all have a role in making this room work") help students see responsibility as shared, not just something imposed by adults.

Middle School

Adolescents grapple with identity, autonomy, and belonging. Accountability becomes more complex:

- Students may resist adult feedback as an attack on their emerging independence.
- Peer approval can outweigh adult expectations.
- Online behavior introduces new arenas of harm.

Effective accountability here requires:

- Collaborative problem-solving ("Let's walk through what happened step by step").
- Opportunities for restorative conferences where students hear directly from those impacted.
- Clear boundaries paired with respect ("I will not allow you to speak to me that way. I'm also not giving up on you.").

High School and Beyond

Older adolescents and young adults are capable of deep reflection but may still default to defensiveness when they feel cornered. In school, work, and relationships, accountability includes:

- Owning complex mistakes (cheating, substance use, betrayal of trust).
- Facing more serious consequences while still being offered pathways back into community.
- Learning to self-advocate: admitting error while also naming unmet needs or systemic barriers.

Throughout adulthood, accountability remains central in employment, parenting, and partnerships. The same patterns learned in childhood—either avoidance and blame or honest repair—tend to resurface in these arenas (Lerner, 2018).

Power, Equity, and "Who Gets Held Accountable?"

Any honest discussion of accountability in schools must confront questions of power and equity. Research consistently shows that Black, Latino, Indigenous, and disabled students are more likely to be labeled "defiant," receive harsher punishments for similar behaviors, and be pushed into exclusionary discipline pathways (Skiba et al., 2014; Ladson-Billings, 2009; Noguera, 2003; Tatum, 2017).

These patterns show up in small ways:

- A Black student's question is read as challenge; a White student's question is read as curiosity.
- A student with an IEP is punished for behavior tied to unmet support needs.
- A bilingual student is marked "non-compliant" for misunderstandings rooted in language.

When schools talk about "holding students accountable" without examining who is being held accountable and how, they risk reinforcing the very inequities this book seeks to address. Accountability must be paired with:

- **Consistent, bias-aware expectations.** Staff examine discipline data, look for disproportionality, and reflect on how implicit bias may be shaping their responses (Skiba et al., 2014; Tatum, 2017).
- **Transparent processes.** Students and families understand how decisions are made and have voice in the process.

- **Contextual understanding.** Behavior is considered in light of trauma, disability, culture, and structural barriers—not to excuse harm, but to inform meaningful repair (Souers & Hall, 2016).

In this sense, accountability also applies to systems. Districts, schools, and municipalities have responsibilities not only to enforce rules, but to examine how policies, budgets, and historical patterns contribute to the conditions under which students live and learn (Bronfenbrenner, 1979; Darling-Hammond, 2010).

Home and School: Dueling Stories About Responsibility

Earlier chapters described the "temporary custodian" mindset: some parents experience schools more like service providers than partners. That mindset intersects directly with accountability.

From the school's perspective, conversations about behavior often sound like:

- "We need your support at home."
- "He needs consistent consequences in both places."

From the parent's perspective, especially when juggling multiple jobs, housing instability, or their own painful school experiences, these messages can sound like blame:

- "You are responsible for his behavior, and you are failing."
- "We did our part; now you fix it."

Likewise, when parents say, "That's your job," educators may hear:

- "I am not responsible for what happens during the school day."
- "You are on your own when things get hard."

Both sides are often reacting to conditions beyond their control (Hoover-Dempsey & Sandler, 1997; Ishimaru, 2019). The goal is not to divide responsibility 50/50 on paper, but to build a shared language:

"We are both accountable to this child. We each have different tools, constraints, and roles. How do we work together?"

Practically, this might mean:

- Sending home descriptive information ("Here is what we are seeing in class and when it tends to happen") rather than verdicts.
- Asking parents what strategies work at home and where they feel stuck, honoring their expertise.
- Avoiding public shaming—at family nights, in emails, or on report cards—about "uninvolved parents" or "unsupportive teachers."

When families and schools align around a common picture of accountability, the child experiences coherence instead of competing narratives.

Adult Modeling: "I Was Wrong, and I'm Still Your Teacher/Parent"

Children take their deepest accountability lessons from how adults respond when *they* make mistakes.

- Does a teacher ever apologize for overreacting?

- Does a principal acknowledge when a policy caused harm?
- Does a parent own losing their temper and explain how they will handle it differently?

When adults model accountability, they show that responsibility is compatible with dignity. A teacher who says, "I spoke too sharply yesterday; I'm sorry," communicates powerful messages:

- Authority can admit error without collapsing.
- Our relationship matters more than my pride.
- You are allowed to make repairs, too (Jennings & Greenberg, 2009; Brackett, 2019).

The "on-stage" metaphor from the previous chapter fits here. Stepping into a professional role does not mean pretending to be infallible. It means being intentional about **how** we show accountability in front of students. The teacher-self can say:

"In my role, I take responsibility for my words and decisions. I expect you to do the same. None of that changes our worth."

When accountability is modeled at every level—classroom, home, leadership, and system—students see it as a normal part of community life, not as a weapon pulled out only when they are in trouble.

Practical Moves: Teaching Accountability Without Humiliation

Although each school and family context is different, several practical moves can support accountable cultures.

1. Shift the questions

Move from:

- "Who started it?"
- "Why did you do that?"

Toward:

- "What happened, from your point of view?"
- "Who has been affected and how?"
- "What needs to happen now to make things as right as possible?"

These questions, often used in restorative practices, invite reflection rather than instant defensiveness (Gregory & Evans, 2020).

2. Separate message from identity

Use language that clearly separates behavior from worth:

- "Throwing the chair is not acceptable. You are not a 'bad kid'; you made a dangerous choice."
- "This grade reflects your work *on this assignment*, not your intelligence."

Over time, this helps students internalize, "I can change my behavior without erasing myself."

3. Build structured opportunities for repair

Instead of only assigning generic consequences (detention, loss of recess), create chances to repair:

- Writing letters or having guided conversations with those harmed.

- Helping restore shared spaces (clean-up, organization) when property is damaged.
- Participating in circles where everyone affected can speak and listen.

Repair should be proportionate and meaningful, not merely symbolic or humiliating.

4. Connect accountability to choice and skills

Help students see that different choices require different skills:

- A child who keeps "lying" might need help tolerating uncomfortable feelings and practicing how to tell the truth.
- A student who repeatedly misses deadlines might need explicit instruction in planning, not just lectures about responsibility (Deci & Ryan, 2000; Durlak et al., 2011).

When adults frame accountability as "you are bad" rather than "you are missing a skill," they miss opportunities to teach.

Conclusion: Accountability as Foundation, Not Weapon

Accountability is the first named pillar in the five lifelong competencies for a reason. Without it, the sandcastle cannot hold its shape. Children who never learn to own their choices struggle with trust, work, and relationships across their lives. Systems that wield accountability as a one-sided tool—aimed at students and families but never at policies or practices—erode their own legitimacy.

In a healthier vision, accountability becomes a shared practice woven into daily interactions:

- A five-year-old cleaning up spilled blocks and saying, "I forgot to be careful."
- A teenager acknowledging hurtful words and sitting in a circle to listen and repair.
- A teacher apologizing for a sarcastic comment and recommitting to respect.
- A principal revising a discipline policy after seeing who it harms.
- A city committing resources to SEL, mental health, and family partnership because it recognizes its own role in preserving sandcastles.

When accountability is grounded in dignity, students do not have to choose between self-protection and honesty. They can learn to say, "I did this, it mattered, and I am still worthy of belonging." That is the kind of accountability that travels with them long after test scores and grades have faded.

In the chapters that follow, we will turn to **respect for self and others** and **conflict resolution**—two competencies tightly intertwined with accountability. Together with emotional intelligence and resilience, they form the relational architecture that allows children and adults to build, preserve, and rebuild sandcastles across a lifetime.

References

Brackett, M. A. (2019). *Permission to feel: Unlocking the power of emotions to help our kids, ourselves, and our society thrive.* Celadon Books.

Bronfenbrenner, U. (1979). *The ecology of human development: Experiments by nature and design.* Harvard University Press.

Brown, B. (2012). *Daring greatly: How the courage to be vulnerable transforms the way we live, love, parent, and lead.* Gotham Books.

Darling-Hammond, L. (2010). *The flat world and education: How America's commitment to equity will determine our future.* Teachers College Press.

Deci, E. L., & Ryan, R. M. (2000). The "what" and "why" of goal pursuits: Human needs and the self-determination of behavior. *Psychological Inquiry, 11*(4), 227–268.

Durlak, J. A., Weissberg, R. P., Dymnicki, A. B., Taylor, R. D., & Schellinger, K. B. (2011). The impact of enhancing students' social and emotional learning: A meta-analysis of school-based universal interventions. *Child Development, 82*(1), 405–432.

Eccles, J. S., & Roeser, R. W. (2011). Schools as developmental contexts during adolescence. *Journal of Research on Adolescence, 21*(1), 225–241.

Gregory, A., & Evans, K. R. (2020). The starts and stumbles of restorative justice in education: Where do we go from here? *National Education Policy Center.*

Hoover-Dempsey, K. V., & Sandler, H. M. (1997). Why do parents become involved in their children's education? *Review of Educational Research, 67*(1), 3–42.

Ishimaru, A. M. (2019). *Just schools: Building equitable collaborations with families and communities*. Teachers College Press.

Jennings, P. A., & Greenberg, M. T. (2009). The prosocial classroom: Teacher social and emotional competence in relation to student and classroom outcomes. *Review of Educational Research, 79*(1), 491–525.

Ladson-Billings, G. (2009). *The dreamkeepers: Successful teachers of African American children* (2nd ed.). Jossey-Bass.

Lerner, R. M. (2018). *Concepts and theories of human development* (4th ed.). Routledge.

Noguera, P. A. (2003). The trouble with Black boys: The role and influence of environmental and cultural factors on the academic performance of African American males. *Urban Education, 38*(4), 431–459.

Skiba, R. J., Arredondo, M. I., & Williams, N. T. (2014). More than a metaphor: The contribution of exclusionary discipline to a school-to-prison pipeline. *Equity & Excellence in Education, 47*(4), 546–564.

Souers, K., & Hall, P. (2016). *Fostering resilient learners: Strategies for creating a trauma-sensitive classroom*. ASCD.

Tatum, B. D. (2017). *"Why are all the Black kids sitting together in the cafeteria?" And other conversations about race* (20th anniversary ed.). Basic Books.

Chapter 9

Respect for Self and Others

Dignity as Daily Practice

More Than "Yes, Ma'am" and "Sit Still"

In many schools, "respect" is written on posters, painted on walls, and printed in handbooks. Yet when students ask what it means, the first answers they hear are often about behavior:

- "Respect means following directions the first time."
- "Respect means sitting quietly and not talking back."
- "Respect means using 'please' and 'thank you.'"

None of these are wrong. Courtesy and cooperation matter in community life. But if we stop there, we reduce respect to politeness and compliance. A classroom can look "respectful" on the surface—students quiet, uniforms neat, eyes forward—while underneath some students feel unseen, stereotyped, or afraid to bring their true selves into the room (Noddings, 2013; Tatum, 2017).

This book takes a broader view. Respect is about dignity: the basic worth of each person, regardless of behavior, ability, identity, or past. Respect for self means internalizing that worth. Respect for others means acting in ways that protect their worth, even when we are tired, stressed, or in conflict (Brown, 2012; Rogers, 1959).

From transitional kindergarten through adulthood, respect is not just a rule. It is a relationship skill, a cultural lens, and a daily practice that shapes whether sandcastles are built on firm ground or on silent resentment.

Respect for Self: "I Matter, Even When I Mess Up"

It is hard to offer genuine respect to others if you quietly believe that you yourself are worthless. Many students arrive at school with long histories of being told, directly or indirectly, that they are "too much," "not enough," or both. They may have absorbed messages about their race, language, disability, or family that erode self-respect:

- "Kids from this neighborhood never make it."
- "You're the bad kid in this family."
- "Your English is wrong."

When self-respect is low, behaviors can swing in two directions:

- **Collapse.** Students withdraw, avoid risk, and say things like "I'm dumb," "I don't care," or "It doesn't matter."
- **Overcompensation.** Students project arrogance, pick fights, or mock others as a shield over their own shame.

Respect for self does not mean never feeling doubt or pain. It means being able to say, consciously or unconsciously, "I am not perfect, but I am worthy of care, protection, and growth." Schools influence this sense of worth every day, through grading practices, feedback, discipline, and the simple question: "Whose stories and successes do we highlight?" (Ladson-Billings, 2009; Osher, Cantor, Berg, Steyer, & Rose, 2020).

Teachers support self-respect when they:

- Give specific, believable praise tied to effort and growth ("You stuck with this, even when it was confusing. That matters.").
- Avoid global labels ("lazy," "troublemaker") and instead describe behaviors.
- Make room for student voice, allowing young people to see themselves as contributors, not just recipients.

Respect for self is not about inflating egos. It is about building an inner sense of worth that can withstand failure, feedback, and conflict.

Respect for Others: Seeing the Human, Not Just the Behavior

Respect for others begins with a simple but demanding practice: seeing the whole human being in front of you, not just the role they play or the behavior they show today.

For students, that might mean:

- Recognizing that a classmate who is always late may be caring for siblings every morning.
- Understanding that a peer who shouts or jokes inappropriately might be managing anxiety or trauma.
- Noticing that someone who "never participates" may be afraid of public humiliation.

For adults, respect for students includes:

- Learning and using names correctly.
- Avoiding sarcasm and public shaming.
- Listening fully before making assumptions.

Respect does not mean allowing harmful behavior. It means addressing behavior in a way that protects dignity: "I will not let you speak to me or others that way, and I will not treat you as if this moment defines you" (Souers & Hall, 2016).

Research on teacher–student relationships shows that when students feel respected and cared for, they are more engaged, more motivated, and more willing to accept correction (Roorda,

Koomen, Spilt, & Oort, 2011). Respect is not a soft extra; it is a core ingredient in academic and social success.

Cultural Respect: Whose Ways "Count" at School?

You cannot claim to respect a student while routinely dismissing their language, culture, or community as inferior. Culturally responsive teaching is not a separate initiative from respect. It is respect in action (Gay, 2018; Ladson-Billings, 2009).

Questions that reveal cultural respect (or lack of it) include:

- Whose history appears in the curriculum, and whose is missing?
- Are students' names, languages, and family structures treated as assets or as problems to fix?
- Do classroom norms make space for different communication styles (more expressive, more reserved) while still holding shared boundaries?

A student may be labeled "disrespectful" for direct eye contact in one cultural context or for avoiding eye contact in another. A loud voice may be normal in one family and taboo in another. When adults interpret all behavior through a narrow cultural lens, students are told, in effect, "Respect looks like acting less like you and more like us."

Culturally respectful classrooms:

- Teach explicit norms, but also explain why they exist and where they come from.
- Invite students to share respectful practices from their own cultures and integrate them where appropriate.

- Acknowledge historical and current injustices that shape families' relationships with schools, policing, and authority (Tatum, 2017).

Respect, in this sense, is not colorblind. It is color-conscious and context-conscious. It recognizes that dignity must be protected *in* culture, not erased *for* culture.

The Respect–Regulation Connection

Earlier chapters emphasized that there is no significant learning without regulation. Respect is one of the fastest ways to either support or shatter regulation.

When students feel respected:

- Their nervous systems are more likely to stay in a window where curiosity and problem-solving are possible.
- Feedback, even tough feedback, is easier to tolerate.
- Limits feel more like guidance and less like attack (Immordino-Yang, 2016; Osher et al., 2020).

When students feel disrespected—mocked, ignored, stereotyped, or treated unfairly—fight, flight, or freeze responses become more likely. A comment about "attitude" may be a reaction to a moment when the student's sense of dignity was threatened and they had few tools to protect it.

The same is true for adults. Teachers who feel disrespected by students, families, or leadership are more prone to dysregulation and burnout (Jennings & Greenberg, 2009; Maslach & Leiter, 2016). Respect is reciprocal: it flows in every direction and influences everyone's capacity to stay present.

Respect, Power, and Equity

Respect is not distributed equally in schools. Decades of research show that Black and Brown students, multilingual learners, Indigenous students, students with disabilities, and LGBTQ+ students are more likely to experience disrespect in the form of:

- Lowered expectations.
- Stereotyping and microaggressions.
- Disproportionate discipline for subjective offenses like "defiance" or "disrespect."

These patterns are not about a few "bad apples." They reflect structural inequities in curriculum, staffing, policies, and broader society (Darling-Hammond, 2010; Noguera, 2003; Skiba, Arredondo, & Williams, 2014).

Equitable respect requires that schools:

- Examine data for patterns: Who is being sent out, suspended, or referred most often, and for what reasons?
- Provide professional learning on implicit bias, stereotype threat, and culturally responsive pedagogy.
- Create spaces where students can safely name experiences of disrespect and be heard without retaliation.

Respect in an equity frame is not politeness alone. It is the institutional willingness to say, "We will look honestly at who is being harmed here, and we will change our practices," not just "You need to be nicer to adults."

Teaching Respect Without Humiliation

The easiest way to produce surface-level respect is fear. A student who has been shamed or punished harshly for speaking out may become quiet. To an untrained eye, this looks like respect. In reality, it is compliance rooted in threat, not dignity.

Teaching respect as a lifelong competency looks different. It includes:

1. Explicitly naming dignity
Teachers and leaders talk openly with students about what it means to protect everyone's dignity, including:

- How we talk to each other in disagreement.
- How we handle private information.
- How we treat people when they are not in the room.

Respect becomes a shared value, not just a teacher demand.

2. Using language that protects the person while challenging behavior

Instead of:

- "You are disrespectful."

Try:

- "The way you spoke just now crossed a line. In this space, we speak to each other without name-calling or threats."

The behavior is clearly confronted, but the student is not collapsed into the behavior.

3. Practicing perspective taking

In conflict, adults can ask students to consider:

- "If someone said that to you, how would you feel?"
- "What do you think I felt when that happened?"

This is not a trap. It is a guided exercise in connecting action, emotion, and impact.

4. Modeling respectful disagreement

Students watch closely when adults disagree with each other. Staff meetings, parent conferences, and hallway conversations are all lessons. When they see adults set boundaries, express strong views, and still treat each other with dignity, they learn that respect is compatible with honesty and firmness (Eisenberg, Spinrad, & Morris, 2014; Roorda et al., 2011).

Respect at Home and in the Community

Respect is not a school-only competency. Families and communities carry their own histories, beliefs, and practices around respect, many of which are shaped by survival in an unequal society.

Some families emphasize strict obedience to elders as a protection in public spaces: "You cannot talk to the police or the teacher that way and still be safe." Others emphasize questioning authority, especially when it has been used unjustly. Many hold both messages at once.

Schools that truly respect families:

- Ask how respect is taught and practiced at home.
- Avoid framing families' practices as "wrong" simply because they do not match middle-class, White norms.

- Share school expectations in a way that invites dialogue: "Here is how we handle disagreement here. How does that compare to what you teach at home?"

Community organizations, faith groups, and youth programs can reinforce or undermine respectful norms. Partnerships that align around dignity—especially in neighborhoods where young people face daily disrespect from institutions—can become powerful protective factors (Adelman & Taylor, 2006; Ishimaru, 2019).

Respect and the "On-Stage" Educator

The earlier chapter on teaching as an on-stage profession connects directly to respect. When educators see themselves as playing a professional role, they are more able to:

- Respond to student disrespect without retaliating.
- Use tone and body language that convey firmness and care simultaneously.
- Separate their own wounded feelings from the task of coaching respectful behavior.

An "on-stage" teacher might think, "Personally, I felt stung by that comment. In my role, my job is to protect dignity in this room, including yours and mine. That means I will address this clearly and calmly" (Hargreaves, 1998; Jennings & Greenberg, 2009).

This stance keeps respect from collapsing into a power struggle. Instead, the teacher becomes a model of how to hold self-respect and respect for others at the same time.

Conclusion: Respect as Daily Architecture of the Sandcastle

If accountability is the foundation of the sandcastle and emotional intelligence the pattern in the sand, respect is the daily architecture—the way walls, doors, and windows are shaped so that people can live inside together.

When respect is thin or conditional, children—and adults—learn to stay small, guarded, or reactive. When respect is deep and consistent, they are more likely to take risks, admit mistakes, and stay in relationship long enough to learn.

Respect for self tells each child: "You are not your worst day. You matter."
Respect for others tells each child: "So does the person next to you."
Cultural respect tells each community: "Your language, history, and way of being belong in this space."

In the chapters that follow, we will look at conflict resolution—how people who respect themselves and each other actually move through disagreement—and return to the systems level: what it would mean for schools and municipalities to treat respect and dignity not as inspirational posters, but as measurable commitments in policy, practice, and risk management.

References

Adelman, H. S., & Taylor, L. (2006). *The school leader's guide to student learning supports: New directions for addressing barriers to learning.* Corwin Press.

Brown, B. (2012). *Daring greatly: How the courage to be vulnerable transforms the way we live, love, parent, and lead.* Gotham Books.

Darling-Hammond, L. (2010). *The flat world and education: How America's commitment to equity will determine our future.* Teachers College Press.

Eisenberg, N., Spinrad, T. L., & Morris, A. S. (2014). Empathy-related responding in children. In M. Killen & J. G. Smetana (Eds.), *Handbook of moral development* (2nd ed., pp. 184–207). Psychology Press.

Gay, G. (2018). *Culturally responsive teaching: Theory, research, and practice* (3rd ed.). Teachers College Press.

Hargreaves, A. (1998). The emotional practice of teaching. *Teaching and Teacher Education, 14*(8), 835–854.

Hoover-Dempsey, K. V., & Sandler, H. M. (1997). Why do parents become involved in their children's education? *Review of Educational Research, 67*(1), 3–42.

Ishimaru, A. M. (2019). *Just schools: Building equitable collaborations with families and communities.* Teachers College Press.

Immordino-Yang, M. H. (2016). *Emotions, learning, and the brain: Exploring the educational implications of affective neuroscience.* W. W. Norton.

Jennings, P. A., & Greenberg, M. T. (2009). The prosocial classroom: Teacher social and emotional competence in relation to student and classroom outcomes. *Review of Educational Research, 79*(1), 491–525.

Ladson-Billings, G. (2009). *The dreamkeepers: Successful teachers of African American children* (2nd ed.). Jossey-Bass.

Maslach, C., & Leiter, M. P. (2016). Understanding the burnout experience: Recent research and its implications for psychiatry. *World Psychiatry, 15*(2), 103–111.

Noddings, N. (2013). *Caring: A relational approach to ethics and moral education* (2nd ed.). University of California Press.

Noguera, P. A. (2003). The trouble with Black boys: The role and influence of environmental and cultural factors on the academic performance of African American males. *Urban Education, 38*(4), 431–459.

Osher, D., Cantor, P., Berg, J., Steyer, L., & Rose, T. (2020). Drivers of human development: How relationships and context shape learning and development. *Applied Developmental Science, 24*(1), 6–36.

Roorda, D. L., Koomen, H. M. Y., Spilt, J. L., & Oort, F. J. (2011). The influence of affective teacher–student relationships on students' school engagement and achievement: A meta-analytic approach. *Review of Educational Research, 81*(4), 493–529.

Rogers, C. R. (1959). A theory of therapy, personality, and interpersonal relationships, as developed in the client-centered framework. In S. Koch (Ed.), *Psychology: A study of a science* (Vol. 3, pp. 184–256). McGraw-Hill.

Skiba, R. J., Arredondo, M. I., & Williams, N. T. (2014). More than a metaphor: The contribution of exclusionary discipline to a school-to-prison pipeline. *Equity & Excellence in Education, 47*(4), 546–564.

Souers, K., & Hall, P. (2016). *Fostering resilient learners: Strategies for creating a trauma-sensitive classroom.* ASCD.

Tatum, B. D. (2017). *"Why are all the Black kids sitting together in the cafeteria?" And other conversations about race* (20th anniversary ed.). Basic Books.

Chapter 10

Conflict Resolution

Learning to Stay at the Table

Conflict Is Not the Problem

In many schools and homes, the word *conflict* carries a negative charge. People talk about "avoiding conflict," "keeping the peace," or "nipping conflict in the bud." When a disagreement breaks out in a classroom, the instinct is often to stop it as quickly as possible so teaching can resume.

But conflict itself is not the problem. Developmental psychologists and conflict theorists have been clear for decades: wherever people have different needs, values, or perspectives, conflict will arise (Deutsch, 1973; Johnson & Johnson, 1995). The question is not *whether* there will be conflict, but *how we handle it.*

For children and adults, conflict is one of the main "labs" where the five lifelong competencies in this book show up at once:

- Accountability: Can I own my part without collapsing or blaming?
- Respect: Can I treat myself and the other person as worthy, even when I am angry?
- Emotional intelligence: Can I notice and manage my feelings enough to stay in the conversation?
- Resilience: Can I come back after a rupture and try again?

Conflict resolution, in this sense, is not the art of making conflict disappear. It is the practice of staying at the table long enough for something better than either/or to emerge.

What Conflict Resolution Really Is (and Is Not)

When people hear "conflict resolution," they sometimes imagine:

- A scripted program that teaches students to say, "I feel… when you… because…"
- Peer mediators in matching shirts.
- Posters about "win–win solutions."

These tools can be useful, but they do not capture the whole picture. At its core, conflict resolution involves three ongoing capacities (Johnson & Johnson, 1995; Jones et al., 2017):

1. **Staying present.**

   Remaining engaged with the person or issue instead of shutting down, running away, or exploding.

2. **Understanding perspectives and impact.**

   Listening to what the other person experienced, recognizing emotional impact, and checking your own assumptions.

3. **Working toward repair or next steps.**

   Collaboratively deciding what needs to happen now: apologies, restitution, boundary-setting, or changes in behavior or systems.

Conflict resolution is *not*:

- Avoiding disagreement to "keep the peace."
- Forcing quick forgiveness without real understanding.
- Making the more vulnerable person "be the bigger person" every time.
- A one-time conversation that erases all past harm.

In schools, the temptation is to solve conflict at the surface level: separate students, assign a consequence, and move on. That may calm the moment, but it does not build the skills students need for friendships, work, or family life later.

Developmental Pathways: Learning to Stay at the Table

Like accountability and respect, conflict resolution develops in stages (Denham, 2006; Eccles & Roeser, 2011). The goal is not to expect a five-year-old to handle disagreement like a twenty-five-year-old. It is to see each age as practice for the next.

Early Childhood (TK–Grade 2)

- Conflicts are often about concrete resources: toys, space, attention.
- Children tend to see only their own perspective; empathy is emerging but fragile.
- Adults do much of the "translation": "You both wanted the same block. When you grabbed it, he got hurt and sad."

At this stage, conflict resolution teaching looks like:

- Using simple language ("We take turns," "Hands are for helping.").
- Naming feelings for both sides ("You're mad; he looks scared.").
- Coaching basic repair ("Can you bring him a tissue?" "Can you ask, 'Do you want to play?'").

The main lessons: "I can use words instead of hurting," and "Relationships can be fixed after something goes wrong."

Upper Elementary (Grades 3–5)

- Conflicts shift toward fairness, rules, and social standing: cheating, exclusion, "who started it."
- Children can better understand multiple viewpoints but are still sensitive to embarrassment.

Here, conflict resolution involves:

- Group problem-solving: "What would be fair here?"
- Introducing simple structures like "talking sticks" or sentence stems: "When you…, I felt…, and I need…"
- Emphasizing private, not public, correction to protect dignity.

Middle School

- Conflicts often revolve around identity, belonging, and peer reputation.
- Social media amplifies conflict and makes it more public and permanent.

Effective conflict teaching includes:

- Helping students recognize escalation patterns—online and offline.
- Teaching them how to pause, seek clarification, and decide whether to engage.
- Creating safe spaces (circles, advisory) to talk about real peer conflicts and practice responses (Eccles & Roeser, 2011; Jones et al., 2017).

High School and Young Adulthood

- Conflicts become more complex: romantic relationships, work obligations, politics, and future plans.
- Power differences become more pronounced in work, law enforcement, and institutional settings.

Here, conflict resolution involves:

- Negotiating boundaries in relationships.
- Advocating for oneself with teachers, employers, or institutions while staying regulated.
- Grappling with conflicts that do not have easy solutions, including moral or political disagreements (Mezirow, 2000).

Adults continue to revisit the same skills in partnerships, parenting, workplaces, and community life. A 45-year-old who never learned to stay at the table may still respond to conflict with stonewalling, rage, or avoidance.

Regulation: The Doorway Into Conflict Resolution

Earlier chapters emphasized that no significant learning happens without regulation. Conflict resolution is a clear example. A dysregulated nervous system is not built for nuanced perspective taking or complex problem-solving (Immordino-Yang, 2016; Siegel, 2012).

When a child—or adult—is in fight/flight/freeze:

- Small slights feel huge.
- Neutral comments sound hostile.

- The body pushes for quick relief: shout, slam, walk out, or shut down.

Trying to teach conflict skills in that moment often backfires. The first step is to help everyone move back toward regulation:

- Breathing, grounding, or movement.
- Physical separation for a short period if safety is at risk.
- An adult modeling calm tone and body language.

Only then can we return to questions like:

- "What happened?"
- "How did you feel?"
- "What needs to happen next?"

In this sense, conflict resolution is emotional intelligence under pressure—using the same awareness and regulation skills, but in a charged situation (Denham, 2006; Jones et al., 2017).

Common Patterns: Attack, Avoid, Appease, or Problem-Solve

Across ages, people tend to fall into familiar conflict responses:

1. **Attack**
    - Insulting, yelling, threatening, or physically lashing out.
    - Feels powerful in the moment but often damages relationships and safety.
2. **Avoid**
    - Walking away, ghosting, staying silent, or pretending nothing happened.

- Protects short-term comfort but leaves issues unresolved.

3. **Appease**
    - Agreeing outwardly to keep the peace, while inwardly feeling resentful or unseen.
    - Often chosen by those with less power or who fear retaliation.

4. **Problem-solve**
    - Naming the issue, listening, expressing needs, and working toward a plan.
    - Requires regulation, practice, and some level of safety.

Most of us use all four at different times. The goal of conflict education is not to shame attack, avoid, or appease responses, but to:

- Help students notice their patterns: "When things get tense, what do you usually do?"
- Expand their options: "What might it look like to stay in this conversation one step longer, safely?"
- Address the conditions that make problem-solving feel dangerous or impossible, especially for students with less social or institutional power (Ladson-Billings, 2009; Tatum, 2017).

Power, Equity, and "Who Can Safely Speak Up?"

Conflict does not happen on a level playing field. Race, class, language, disability, immigration status, and gender identity all shape who feels safe to speak honestly and who does not.

For example:

- A Black student may hesitate to challenge a teacher's unfair comment, knowing they are already seen as "defiant."
- A bilingual student may avoid conflict in English because they cannot express themselves fully and fear being misunderstood.
- A student with a disability may be labeled "aggressive" for behaviors connected to sensory overload or communication differences.

If schools teach conflict resolution in a way that ignores these realities—telling all students simply to "use I-statements" or "talk it out"—they risk placing additional burden on those who are already at higher risk of harm (Skiba et al., 2014; Noguera, 2003).

Equity-minded conflict work asks:

- Who gets to initiate conflict conversations without being punished?
- Whose feelings and perspectives are taken seriously, and whose are minimized?
- How do discipline policies respond differently to the same behavior depending on who is involved?

Restorative practices, when done well, can address some of these questions by centering voice, impact, and repair rather than focusing solely on rule-breaking (Gregory & Evans, 2020). But they must be implemented with attention to power and bias, not as a quick replacement for suspension.

Practical Tools: Building Conflict Skills in Schools

There is no single program that "fixes" conflict. But there are concrete practices that help students and adults learn to stay at the table.

1. Conflict as curriculum, not just disruption

- Use real but anonymized scenarios from classroom life in advisory or SEL time.
- Have students analyze what happened, how people felt, and what other choices were possible.
- Treat these discussions as seriously as academic content, not as time-fillers (Jones et al., 2017).

2. Sentence stems and scripts

Provide and practice phrases like:

- "When you ___, I felt ___. I need ___."
- "Can we talk about what happened earlier?"
- "I'm too upset to talk right now; can we try again later?"

Practice them in low-stakes role plays so students have the words ready when real conflict hits.

3. Circles and structured dialogues

- Proactive circles build relationships before conflict.

- Restorative circles or conferences, facilitated by trained staff, can help students and adults hear impact and plan repair (Gregory & Evans, 2020).

4. Problem-solving conferences

One-on-one or small-group conversations that walk through:

- What happened?
- What were you thinking and feeling at the time?
- Who has been affected and how?
- What needs to happen now to make things as right as possible?

These questions shift the focus from fault to responsibility and repair.

5. Adult learning and support

Teachers and staff need training and coaching in conflict skills, not just management techniques:

- De-escalation strategies.
- How to set firm boundaries without humiliation.
- How to repair when they misstep with students or families (Jennings & Greenberg, 2009; Souers & Hall, 2016).

When adults experience conflict resolution as something that protects their dignity, they are more likely to offer the same experience to students.

Home and Community: The First Conflict Classroom

Children's first conflict lessons usually come at home: how caregivers argue, apologize (or do not), and talk about disagreement.

Some families model open, respectful conflict:

- "We are both upset; let's take a break and talk later."
- "I was wrong to say that. I'm sorry."

Others, often for understandable historical reasons, model:

- "Don't talk back to adults."
- "We don't air our dirty laundry."
- "Keep your head down and stay out of trouble."

Communities also teach conflict lessons: how neighbors handle disputes, how police and schools treat youth, how social media drama is handled.

Schools that respect families as partners in conflict education:

- Ask caregivers how they were taught to handle conflict and what they hope for their children.
- Share strategies in workshops or newsletters that families can adapt, not scripts they "must" use.
- Recognize that in some communities, being cautious about conflict with institutions is a survival strategy, not a character flaw (Ishimaru, 2019; Tatum, 2017).

When schools and families build a shared language around conflict—"staying at the table," "repair," "impact"—students experience more consistent guidance across settings.

The "On-Stage" Educator in Moments of Conflict

The earlier chapter on teaching as an on-stage profession comes into sharp focus here. In conflict moments, students watch their teachers closely:

- Does the adult retaliate when insulted?
- Do they shut down and withdraw?
- Or do they model staying in the conversation with calm firmness?

An educator who sees themselves as playing a professional role can think, "Personally, I feel hurt and angry. In my role, my job is to protect safety and dignity and to coach conflict skills." That mindset makes it easier to:

- Lower their voice instead of raising it.
- Set clear limits: "I will not let you speak to me that way," without attacking the student.
- Return to the conversation later to repair, if needed (Hargreaves, 1998; Jennings & Greenberg, 2009).

In those moments, students are not just learning whether they will be punished. They are learning *how adults who care about them handle conflict.* Those lessons last far longer than the specific incident.

Conclusion: Staying at the Table as a Lifelong Skill

Conflict resolution may be the competency that most clearly shows whether the foundations we have been building in this book are holding.

- Without accountability, conflict turns into endless blame.

- Without respect, it becomes dehumanizing.
- Without emotional intelligence, it spins into reactivity.
- Without resilience, people give up on relationships after the first big wave.

Learning to stay at the table does not mean tolerating abuse or ignoring injustice. Sometimes safety or integrity requires walking away, setting firm boundaries, or challenging systems. But even those decisions can be made with more clarity and less collateral damage when people have experience naming feelings, recognizing impact, and seeking repair where possible.

In the long arc from transitional kindergarten to later adulthood, conflict is inevitable: in classrooms, on playgrounds, in families, at city council meetings, and in workplaces. The question for schools and families is whether we treat each conflict as a random disruption—or as an opportunity to practice one of the central human skills we claim to value.

In the next chapter, we will look more closely at emotional intelligence in action: how children and adults "read the room" and "read themselves" in the everyday micro-conflicts and misunderstandings that either quietly erode or steadily strengthen our sandcastles over time.

References

Darling-Hammond, L. (2010). *The flat world and education: How America's commitment to equity will determine our future.* Teachers College Press.

Deutsch, M. (1973). *The resolution of conflict: Constructive and destructive processes.* Yale University Press.

Denham, S. A. (2006). Social–emotional competence as support for school readiness: What is it and how do we assess it? *Early Education and Development, 17*(1), 57–89.

Durlak, J. A., Weissberg, R. P., Dymnicki, A. B., Taylor, R. D., & Schellinger, K. B. (2011). The impact of enhancing students' social and emotional learning: A meta-analysis of school-based universal interventions. *Child Development, 82*(1), 405–432.

Eccles, J. S., & Roeser, R. W. (2011). Schools as developmental contexts during adolescence. *Journal of Research on Adolescence, 21*(1), 225–241.

Eisenberg, N., Spinrad, T. L., & Morris, A. S. (2014). Empathy-related responding in children. In M. Killen & J. G. Smetana (Eds.), *Handbook of moral development* (2nd ed., pp. 184–207). Psychology Press.

Gregory, A., & Evans, K. R. (2020). The starts and stumbles of restorative justice in education: Where do we go from here? *National Education Policy Center.*

Hargreaves, A. (1998). The emotional practice of teaching. *Teaching and Teacher Education, 14*(8), 835–854.

Immordino-Yang, M. H. (2016). *Emotions, learning, and the brain: Exploring the educational implications of affective neuroscience.* W. W. Norton.

Ishimaru, A. M. (2019). *Just schools: Building equitable collaborations with families and communities.* Teachers College Press.

Jennings, P. A., & Greenberg, M. T. (2009). The prosocial classroom: Teacher social and emotional competence in relation to student and classroom outcomes. *Review of Educational Research, 79*(1), 491–525.

Johnson, D. W., & Johnson, R. T. (1995). Teaching students to be peacemakers. *Edina, MN: Interaction Book Company.*

Jones, S. M., Brush, K. E., Bailey, R., Brion-Meisels, G., McIntyre, J., Kahn, J., Nelson, B., & Stickle, L. (2017). *Navigating SEL from the inside out: Looking inside & across 25 leading SEL programs.* The Wallace Foundation.

Ladson-Billings, G. (2009). *The dreamkeepers: Successful teachers of African American children* (2nd ed.). Jossey-Bass.

Maslach, C., & Leiter, M. P. (2016). Understanding the burnout experience: Recent research and its implications for psychiatry. *World Psychiatry, 15*(2), 103–111.

Mezirow, J. (2000). *Learning as transformation: Critical perspectives on a theory in progress.* Jossey-Bass.

Noguera, P. A. (2003). The trouble with Black boys: The role and influence of environmental and cultural factors on the academic performance of African American males. *Urban Education, 38*(4), 431–459.

Osher, D., Cantor, P., Berg, J., Steyer, L., & Rose, T. (2020). Drivers of human development: How relationships and context shape learning and development. *Applied Developmental Science, 24*(1), 6–36.

Siegel, D. J. (2012). *The developing mind: How relationships and the brain interact to shape who we are* (2nd ed.). Guilford Press.

Skiba, R. J., Arredondo, M. I., & Williams, N. T. (2014). More than a metaphor: The contribution of exclusionary discipline to a school-to-prison pipeline. *Equity & Excellence in Education, 47*(4), 546–564.

Souers, K., & Hall, P. (2016). *Fostering resilient learners: Strategies for creating a trauma-sensitive classroom.* ASCD.

Tatum, B. D. (2017). *"Why are all the Black kids sitting together in the cafeteria?" And other conversations about race* (20th anniversary ed.). Basic Books.

Chapter 11

Emotional Intelligence in Action

Reading the Room, Reading Yourself

When the Message and the Meaning Do Not Match

A seventh-grader slams their binder shut when a teacher says, "Let's check this one more time." The teacher hears disrespect and noncompliance. The student hears, "You're stupid; you never get it right."

A parent receives a brief email from the school: "We need to talk about your child's behavior." The administrator meant, "Let's problem-solve together." The parent, based on years of negative school experiences, reads it as, "You are a bad parent, and we are blaming you."

A principal walks into a classroom with a neutral expression, just checking on something. Students whisper, "Somebody's in trouble." The teacher's heart rate jumps, even though nothing is wrong.

In each scenario, the same observable event carries different emotional meanings for different people. Emotional intelligence is the set of skills that helps us navigate this gap between **what is happening** and **what we think it means** (Mayer, Salovey, & Caruso, 2008; Brackett, 2019). Earlier in the book, we defined emotional intelligence as the ability to notice, name, understand, and manage emotions in ourselves and others. This chapter focuses on how those skills show up in daily practice: *reading the room, reading yourself, and adjusting your response in real time.*

Emotional Intelligence as a Process, Not a Label

Since the 1990s, emotional intelligence (EI) has been framed both as a measurable ability and, in popular culture, as a personality label ("She's really high in EQ") (Goleman, 1995; Mayer et al., 2003). For practical purposes in schools and families, it is more useful to treat EI as a **process** that unfolds in three steps:

1. **Perception.**
   - Noticing emotional cues in yourself and others: facial expressions, tone, posture, energy level, and physical sensations (tight chest, rapid heartbeat).
2. **Interpretation.**
   - Making sense of those cues: "She looks annoyed," "He seems nervous," "I am starting to feel overwhelmed."
3. **Response.**
   - Choosing what to do with that information: ask a question, pause, set a boundary, offer support, or change course.

Breakdowns can occur at any step:

- We **miss** cues (a student's withdrawn posture, our own rising frustration).
- We **misinterpret** cues ("She's rolling her eyes at me," when she is actually anxious; "He's fine," when he is shutting down).

- We overreact or under-respond because our own emotional state is driving us more than the situation itself (Denham, 2006; Immordino-Yang, 2016).

The goal is not to become perfectly accurate or perfectly calm. It is to become more *aware* and *intentional* about how we are reading the room and ourselves, especially in high-stakes moments.

Reading the Room: Collective Emotion in Classrooms and Homes

Every classroom, family gathering, or staff meeting has an emotional climate—a mix of feelings in the space at any given time. "Reading the room" means paying attention to that climate, not just the content or task.

In a classroom, this might sound like:

- "The energy just dropped after that quiz. We need a quick reset before moving on."
- "Half of you look confused; let's check in before I add another layer."
- "I am noticing a lot of side conversations and some eye rolls. Something about this conversation is not landing."

For a parent or caregiver, reading the room might mean noticing:

- Tension around the dinner table after a stressful day.
- A child who is unusually quiet in the car.
- A teenager whose sarcasm is sharper than usual.

Effective "room reading" involves:

- Scanning faces and bodies, not just hands raised.

- Noticing patterns over time, not just one moment ("This class always gets restless right before lunch.").
- Being curious rather than defensive when the climate shifts ("Did something happen before my class today?").

Research on classroom climate shows that students' perceptions of emotional safety, care, and fairness are strongly associated with engagement, motivation, and achievement (Pianta, Hamre, & Allen, 2012; Roorda, Koomen, Spilt, & Oort, 2011). Reading the room is not "extra"; it is a core teaching and parenting skill.

Reading Yourself: The Internal Dashboard

Reading the room is only half of emotional intelligence in action. The other half is reading **yourself**. Many escalated situations begin not because a child's behavior changed dramatically, but because an adult's internal state shifted in ways they did not notice.

Common cues include:

- Physical: clenched jaw, shallow breathing, tight shoulders, racing heart.
- Cognitive: "always" and "never" thoughts ("They *always* do this," "This is *never* going to change.").
- Emotional: sudden spikes of irritation, shame, hopelessness, or fear.

Without awareness, these cues drive automatic responses: snapping at a student, sending a harsh email, or withdrawing from a conversation. With awareness, they become early warning signals:

- "My patience is wearing thin; I need a 30-second reset before I respond."

- "I am taking this student's behavior personally; what story am I telling myself?"
- "I am exhausted today; I may need extra support or simpler plans."

Self-awareness is not self-blame. It is simply admitting that our nervous systems and histories are part of the room. Educators and caregivers bring their own experiences of school, trauma, identity, and authority to every interaction (Jennings & Greenberg, 2009; Perry & Szalavitz, 2017). Reading yourself is an act of professional and personal responsibility: "My state affects their state."

When Stories Run Ahead of Facts

One of the most powerful ideas in emotional intelligence work is that we respond less to events themselves and more to the stories we tell about them (Brackett, 2019; Gross, 2015).

For example:

- Event: A student puts their head down during instruction.
    - Story A: "They are disrespecting me and my lesson."
    - Story B: "They might be tired, overwhelmed, or ashamed about not understanding."
- Event: A parent does not respond to multiple emails.
    - Story A: "They do not care about their child's education."
    - Story B: "They may be overwhelmed, working multiple jobs, or avoiding school because of past negative experiences."

- Event: A principal gives brief, critical feedback.
    - Story A: "They think I am incompetent."
    - Story B: "They are under pressure themselves and may not realize how they sound."

Emotional intelligence does not mean assuming the most positive story every time. It means recognizing that there are multiple possible interpretations and checking them before acting. Questions like, "What else could be true?" or "What don't I know yet?" create space between story and response (Beck, 2011; Brackett, 2019).

This is especially important in cross-cultural contexts, where behaviors are easily misread through a limited lens (Tatum, 2017).

Culture, Identity, and Emotional "Accents"

Emotions are universal, but the way we express and read them is deeply shaped by culture, race, gender, language, disability, and history (Matsumoto, 2001; Tatum, 2017). What looks like anger in one context might be enthusiasm in another; what looks like respect in one family might look like avoidance in another.

Examples:

- Direct eye contact may be considered respectful in some communities and disrespectful in others.
- A loud, animated tone may be normal family communication for one student and read as "aggressive" by an adult from a quieter background.
- A student on the autism spectrum might avoid eye contact or show flat affect while feeling intense emotion internally.

When educators and caregivers interpret all emotional cues through one cultural template, they risk mislabeling students as "disrespectful," "cold," or "oversensitive," when in fact they are communicating within their own emotional norms (Gay, 2018; Ladson-Billings, 2009).

Culturally aware emotional intelligence includes:

- Asking, not assuming: "When you talk like that at home, how do people see it?"
- Learning from families about how emotions are expressed and handled.
- Examining discipline data for patterns that suggest some students' emotional styles are penalized more than others (Skiba, Arredondo, & Williams, 2014).

In this way, EI becomes an equity tool, not just a personal growth project.

Emotional Intelligence in Micro-Moments

It is tempting to think of emotional intelligence only in big, dramatic situations—crises, fights, or major life events. In reality, the most powerful practice happens in **micro-moments**: the hundred small decisions each day that either escalate or soothe, connect or disconnect.

A few examples:

- A student answers incorrectly.
    - Low EI response: "No, that's wrong; anyone else?" (Student feels exposed; others become more hesitant.)

  - Higher EI response: "You're close—you're thinking about ___. Let's build on that," or "Thanks for taking a risk; who wants to add another idea?"

- A teenager mutters something under their breath while walking away.
  - Low EI response: "Get back here right now; you don't talk to me like that!" (Public power struggle.)
  - Higher EI response: Make a note, breathe, and circle back privately: "Earlier you said ___. I want to talk about that because our relationship matters."

- A colleague seems unusually short in an email.
  - Low EI response: Firing back a defensive reply.
  - Higher EI response: "I might be reading tone into this; let me ask for clarity," or "Can we talk briefly? I want to make sure I understood your message."

Over time, these micro-choices shape classroom climates, family relationships, and staff cultures. Emotional intelligence is the quiet architecture underneath whether people feel safe enough to learn and work together (Osher, Cantor, Berg, Steyer, & Rose, 2020; Pianta et al., 2012).

Teaching and Practicing Emotional Intelligence

EI can be taught and practiced explicitly, not just hoped for. Across ages, some practical approaches include:

1. Emotion vocabulary and check-ins

- Using feelings charts, mood meters, or simple "How are you *really* coming in today?" routines helps students and adults build language for inner states (Brackett, 2019; Denham, 2006).
- Normalizing a wide range of emotions ("It's okay to feel frustrated, scared, or bored; what matters is what we do with those feelings.").

2. Think-alouds by adults

Educators and caregivers can narrate their own EI process in age-appropriate ways:

- "I am starting to feel rushed, and when I feel rushed, I get impatient. I'm going to take a breath so I can listen better."
- "I noticed your face changed when I said that. I wonder how that landed for you."

These think-alouds demystify emotional processes and model regulation without pretending adults are always calm (Jennings & Greenberg, 2009).

3. Scenario practice and role plays

Using real, anonymized situations:

- "Imagine your friend posts something embarrassing about you online. What are three possible ways you might feel, three stories you might tell yourself, and three responses you could choose?"

- "Your teacher corrects you in front of the class. What might they be feeling? What might you be feeling? How could each of you respond?"

This strengthens the "perception–interpretation–response" chain before students face high-stakes decisions in real life (Jones et al., 2017).

4. Reflection after incidents

Instead of only asking, "What rule was broken?" teachers and parents can ask:

- "What were you feeling right before this happened?"
- "What were you telling yourself?"
- "Looking back, what other options did you have?"

These questions train students' internal observers, helping them see their own patterns and build self-management over time (Durlak, Weissberg, Dymnicki, Taylor, & Schellinger, 2011).

Emotional Intelligence, Risk, and Long-Term Outcomes

From a risk management perspective, emotional intelligence is not a soft extra; it is a protective factor. Students and adults with stronger EI skills are:

- Less likely to engage in aggressive or risky behavior.
- More likely to maintain supportive relationships with peers and adults.
- Better able to navigate stress, change, and feedback (Durlak et al., 2011; Masten, 2014).

For municipalities and school systems, investing in EI is a long-term strategy for reducing incidents, conflicts, and costly crises—from suspensions and dropouts to workplace grievances and staff burnout. Emotional intelligence sits underneath safer classrooms, healthier workplaces, and more resilient communities.

Connecting Back to the Five Lifelong Competencies

Emotional intelligence in action pulls together themes from earlier chapters:

- **Accountability:** We need EI to recognize our feelings when we are confronted and still choose to own our actions.
- **Respect:** We need EI to notice when someone's dignity is at risk and adjust our words or tone.
- **Conflict resolution:** We need EI to stay regulated enough to listen and seek repair rather than win.
- **Resilience:** We need EI to make meaning of setbacks and connect with others instead of withdrawing or attacking.

For educators operating in an "on-stage" role, emotional intelligence is the backstage rehearsal that makes the front-stage performance sustainable and authentic. For families navigating work, stress, and structural inequities, EI is a tool for surviving daily waves without letting them erode relationships.

Conclusion: Seeing With Softer Eyes

Emotional intelligence, practiced over years, teaches us to see with "softer eyes"—eyes that notice more, assume less, and respond with a little more wisdom each time. The sandcastle metaphor reminds us that we cannot control every tide. But we can shape how we interpret the waves and how we respond to each other when the water comes in.

Teaching children and adults to read the room and read themselves is not about perfection. It is about building a shared habit of pausing, checking our stories, and choosing responses that align with our deepest values rather than our most immediate impulses. That habit, practiced across TK classrooms, living rooms, staff meetings, and city offices, is one of the quiet ways we preserve sandcastles—not by stopping the tide, but by helping the builders see clearly, feel deeply, and act with intention.

In the next part of the book, we turn more directly to the relationship between families and schools: how mindsets about "custodianship," partnership, and blame shape whether emotional intelligence and the other competencies can take root across home and school, or whether they remain isolated efforts on either side of the shoreline.

References

Beck, J. S. (2011). *Cognitive behavior therapy: Basics and beyond* (2nd ed.). Guilford Press.

Brackett, M. A. (2019). *Permission to feel: Unlocking the power of emotions to help our kids, ourselves, and our society thrive.* Celadon Books.

Denham, S. A. (2006). Social–emotional competence as support for school readiness: What is it and how do we assess it? *Early Education and Development, 17*(1), 57–89.

Durlak, J. A., Weissberg, R. P., Dymnicki, A. B., Taylor, R. D., & Schellinger, K. B. (2011). The impact of enhancing students' social and emotional learning: A meta-analysis of school-based universal interventions. *Child Development, 82*(1), 405–432.

Gay, G. (2018). *Culturally responsive teaching: Theory, research, and practice* (3rd ed.). Teachers College Press.

Goleman, D. (1995). *Emotional intelligence: Why it can matter more than IQ*. Bantam Books.

Gross, J. J. (2015). Emotion regulation: Current status and future prospects. *Psychological Inquiry, 26*(1), 1–26.

Immordino-Yang, M. H. (2016). *Emotions, learning, and the brain: Exploring the educational implications of affective neuroscience.* W. W. Norton.

Jennings, P. A., & Greenberg, M. T. (2009). The prosocial classroom: Teacher social and emotional competence in relation to student and classroom outcomes. *Review of Educational Research, 79*(1), 491–525.

Jones, S. M., Brush, K. E., Bailey, R., Brion-Meisels, G., McIntyre, J., Kahn, J., Nelson, B., & Stickle, L. (2017). *Navigating SEL from the inside out: Looking inside & across 25 leading SEL programs*. The Wallace Foundation.

Ladson-Billings, G. (2009). *The dreamkeepers: Successful teachers of African American children* (2nd ed.). Jossey-Bass.

Masten, A. S. (2014). *Ordinary magic: Resilience in development.* Guilford Press.

Matsumoto, D. (2001). Culture and emotion. In D. Matsumoto (Ed.), *The handbook of culture and psychology* (pp. 171–194). Oxford University Press.

Mayer, J. D., Salovey, P., & Caruso, D. R. (2008). Emotional intelligence: New ability or eclectic traits? *American Psychologist, 63*(6), 503–517.

Osher, D., Cantor, P., Berg, J., Steyer, L., & Rose, T. (2020). Drivers of human development: How relationships and context shape learning and development. *Applied Developmental Science, 24*(1), 6–36.

Pianta, R. C., Hamre, B. K., & Allen, J. P. (2012). Teacher–student relationships and engagement: Conceptualizing, measuring, and improving the capacity of classroom interactions. In S. L. Christenson et al. (Eds.), *Handbook of research on student engagement* (pp. 365–386). Springer.

Perry, B. D., & Szalavitz, M. (2017). *The boy who was raised as a dog: And other stories from a child psychiatrist's notebook* (Rev. ed.). Basic Books.

Roorda, D. L., Koomen, H. M. Y., Spilt, J. L., & Oort, F. J. (2011). The influence of affective teacher–student relationships on students' school engagement and achievement: A meta-analytic approach. *Review of Educational Research, 81*(4), 493–529.

Skiba, R. J., Arredondo, M. I., & Williams, N. T. (2014). More than a metaphor: The contribution of exclusionary discipline to a school-to-prison pipeline. *Equity & Excellence in Education, 47*(4), 546–564.

Tatum, B. D. (2017). *"Why are all the Black kids sitting together in the cafeteria?" And other conversations about race* (20th anniversary ed.). Basic Books.

Chapter 12

Is School Your Partner or Your Babysitter?

The Custodian Mindset

Naming the Custodian Mindset

In earlier chapters, we explored the paradox of schools being asked to build stable outcomes on unstable foundations and the way social and emotional learning (SEL) undergirds all academic work (Durlak, Weissberg, Dymnicki, Taylor, & Schellinger, 2011; Immordino-Yang, 2016). This chapter turns toward a quieter but equally influential dynamic: how parents and caregivers *think about* the role of school in their child's life.

For some families, school is a partner. Educators are extensions of the caregiving network, trusted adults who walk alongside parents over many years. Communication, even when tense, happens inside an assumption of shared purpose.

For others, school is more like a custodian or coach for hire. Educators are professionals who temporarily "hold" or "train" the child during specified hours, similar to a sports league or after-school program. When the season is over, the relationship ends. In this framing, asking families to invest additional time or emotional labor can feel like a category error: *Isn't that your job?*

We call this the custodian mindset. It is not an insult. It is a metaphor that describes how many families, especially those stretched thin by work, economic instability, or prior negative experiences with schools, practically navigate a system that feels distant or judgmental (Hoover-Dempsey & Sandler, 1997; Ishimaru, 2019).

The custodian mindset shapes how adults interpret everything from a homework request to a discipline call. It influences whether "We are worried about your child" is heard as collaboration or accusation. It is not the only mindset in play, but it is a powerful one.

Where the Custodian Mindset Comes From

The custodian mindset rarely emerges from a single event. It is the product of overlapping forces.

Historical and Structural Roots

Families do not meet schools as blank slates. For generations, schooling in the United States has functioned as both a gateway to opportunity and a site of exclusion, particularly for Black, Brown, Indigenous, immigrant, and low-income communities (Darling-Hammond, 2010; Noguera, 2003; Tatum, 2017).

Parents who remember being tracked into low-level classes, punished for language use, or dismissed when they raised concerns carry those experiences into interactions about their own children. When schools now say, "We want to partner with you," it can sound like a new slogan layered over unresolved harm.

Sociological work on family–school relationships shows that schools often privilege "middle-class" forms of involvement: attending meetings at specific times, navigating written communication comfortably, and engaging in extended verbal negotiation (Lareau, 2011). Families who support learning through late-night conversations, shared stories, or modeling hard work may not see those efforts recognized as partnership. Over time, the message can be internalized: *School is their world. Home is ours. We hand the child over and hope for the best.*

In that context, seeing educators as custodians of the school day rather than co-architects of the child's life is understandable, even rational.

Economic Pressures and Time Poverty

The custodian mindset is also a response to time poverty. Many caregivers are navigating multiple jobs, shift work, transportation challenges, or elder care responsibilities. When every hour has a cost, the idea of attending yet another meeting, monitoring online portals, or volunteering in class can feel impossible, even if they want to be more involved (Maier, Daniel, Oakes, & Lam, 2017).

From this vantage point, school functions as a necessary and sometimes welcome holding environment: a place where children are physically safe, fed, and supervised while adults work. Parents may deeply appreciate individual teachers and still experience the institution primarily as a practical necessity. When educators then ask, "Can you come in for a meeting at 2:00 p.m.?" the request can land as both unrealistic and vaguely judgmental.

Research on parent involvement suggests that when families feel they lack the skills, time, or status to participate in "school-defined" ways, they are more likely to withdraw from formal engagement even while continuing to support learning privately at home (Hoover-Dempsey & Sandler, 1997; López, 2001). The result is that schools may misread constrained capacity as indifference.

Racialized and Classed Experiences with Institutions

Trust in schools is tied to trust in institutions more broadly. Communities that have experienced discriminatory policing, housing, or child welfare interventions may reasonably approach any institution—schools included—with caution (Ishimaru, 2019; Noguera, 2003).

When a school calls, the phone may carry not just the voice of a teacher but the echo of prior institutional encounters: social workers, probation officers, or case managers. In this climate, keeping school at arm's length—treating it as a bounded service rather than a full partner—can be a protective strategy.

For educators, recognizing these histories does not mean abandoning expectations. It means understanding that "custodian mindset" is not about families refusing to care. It is often about families trying to survive.

How Custodian Thinking Shows Up in Daily Life

The custodian mindset is rarely spoken aloud. It shows up in pattern, tone, and assumptions.

For Families

From a custodian frame, statements like these make sense:

- "I send my child to school to learn. That's what you're paid for."
- "I can't be at every conference; that's why we have teachers."
- "If there's a problem, call me. Otherwise, I have to work."

Families may still help with homework, ask their children about school, and value education deeply. But they conceptualize their role as distinct from the school's. Their responsibility is to provide shelter, food, and values; the school's responsibility is to provide instruction, structure, and credentials.

When teachers invite more active collaboration—such as co-creating behavior plans, practicing SEL skills at home, or attending workshops—some parents may feel that the school is pushing work back onto them. The phrase "That's your job" is not always spoken, but it often sits under the surface.

For Educators

Educators also carry mental models about families. When they experience repeated no-shows, hostile comments, or limited follow-through, they may begin to see parents as "uninvolved," "hard to reach," or "not interested." These deficit framings can harden over time, especially when staff are overwhelmed (Jennings & Greenberg, 2009; Santoro, 2018).

From this vantage point, it can be tempting to think of school as the *primary* site of development and home as a variable to be managed. The language shifts subtly from "our students and families" to "our kids and their parents." That one word, *their*, can signal distance.

In some cases, educators unconsciously adopt their own version of a custodian mindset, seeing themselves as responsible for holding the child's progress together while assuming little will change at home. This stance can be simultaneously compassionate and paternalistic, carrying both real care and an implicit judgment.

Two Conversations, Two Metaphors

Consider two versions of the same parent–teacher conference.

Conversation A: Custodian Frame

Teacher: "We've been having a lot of behavior issues with Jayden. He's not following directions and it's disrupting the class. We need you to reinforce expectations at home."

Parent (thinking): *So you want me to fix what happens at school when I'm not there? Isn't that your job?*

Parent (out loud): "Well, you're the teacher. That's what you're supposed to handle."

In this exchange, both adults locate responsibility primarily at school. The teacher is asking for home support but frames it as an extension of school discipline. The parent hears a critique of their parenting and responds defensively. No one articulates a larger shared goal beyond "getting behavior under control."

Conversation B: Partnership Frame

Teacher: "I wanted to talk with you because Jayden is having trouble staying regulated in the afternoon. We're seeing a lot of calling out and leaving his seat. My goal is for him to feel successful and safe here. What are you noticing at home around this time of day?"

Parent: "Honestly, by the time he gets home, he's exhausted and wired. I'm working late, and my mom is with him. We've been arguing about bedtime."

Teacher: "That makes sense. Could we work together on a plan that helps him practice calming skills in both places? I can teach and reinforce some strategies at school, and maybe we can pick one or two you're willing to try at home. We'll both keep an eye on what helps."

Here, the teacher explicitly names shared goals ("feel successful and safe"), invites the parent's expertise, and frames the problem as one of regulation across contexts, not simply compliance in the classroom. The parent is positioned as a co-designer, not an evaluator or subcontractor. The mental model shifts from custody to co-construction.

The content of the plan may be similar in both cases. The difference lies in the metaphor of the relationship.

Risks of the Custodian Mindset

The custodian mindset is not morally wrong, but it carries real risks for children, adults, and systems.

Fragmented Accountability

When parents and educators see themselves as operating in separate spheres, accountability for the five lifelong competencies—accountability, respect, emotional intelligence, conflict resolution, and resilience—becomes fragmented.

A child may receive one set of expectations at school ("own your mistakes") and another at home ("never admit weakness") without any explicit integration. Adults may blame each other when the child struggles: educators see "lack of home support," while parents see "school not doing its job."

Research on family–school partnerships suggests that such fragmentation undermines both academic and social outcomes, particularly for students navigating multiple stressors (Mapp & Kuttner, 2013; Osher, Cantor, Berg, Steyer, & Rose, 2020). Children learn to read the gap and sometimes exploit it, but more often they simply feel caught in the middle.

Erosion of Trust and Relational Safety

If educators perceive families as disengaged and families experience schools as judgmental, relational safety erodes on both sides. Over time, this can lead to:

- Less proactive communication (contact only when there is a problem).
- Increased reliance on formal, legalistic language.

- Greater use of exclusionary discipline and referrals to outside agencies.

These responses may protect adults in the short term but often deepen the very problems they are intended to address, including disengagement, absenteeism, and conflict (Skiba, Arredondo, & Williams, 2014).

Burnout and Moral Distress

For educators who care deeply, living inside a custodian frame can produce moral distress—the pain of knowing what students need but feeling unable to provide it within current structures (Santoro, 2018). When families repeatedly signal, "That's your job," and systems do not adjust resources, the emotional weight of responsibility becomes unsustainable.

Similarly, parents who feel they are being silently measured by school expectations they cannot meet may experience chronic guilt and resentment. Both groups are "doing their best with the conditions they live in" but are rarely invited to name those conditions together.

From Custodian to Co-Builder: Shifting the Frame

Moving beyond the custodian mindset is not about demanding more from exhausted families or asking educators to absorb infinite responsibility. It is about reframing the relationship around shared goals and more realistic structures.

Several practices can help.

1. Explicitly Naming the Partnership

Schools that are serious about partnership move beyond generic slogans and specify what "co-building" looks like. For example:

- "Our shared goal is to help every child grow in accountability, respect, emotional intelligence, conflict resolution, and resilience."
- "Here is what you can expect from us, and here is what we will ask from you, knowing your time is limited."

These statements, when backed by consistent action, can signal that partnership is about aligned purpose, not constant presence. Research on dual capacity-building frameworks emphasizes that families are more likely to engage when they understand *how* their contributions matter and feel their existing strengths are acknowledged (Mapp & Kuttner, 2013).

2. Designing for Time and Access

If partnership requires families to attend meetings at 2:00 p.m. on weekdays, it is structurally limited to those with flexible schedules. Co-building demands redesign. Options include:

- Offering conferences at varied times, including evenings or weekends.
- Providing virtual meeting options and phone check-ins.
- Using brief, multilingual communication tools that respect caregivers' time.
- Compensating community members or parent leaders who act as cultural brokers.

These changes are not merely conveniences; they are structural signals that schools recognize the realities of work, transportation, and childcare.

3. Using the Five Competencies as Shared Language

When educators and families use the same vocabulary—accountability, respect, emotional intelligence, conflict resolution, resilience—incidents can be reframed from "behavior problems" to opportunities to practice named skills.

Instead of saying, "He keeps talking back," a teacher might say, "He's struggling with respectful communication when he feels embarrassed." A caregiver might respond, "We've seen that too at home. Let's both focus this week on how he can use respectful words even when he's upset."

Shared language does not erase conflict, but it can keep both sides focused on growth rather than blame.

4. Honoring Family Expertise

A partnership frame requires genuine respect for what families know about their children. This includes:

- Asking open-ended questions about routines, triggers, and strengths.
- Inviting families to share cultural practices around discipline and respect.
- Treating parents' observations as data, not anecdote.

Research on community-based and equity-centered family engagement highlights that when schools position families as co-experts, trust increases and students benefit (Ishimaru, 2019; López, 2001).

Implications for Risk Management and Systems

From a risk management perspective, the custodian mindset is not just a relational issue; it is a systems issue. When schools operate as isolated service providers, they bear disproportionate responsibility for outcomes related to safety, behavior, and long-term well-being.

City leaders, risk managers, and district administrators concerned with claims, incidents, and long-term costs have a stake in shifting the frame. Investments in family engagement, SEL, and relational safety are not "extras"; they are preventive measures that reduce conflict, exclusionary discipline, and downstream involvement with more intensive systems such as juvenile justice and mental health services (Adelman & Taylor, 2006; Maier et al., 2017).

Framing families as co-builders also aligns with broader efforts to create trauma-sensitive schools and communities. Adults cannot co-regulate children effectively when they are locked in adversarial relationships with each other (Souers & Hall, 2016). Partnership is itself a protective factor.

Conclusion: Sharing the Sandcastle

The custodian mindset is, at its core, a story about who owns the sandcastle.

In one version, school builds during the day, home builds at night, and each side critiques the other's work from a distance. When the tide comes in, poverty, stress, racism, illness, policy shifts, each adult group stands on a different stretch of beach, pointing at the ruins.

In another version, parents and educators stand closer together. They acknowledge the tide. They acknowledge their limited resources and their different histories with institutions. They stop pretending the hill is level or that anyone can do this alone. And they decide, as best they can, to share ownership of both the sandcastle and the scaffolding around it.

Reframing school from "babysitter" to "partner" does not happen through a single workshop or slogan. It happens through repeated conversations, redesigned structures, and the steady use of shared language about what we are really trying to build: young people who can take responsibility, treat others with dignity, navigate conflict, understand themselves, and stand back up when life knocks them down.

In the chapters that follow, we will look more closely at how this partnership plays out in the emotionally charged moments when educators say, "I love your child," parents think "You don't even know them," and both are right in different ways. The goal is not to erase tension, but to hold it with enough honesty and care that the sandcastles we build together have a better chance of surviving the tide.

References

Adelman, H. S., & Taylor, L. (2006). *The school leader's guide to student learning supports: New directions for addressing barriers to learning.* Corwin Press.

Darling-Hammond, L. (2010). *The flat world and education: How America's commitment to equity will determine our future.* Teachers College Press.

Durlak, J. A., Weissberg, R. P., Dymnicki, A. B., Taylor, R. D., & Schellinger, K. B. (2011). The impact of enhancing students' social and emotional learning: A meta-analysis of school-based universal interventions. *Child Development, 82*(1), 405–432.

Hoover-Dempsey, K. V., & Sandler, H. M. (1997). Why do parents become involved in their children's education? *Review of Educational Research, 67*(1), 3–42.

Immordino-Yang, M. H. (2016). *Emotions, learning, and the brain: Exploring the educational implications of affective neuroscience.* W. W. Norton.

Ishimaru, A. M. (2019). *Just schools: Building equitable collaborations with families and communities.* Teachers College Press.

Jennings, P. A., & Greenberg, M. T. (2009). The prosocial classroom: Teacher social and emotional competence in relation to student and classroom outcomes. *Review of Educational Research, 79*(1), 491–525.

Lareau, A. (2011). *Unequal childhoods: Class, race, and family life* (2nd ed.). University of California Press.

López, G. R. (2001). The value of hard work: Lessons on parent involvement from an (im)migrant household. *Harvard Educational Review, 71*(3), 416–437.

Maier, A., Daniel, J., Oakes, J., & Lam, L. (2017). *Community schools as an effective school improvement strategy: A review of the evidence.* Learning Policy Institute.

Mapp, K. L., & Kuttner, P. J. (2013). *Partners in education: A dual capacity-building framework for family–school partnerships.* SEDL.

Noguera, P. A. (2003). The trouble with Black boys: The role and influence of environmental and cultural factors on the academic performance of African American males. *Urban Education, 38*(4), 431–459.

Osher, D., Cantor, P., Berg, J., Steyer, L., & Rose, T. (2020). Drivers of human development: How relationships and context shape learning and development. *Applied Developmental Science, 24*(1), 6–36.

Santoro, D. A. (2018). *Demoralized: Why teachers leave the profession they love and how they can stay.* Harvard Education Press.

Skiba, R. J., Arredondo, M. I., & Williams, N. T. (2014). More than a metaphor: The contribution of exclusionary discipline to a school-to-prison pipeline. *Equity & Excellence in Education, 47*(4), 546–564.

Souers, K., & Hall, P. (2016). *Fostering resilient learners: Strategies for creating a trauma-sensitive classroom.* ASCD.

Tatum, B. D. (2017). *"Why are all the Black kids sitting together in the cafeteria?" And other conversations about race* (20th anniversary ed.). Basic Books.

Chapter 13

The Parent Side

Exhaustion, Guilt, and Overcompensation

The Weight Parents Carry That Schools Often Do Not See

From the hallway, it can look simple. A parent misses a conference, does not reply to an email, or responds sharply when a teacher calls about behavior. On paper, it reads as "unavailable," "hostile," or "not engaged."

Inside the parent's life, the picture is very different.

There is the mother working an early shift who reads the school's email on her phone in a parking lot, glancing at the clock because she cannot risk being late to work again. There is the father whose own schooling was filled with humiliation and who feels his chest tighten every time he walks past the front office. There is the grandmother caring for three grandchildren, scanning a letter she struggles to fully understand and telling herself, "I'll deal with this later," because right now she has dinner to cook and a teenager in crisis.

When educators and parents meet around the sandcastle of a child's life, they bring very different daily realities with them. This chapter stays with the parent side of that meeting: the exhaustion, guilt, and overcompensation that shape how families hear the school's voice and how they respond when their child is discussed.

The goal is not to romanticize hardship or excuse harmful behavior. It is to widen the lens so that what looks like "non-cooperation" or "over-defensiveness" is understood as a complex mix of love, fear, shame, and survival.

Time Poverty and the Myth of the "Uninvolved Parent"

Research on family engagement has repeatedly found that parents across income and education levels value their children's schooling and want them to succeed (Hoover-Dempsey & Sandler, 1997;

Jeynes, 2010). What varies is not the desire, but the capacity to participate in ways schools are set up to recognize.

Middle-class norms of "good involvement" often include:

- Attending events and conferences during set hours.
- Responding promptly to emails or online portals.
- Helping with homework in specific ways.
- Volunteering in classrooms or on field trips.

Families juggling multiple jobs, non-traditional work hours, transportation barriers, or caregiving for other relatives may not be able to meet these expectations, even if they care deeply. Sociologist Annette Lareau describes how middle-class caregivers tend to practice "concerted cultivation"—actively managing school relationships and activities—while many working-class and poor families practice a more trust-based or hands-off approach, in part because of time, resources, and culture (Lareau, 2011).

When all of this is filtered through the school's lens, constrained capacity can show up as:

- Late or missing forms.
- Missed meetings.
- Irregular communication.
- Limited visible presence on campus.

It is easy, especially for stressed educators, to interpret these patterns as not caring. But as family engagement research has emphasized, many parents are doing academic and character work off the school's radar: talking with children about effort, discipline, respect, and faith late at night or on long car rides (López, 2001; Hoover-Dempsey & Sandler, 1997).

Time poverty also heightens the stakes of every school interaction. When a parent has had to swap shifts, borrow money for gas, or find last-minute childcare just to attend a meeting, even a small perceived insult can cut deeply. School becomes not just a place of learning, but another arena where they feel graded.

Guilt as a Constant Background Noise

Many caregivers carry a quiet, persistent guilt soundtrack:

- "I'm not home enough."
- "I yell more than I want to."
- "I can't help with the homework."
- "I wish I could afford better."

Cultural expectations of "intensive parenting" tell adults that good parents attend every event, monitor every assignment, and always know the right response (Hays, 1996; Johnston & Swanson, 2006). For parents living under economic or emotional strain, those expectations are impossible to meet. The gap between ideal and reality becomes a source of chronic shame.

When a teacher calls and says, "I'm concerned about your child's behavior," the parent does not hear this in a vacuum. It lands on top of that existing guilt. The message can quickly become, "You are not doing enough" or "You are failing."

Some common responses follow:

- **Minimizing**: "It's not that bad. Kids are kids."
- **Deflecting**: "Well, what are you doing about it at school?"

- **Avoiding**: Not answering calls or opening emails.
- **Overexplaining**: Sharing detailed stories about home stress to justify the child's behavior.

These responses are not signs that parents do not care. They are signs that their sense of adequacy is already fragile. Each new concern can feel like proof that the worst things they fear about themselves are true.

In this emotional environment, accountability conversations about the child can easily slide into unspoken judgment of the parent. Without care, the very discussions that could help build the five competencies become minefields instead.

Overcompensation and Fierce Defense

One of the most confusing experiences for educators is when a parent reacts with intense defensiveness or even anger when a behavior concern is raised. From the school's perspective, the situation may seem straightforward: a clear pattern, documented incidents, and a reasonable request for change.

From the parent's side, several layers often intersect:

1. **Love and Protection**

   Many caregivers see themselves, consciously or not, as the last line of defense between their child and a world they perceive as harsh, racist, classist, or unforgiving (Noguera, 2003; Tatum, 2017). When a school labels their child "a problem," it can feel like the first step toward a pipeline of exclusion, from special education misplacement to suspension to juvenile justice.

2. **Internalized Blame**

   If behavior is framed in ways that suggest poor parenting "There's no discipline at home," "They clearly have no structure" parents may defend their child as a way of defending their own dignity. Criticizing the sandcastle can feel like criticizing the builder.

3. **Fear of Losing Control**

   For families who have had negative experiences with institutions, any hint that the school might "write up," "evaluate," or "refer" their child can trigger fears about systems getting involved in ways they cannot control, including child welfare agencies. Over-defense becomes a pre-emptive attempt to keep authority at bay (Ishimaru, 2019).

This is where overcompensation shows up. Parents might insist, "My child would never do that," even in the face of clear evidence, or demand that all responsibility be placed on peers, teachers, or the system. They may threaten to go to the district, call a lawyer, or pull the child from school.

While these reactions can be deeply challenging, it is important to see the function beneath them. Overcompensation often tries to accomplish three things at once: protect the child, preserve the parent's sense of worth, and push back against systems they do not fully trust.

If educators respond only with more data and firmer tones, the underlying fear and shame go unaddressed, and both sides become more entrenched.

Race, Class, and Who Gets Judged

Exhaustion, guilt, and overcompensation are not evenly distributed. They intersect with race, class, language, and disability in ways that matter.

Decades of research have shown that Black, Brown, Indigenous, and immigrant families often encounter schools through a lens of surveillance rather than welcome (Darling-Hammond, 2010; Noguera, 2003; Tatum, 2017). For these families, interactions with educators are shaped by:

- Historical patterns of tracking and exclusion.
- Disproportionate discipline and special education referrals.
- Language barriers and fears related to immigration status.
- Stereotypes about "uninvolved" or "aggressive" parents.

A White, middle-class parent who questions a teacher's decision may be seen as "advocating." A Black or Latina mother who responds in the same tone and volume may be labeled "hostile" or "noncompliant" (López, 2001; Ishimaru, 2019). The same protective instinct is filtered through different assumptions.

Class also shapes whose exhaustion is considered legitimate. A professional parent who misses an event because of a business trip may be met with understanding. A parent who misses the same event due to a late shift at a warehouse may be quietly judged as disorganized or apathetic.

These inequities are not simply personal biases; they are woven into broader narratives about which families are seen as "good partners" and which are seen as problems to be managed. Naming this dynamic is essential if we want to build the kind of partnerships described in earlier chapters rather than inadvertently reproducing harm.

Parents as Learners and Cycle-Breakers

One of the most powerful shifts educators can make is to see parents not only as caregivers, but as learners and cycle-breakers in their own right. Many adults are trying to do something different from what they experienced growing up, often with little guidance.

Consider:

- A parent who grew up in a household where feelings were shamed but now wants their children to talk openly.
- A father who experienced corporal punishment and is trying to adopt non-violent discipline.
- A caregiver who left school early and is now trying to navigate IEP meetings filled with acronyms.

These adults are building their own competencies in accountability, respect, emotional intelligence, conflict resolution, and resilience at the same time they are trying to support their children. They are, in a real sense, students in a parallel classroom.

When schools treat parents as fixed "that kind of parent" they miss the chance to support this growth. When they instead approach families with respectful curiosity and a belief in their capacity to learn and adapt, the relationship changes (Mapp & Kuttner, 2013; Ishimaru, 2019).

This might sound like:

- "What did discipline look like when you were a child, and what are you hoping to do similarly or differently?"

- "What feels hardest about supporting homework right now?"
- "What would make you feel more confident in communicating with the school?"

These questions position parents as reflective agents, not just recipients of school directives.

Reframing "Difficult Parents" as Protective Parents

From a practical standpoint, one of the most useful mental shifts for educators is to translate "difficult" into "protective" in their internal narratives.

- The parent who shows up angry and accusatory may be fiercely protective.
- The parent who refuses to sign a discipline plan may be trying to avoid labeling their child.
- The parent who demands that their child be moved from a class may be trying to preempt what they see as a pattern of unfair treatment.

This reframing does not mean agreeing with every demand or avoiding necessary boundaries. It does mean that behind almost every heated interaction is a parent who is afraid, ashamed, or both. When educators recognize that, they can choose responses that lower defenses instead of raising them.

For example, a principal might say:

"I can see how much you care about your daughter. I want that energy on the same side as the school, not against it. Can we slow down and talk about what you're most worried about?"

Or a teacher might say:

"I know these conversations are hard. When we talk about his behavior, it can feel like we're judging you. That's not my intent. I want us to work together so he can feel successful and respected here."

These statements do not solve everything, but they acknowledge the emotional undercurrent rather than pretending it is not there.

Implications for the Five Lifelong Competencies

The parent side of exhaustion, guilt, and overcompensation directly affects how the five competencies are taught and received.

- **Accountability**: Parents who feel blamed may resist conversations about their child's responsibility because they hear it as an indictment of their own. Schools that frame accountability in shared, non-shaming ways ("What can each of us do differently?") make it easier for parents to engage.
- **Respect**: When families experience subtle or overt disrespect, they are less likely to support school expectations around respectful behavior. Modeling respect in tone, timing, and follow-through is not just good manners; it is part of the curriculum.
- **Emotional Intelligence**: Parents who have had little room for their own emotions may struggle to help children name and manage theirs. Inviting parents into simple emotion-language tools (like the same feeling charts or scripts used at school) can support parallel growth.
- **Conflict Resolution**: Every tense meeting between home and school can either reinforce "When we disagree,

someone must win and someone must lose" or demonstrate "We can stay at the table and look for a path that, while imperfect, honors everyone's voice."

- **Resilience**: Parents are often models of resilience in ways schools rarely see. Making space in school events or communications to honor family stories of perseverance can strengthen mutual respect and give children a richer picture of their own legacy.

Practical Steps for Schools and Systems

To respond wisely to the realities described in this chapter, schools and systems can:

1. **Design communication for real lives, not ideal schedules**
    - Offer flexible meeting times and virtual options.
    - Use concise, jargon-free, multilingual communication.
    - Ask parents their preferred communication method and honor it when possible.
2. **Train staff in trauma-informed and culturally responsive family engagement**
    - Help educators recognize signs of time poverty, shame, and mistrust.
    - Provide scripts and coaching for de-escalating tense conversations.

- Examine discipline and referral patterns for racial and class bias (Darling-Hammond, 2010; Skiba, Arredondo, & Williams, 2014).

3. **Create roles for parent leaders and cultural brokers**
    - Partner with trusted community members who can bridge language and cultural gaps.
    - Compensate these roles rather than relying solely on volunteer labor, which often excludes the most time-stressed families.

4. **Normalize parent learning and growth**
    - Offer workshops that focus on shared challenges (bedtime routines, screen time, conflict with teens) rather than only on compliance topics.
    - Emphasize that everyone, including staff, is learning about SEL and the five competencies.

These steps are not quick fixes. They are ways of slowly changing the conditions in which parents and educators meet each other, so that sandcastles have a better chance of being built together rather than in parallel.

Conclusion: Seeing Parents as Partners in the Tide

Parents stand at the water's edge with their own histories, fears, and hopes. Many are tired in ways that are hard to put into words. Many carry guilt that they are not doing enough, even as they are doing all they can. Many overprotect or overdefend because they know how quickly institutions can turn on families like theirs.

When educators see only the outward behavior—missed meetings, sharp emails, raised voices—they risk misreading the people they need most as adversaries rather than co-builders. When parents see only the school's demands and not the strain educators are under, they risk missing potential allies.

The work of preserving sandcastles requires both sides to see the other in fuller detail. For schools, that means recognizing exhaustion, guilt, and overcompensation not as evidence of apathy, but as signals of how much is already on families' shoulders. For parents, it means recognizing that educators who ask hard questions may be doing so not out of judgment, but out of a desire to help the child stand stronger between tides.

In the next chapter, we turn the lens toward the educator side of this relationship: the invisible labor, emotional weariness, and moral distress that shape how teachers and staff show up in these same conversations. Only by holding both sides in view can we begin to build the kind of home–school partnerships that give children a stable shoreline to grow on.

References

Darling-Hammond, L. (2010). *The flat world and education: How America's commitment to equity will determine our future.* Teachers College Press.

Hays, S. (1996). *The cultural contradictions of motherhood.* Yale University Press.

Hoover-Dempsey, K. V., & Sandler, H. M. (1997). Why do parents become involved in their children's education? *Review of Educational Research, 67*(1), 3–42.

Ishimaru, A. M. (2019). *Just schools: Building equitable collaborations with families and communities.* Teachers College Press.

Jeynes, W. H. (2010). The salience of parental involvement and student achievement: A meta-analysis. *Urban Education, 45*(3), 370–394.

Johnston, D. D., & Swanson, D. H. (2006). Constructing the "good mother": The experience of mothering ideologies by work status. *Sex Roles, 54*(7–8), 509–519.

Lareau, A. (2011). *Unequal childhoods: Class, race, and family life* (2nd ed.). University of California Press.

López, G. R. (2001). The value of hard work: Lessons on parent involvement from an (im)migrant household. *Harvard Educational Review, 71*(3), 416–437.

Mapp, K. L., & Kuttner, P. J. (2013). *Partners in education: A dual capacity-building framework for family–school partnerships.* SEDL.

Noguera, P. A. (2003). The trouble with Black boys: The role and influence of environmental and cultural factors on the academic performance of African American males. *Urban Education, 38*(4), 431–459.

Skiba, R. J., Arredondo, M. I., & Williams, N. T. (2014). More than a metaphor: The contribution of exclusionary discipline to a school-to-prison pipeline. *Equity & Excellence in Education, 47*(4), 546–564.

Tatum, B. D. (2017). *"Why are all the Black kids sitting together in the cafeteria?" And other conversations about race* (20th anniversary ed.). Basic Books.

Chapter 14

The Educator Side

Invisible Labor and Emotional Weariness

The Work Everyone Sees vs. the Work No One Sees

When people think about teaching, they often picture what is visible: direct instruction, grading, classroom management, emails, meetings. Those pieces are real. But they are only the surface of the sandcastle. Underneath lie layers of cognitive and emotional labor that are harder to quantify and easier to overlook.

Every day, most educators are:

- Tracking the emotional temperature of 25–180 students.
- Anticipating conflict and quietly preventing it before it starts.
- Translating curriculum into something that makes sense for wildly different learners.
- Absorbing students' stories about poverty, violence, racism, and family stress.
- Navigating shifting expectations from administrators, districts, families, and the public.

Sociologist Andy Hargreaves called this the emotional practice of teaching: work where feelings are not side effects but central to the job (Hargreaves, 1998). Teachers are expected to care deeply, show up fully, and keep caring even when they are exhausted, under-resourced, or under attack.

This chapter stays with the educator side of the paradox. If earlier chapters asked families and communities to see the child's sandcastle more fully, this one asks those same groups to look more closely at the builders: the people who step onto the stage every day to teach in conditions they did not design.

Teaching as Emotional Labor

"Emotional labor" is a term from organizational research that describes the requirement to manage one's feelings and expressions as part of a job (Hochschild, 1983). Flight attendants, nurses, social workers, and customer service representatives all perform emotional labor when they stay calm and kind in the face of anger or fear.

Teachers, too, are emotional laborers. They are expected to:

- Greet students with warmth, even after personal crises.
- Respond to disrespect with calm authority rather than retaliation.
- Show enthusiasm for content regardless of sleep, health, or morale.
- Absorb parents' frustration without collapsing or attacking.

Over time, this can create a gap between how educators feel and how they must appear. Many describe "putting on their teacher face" when they step into the classroom, regardless of what is happening in their own lives.

Research suggests that chronic, unmanaged emotional labor contributes to burnout: a state of emotional exhaustion, depersonalization, and reduced sense of accomplishment (Maslach & Leiter, 2016). When teachers have to constantly "act okay" without spaces where they can be real, they may begin to protect themselves by numbing, withdrawing, or becoming more rigid.

This is where the on-stage actor metaphor from earlier chapters cuts both ways. Seeing oneself as an actor can help teachers step into a professional role and not take student behavior personally.

But if the performance never ends and there is no backstage where the person behind the role can breathe, the cost becomes unsustainable.

When Your Job Becomes Your Identity

In the United States, work and identity are often fused. One of the first questions adults ask each other is, "What do you do?" and the answer is usually a job, not a hobby or relationship. Many teachers internalize this early and deeply. Being "a teacher" is not just employment; it is a calling, a moral identity, a way of being in the world (Santoro, 2018).

This fusion has benefits. It can:

- Motivate educators to keep learning and improving.
- Provide a sense of purpose and meaning.
- Create solidarity with colleagues.

But it also creates vulnerability. When lessons flop, students disengage, test scores dip, or relationships with families strain, the story in a teacher's head can quickly move from "Today was rough" to "I am failing as a person."

In this environment, every conflict with a student or parent becomes more than a disagreement about behavior or assignments. It becomes an implicit referendum on the teacher's worth. That pressure is intensified when public narratives about education swing between praising "heroes" and blaming "bad teachers" for systemic failures (Darling-Hammond, 2010).

The acting metaphor introduced earlier can help loosen this fusion. Seeing yourself as playing a professional role on stage offers some distance: "My role is under critique here, not my core humanity."

Still, this mental shift works best when it is supported by policies and leadership messages that reinforce it. Otherwise, teachers are asked to detach internally while being evaluated externally on metrics that feel deeply personal.

Invisible Loads: Secondary Trauma, Moral Distress, and Decision Fatigue

On top of emotional labor and identity fusion, modern educators carry several other invisible loads.

Secondary Trauma

Teachers who work with students experiencing violence, abuse, loss, or chronic instability often absorb those stories into their own nervous systems. Over time, this can lead to secondary traumatic stress: symptoms similar to post-traumatic stress that arise from exposure to others' trauma (Hydon, Wong, Langley, Stein, & Kataoka, 2015).

Signs include:

- Intrusive thoughts about students' situations.
- Emotional numbing or hypervigilance.
- Difficulty sleeping or relaxing.

Yet many educators receive no formal training in recognizing or managing secondary trauma, and few systems build in regular spaces for debriefing and support.

Moral Distress and Demoralization

Moral distress occurs when professionals know what would be right for those they serve but feel prevented from doing it by systemic constraints (Santoro, 2018). Teachers describe:

- Wanting to slow down for a dysregulated student but being required to "cover" a scripted curriculum.
- Believing that zero-tolerance discipline is harmful yet feeling pressured to use it.
- Wanting to build deep relationships while juggling large class sizes and constant testing.

This mismatch can lead to demoralization: not just feeling tired, but feeling that one's ability to do good work has been compromised (Santoro, 2018).

Decision Fatigue

Teachers make hundreds of decisions per day: how to respond to a comment, whether to move on or reteach, when to call home, whether a behavior needs a consequence or a conversation. Over time, this constant decision-making drains mental resources and can lead to defaulting to rigid rules or avoidance (Baumeister & Tierney, 2011).

Put together, these factors make emotional weariness almost inevitable without intentional supports.

How Exhaustion Shows Up in Classrooms and Meetings

Emotional weariness rarely announces itself with a sign around someone's neck. It shows up sideways.

In classrooms, it can look like:

- A teacher who used to greet every student now starting class without eye contact.
- Less patience for small misbehaviors and quicker moves to removal or referrals.

- Reduced creativity and risk-taking in instruction.

In meetings with families, it can look like:

- Relying on jargon or scripts instead of real conversation.
- Defensive tone when concerns are raised.
- Avoidance of difficult topics because there is "no energy left" to handle blowback.

From the outside, these behaviors can be interpreted as not caring, being rigid, or being "burned out and checked out." Inside, they are often survival strategies: ways to keep functioning when the emotional tank is empty.

None of this means that harmful actions should be excused. Adults remain responsible for how they treat children and families. It does mean that if we want better outcomes for students, we have to look honestly at the conditions under which educators are being asked to perform.

The On-Stage Role Revisited: Protection, Not Pretending

Earlier in the book, we explored the benefits of educators viewing themselves as performers or characters on stage:

- It can create healthy separation between role and self.
- It can reduce the tendency to take student behavior personally.
- It can help teachers intentionally choose their "character" for a given group (warm demander, calm guide, enthusiastic coach).

For this lens to be healthy, though, it must be framed as protection, not pretense.

Protection means:

- Recognizing that you are more than your job.
- Using role language in your own head ("Right now I am in my facilitator role.").
- Allowing yourself to step out of character when the day ends.

Pretense means:

- Feeling forced to smile or over-care without support.
- Hiding distress and never having safe spaces to be real.
- Using acting language to shame yourself ("If I were a better actor, this wouldn't get to me").

The acting metaphor becomes sustainable when paired with structures that respect teachers as human beings: mentoring, counseling, manageable workloads, and leaders who acknowledge emotional labor openly (Jennings & Greenberg, 2009; Hargreaves, 1998).

Educators as Everyday Risk Managers

From a risk management perspective, teachers and school staff are frontline risk managers whether anyone names them that way or not. Every day, they:

- Assess physical and emotional safety risks in real time.
- Make decisions that affect liability, health, and long-term outcomes.
- Document incidents, follow protocols, and adjust environments.

Yet most are not given the language, training, or support that formal risk professionals receive. Instead, risk work is embedded in "classroom management" and informal expectations.

When educators are emotionally worn down, their ability to perform this risk role is compromised. They may:

- Miss early warning signs of distress.
- React punitively instead of preventively.
- Avoid documenting or reporting because it feels like "one more thing."

Investing in educator well-being is therefore not just a kindness issue. It is a risk management strategy for schools, districts, and municipalities concerned with incidents, claims, turnover, and public trust.

Supporting Educator Resilience: Personal and Systemic Moves

It is tempting to respond to all of this by offering individual self-care advice: yoga, mindfulness apps, gratitude journals. Personal practices can help, but they are not enough on their own. Resilience is shaped by both individual skills and system conditions (Masten, 2014).

Personal Supports

- **Emotional awareness and regulation**

  Educators benefit from the same skills we teach students: noticing body cues, naming feelings, and choosing responses instead of reacting automatically (Brackett, 2019; Jennings & Greenberg, 2009).

- **Professional boundaries**

  Learning to say "no" to extra tasks when possible, setting email hours, and defining what *is* and *is not* in your role can reduce identity overload.

- **Peer support**

  Regular, structured time with colleagues to debrief, share strategies, and normalize struggles is protective. Informal venting helps, but intentional support groups or professional learning communities can go further.

Systemic Supports

- **Reasonable workloads and class sizes**

  No amount of individual resilience can compensate for chronic overload. Adjusting ratios, duties, and documentation requirements is central to any serious well-being plan.

- **Trauma-informed supervision**

  Leaders who understand secondary trauma and moral distress can create spaces where educators can speak honestly without fear of judgment or retaliation (Hydon et al., 2015).

- **Integrated SEL for adults and students**

  Social and emotional learning that includes adult competencies, not just student lessons, has stronger and more sustainable effects (Durlak et al., 2011; Jennings & Greenberg, 2009).

- **Clear, fair discipline and safety policies**

When educators trust that systems are consistent and just, they do not have to carry the emotional burden of patching over unfairness with personal heroics.

Conclusion: Caring for the Builders

If this book is about preserving sandcastles—helping children develop the competencies they need to stand in a world of shifting tides—then we have to ask hard questions about the condition of the builders.

What happens when the people responsible for teaching accountability feel trapped in systems that do not own their mistakes?
What happens when those asked to model respect are routinely disrespected in public discourse? What happens when those tasked with building emotional intelligence for children are given no time or support to process their own emotions?

The answer is not to blame educators for "burning out" or to scold families for not understanding how hard teaching is. It is to recognize that emotional weariness is a predictable outcome of certain working conditions, and to treat educator well-being as central to any serious plan for student success.

The acting metaphor is helpful here. On stage, the performance depends on the actor's preparation, support, and ability to step out of role and rest. Off stage, the actor must be allowed to be fully human. If we want classrooms where children can learn to be accountable, respectful, emotionally intelligent, conflict-capable, and resilient, we must build schools where educators can practice those same skills without constant depletion.

In the next chapter, we will bring the parent and educator perspectives together more explicitly, looking at how two groups of tired adults—each carrying their own history, fears, and hopes—can meet at the shoreline not as enemies or customers, but as co-authors of the sandcastle they share.

References

Baumeister, R. F., & Tierney, J. (2011). *Willpower: Rediscovering the greatest human strength*. Penguin.

Brackett, M. A. (2019). *Permission to feel: Unlocking the power of emotions to help our kids, ourselves, and our society thrive.* Celadon Books.

Darling-Hammond, L. (2010). *The flat world and education: How America's commitment to equity will determine our future.* Teachers College Press.

Durlak, J. A., Weissberg, R. P., Dymnicki, A. B., Taylor, R. D., & Schellinger, K. B. (2011). The impact of enhancing students' social and emotional learning: A meta-analysis of school-based universal interventions. *Child Development, 82*(1), 405–432.

Hargreaves, A. (1998). The emotional practice of teaching. *Teaching and Teacher Education, 14*(8), 835–854.

Hochschild, A. R. (1983). *The managed heart: Commercialization of human feeling.* University of California Press.

Hydon, S., Wong, M., Langley, A. K., Stein, B. D., & Kataoka, S. H. (2015). Preventing secondary traumatic stress in educators. *Child and Adolescent Psychiatric Clinics of North America, 24*(2), 319–333.

Jennings, P. A., & Greenberg, M. T. (2009). The prosocial classroom: Teacher social and emotional competence in relation to student and classroom outcomes. *Review of Educational Research, 79*(1), 491–525.

Maslach, C., & Leiter, M. P. (2016). Understanding the burnout experience: Recent research and its implications for psychiatry. *World Psychiatry, 15*(2), 103–111.

Masten, A. S. (2014). *Ordinary magic: Resilience in development.* Guilford Press.

Santoro, D. A. (2018). *Demoralized: Why teachers leave the profession they love and how they can stay*. Harvard Education Press.

Chapter 15

"I Love Your Son" vs. "You Don't Even Know Him"

When Love Sounds Like a Script

The Moment in the Meeting

A teacher sits across from a parent in a small conference room. The data are on the table: attendance, grades, behavior notes. Everyone knows this conversation might be tense.

Trying to reassure, the teacher leans forward and says, "I want you to know I love your son. I care about him like he's one of my own."

There is a pause. The parent's face tightens.

"You don't even know him," they say. "You see him for a few hours a day. You don't see what he's been through. You don't see how hard we're working. Don't tell me you love him."

The air in the room changes. The teacher feels stung, misunderstood. The parent feels defensive, misunderstood. Both believe they are the one who is truly seeing the child.

This chapter stays with that moment. Not because the words themselves are magic, but because they reveal deeper layers of how love, care, and authority get tangled in school–family relationships, especially in communities shaped by racism, poverty, and historical mistrust of institutions (Darling-Hammond, 2010; Ishimaru, 2019; Tatum, 2017).

What Educators Mean When They Say "I Love Your Child"

For many teachers, saying "I love your child" is not a casual line. It comes from real affection, long hours, and a sense of sacred responsibility. They:

- Laugh at students' jokes and quirks.
- Worry about them on weekends.

- Celebrate their breakthroughs and hurt when they stumble.
- Feel called, not just employed, to be in this work (Hargreaves, 1998; Santoro, 2018).

In that context, "I love your son" is shorthand for:

- "I see something in him."
- "He matters to me."
- "I am not writing him off."

It is also a way of countering the stereotype of the "uncaring school." Teachers may fear that families see them only as disciplinarians or bureaucrats. Saying "I love him" is an attempt to stand on the same emotional ground as the parent.

There is nothing inherently wrong with this impulse. The problem is not that educators care too much. It is that those words land in a context far bigger than the classroom.

What Parents Hear: Scripts, Conditions, and History

When a parent responds, "You don't even know him," it can sound like rejection of the teacher's heart. Underneath, there are often older stories talking.

Parents may hear "I love your son" as:

- **A script**: a line they have heard before in meetings right before harsh discipline, special education referral, or exclusion "We love him, but we can't have him here if he keeps doing this."
- **Conditional affection**: warmth that seems tied to compliance, easy temperament, or performance.

- **Institutional voice**: not just one teacher, but the weight of a system that has routinely misread, over-disciplined, or underserved children like theirs (Noguera, 2003; Skiba, Arredondo, & Williams, 2014).

For families of color, immigrant families, or families of students with disabilities, there is often a long memory of schools saying they "care" while simultaneously:

- Lowering expectations.
- Ignoring racism or bullying.
- Treating their concerns as overreactions.
- Removing their children from classrooms rather than adapting environments (Darling-Hammond, 2010; Tatum, 2017).

In that light, "You don't even know him" is less about an individual teacher's sincerity and more about a structural truth: school staff see children in one setting, for a slice of the day, through the lens of institutional norms. Families see the same child across nights, weekends, crises, and years.

The two know different sides of the same person. Conflict arises when either side claims the full truth.

The Many Meanings of "Knowing" a Child

Knowing a child is not a single act. It is layered:

- **Contextual knowing**: how a student behaves in a specific environment—classroom, playground, church, sports field.

- **Historical knowing**: understanding the child's story over time; their moves, losses, diagnoses, cultural traditions, and joys.
- **Relational knowing**: the felt sense of connection, trust, and mutual recognition.

Educators tend to have deep contextual knowing in school settings and partial historical knowing if trust has grown with the family. Parents and caregivers often hold extensive historical and relational knowledge that schools rarely fully see or validate (Hoover-Dempsey & Sandler, 1997; López, 2001).

When a teacher says, "I know him," they are usually referring to contextual knowing: "I know what he is like in my class, with peers, under the demands of school." When a parent says, "You don't know him," they are pointing to historical and relational knowing: "You don't know his nights, his fears, his tenderness, his history with adults."

Both are right. Both are incomplete. Trouble comes when either kind of knowing is treated as the whole picture.

Love, Power, and Conditional Care

Love in schools is never neutral. It moves through power.

Educators have power to:

- Grade, refer, and recommend.
- Remove students from classrooms.
- Shape narratives about a child in records and staff discussions.

Families have power to:

- Withdraw consent or participation.
- Escalate concerns to higher authorities.
- Frame the school in community conversations.

When a person with institutional power says, "I love your child," families may listen closely for whether that love is unconditional or conditional:

- "We love your child *as long as* he follows our rules."
- "We love your child *as long as* she fits our expectations."

If love seems to evaporate when a child is disruptive, traumatized, resistant, or different, it does not feel like love. It feels like tolerance with a limit. For communities who have experienced schools as gatekeepers rather than allies, this conditionality is especially painful (Ladson-Billings, 2009; Noddings, 2013).

At the same time, teachers are human. They have capacity limits. They cannot single-handedly hold infinite patience or unconditional positive regard in systems that undercut their efforts. Love in this context cannot be purely sentimental. It has to be anchored in structure, boundaries, and shared responsibility.

When Caring Words Outrun Caring Structures

The tension between "I love your son" and "You don't even know him" is a tension between words and structures.

Schools may say:

- "We are a family."
- "We care about every child."

- "We are here for you."

Yet families notice:

- Rushed conferences where nobody seems to have read the file.
- Discipline decisions that do not account for trauma or disability.
- Inconsistent responses to bullying or racist incidents.
- Lack of interpreters or translated materials.

When caring language is not backed by dependable action, it begins to sound hollow. Parents are not unreasonable to ask, "If you love him, why does love look like this?"

Educators feel this too. Many experience what Santoro (2018) calls demoralization, the pain of wanting to do right by students while working inside systems that undermine their efforts. Teachers may say "I love your child" while privately feeling that time, class size, mandates, or policies make it impossible to show that love in the way the child deserves.

The result is emotional dissonance on both sides.

Toward Authentic Language: "I Care and I'm Still Learning Him"

So what does more authentic communication sound like in that conference room? There is no perfect script, but there are healthier patterns.

Instead of asserting full knowledge or total love, educators can lean into:

- **Care**: "I care a lot about your child's well-being and success."
- **Humility**: "I know I am seeing him in one context, and you have a much fuller picture."
- **Curiosity**: "Help me understand him better so I can support him more effectively."

For example:

"I want you to know that your son matters to me. I care about him and I'm invested in his success here. I also know I'm seeing him in just one slice of his life. You know him in ways I don't. Could you tell me what you wish teachers understood about him?"

Or:

"When I say I care about your daughter, I mean I think about her when I plan, I worry when she seems off, and I want her to feel safe and respected here. I know I can still get things wrong. If I've misunderstood her or your family, I want to hear that."

These statements avoid claiming ownership of the word *love* in a way that might collide with trauma or history. They leave room for the parent's experience to stand alongside the educator's.

Listening When Families Push Back

When a parent responds with "You don't even know him," the reflex might be to defend: "Yes I do. I spend all day with him." A more constructive move is to treat that sentence as an opening, not an insult.

Possible responses include:

- "You're right that I don't know everything about him. Tell me what I'm missing."
- "I can hear there's a lot I haven't seen. What feels most important for me to understand?"
- "It sounds like my words didn't land the way I intended. I'm listening."

This kind of response does not require the teacher to abandon their observations or concerns. It simply pauses to honor the family's expertise and pain. Often, once a parent feels heard about the *mis*knowing they have experienced, they are more able to engage in problem-solving about current behavior or academics (Ishimaru, 2019; Mapp & Kuttner, 2013).

Listening does not mean agreeing with everything said. It means acknowledging that "knowing" a child is a shared, ongoing project.

Shared Love, Different Lenses

One way to reframe these moments is to assume that both sides **love the child**, but from different positions and with different tools.

Parents' love is:

- Rooted in history, biology, or chosen family ties.
- Intertwined with their own identity and life story.
- Carried through sleepless nights, bills, and milestones.

Educators' love (or deep care) is:

- Rooted in daily interaction, observation, and professional commitment.

- Intertwined with their sense of purpose and craft.
- Carried through lesson planning, advocacy, and countless small adjustments.

Conflict arises when one form of love claims legitimacy by denying the other. A more generative perspective says:

"We both love this child. We love him differently. Together, our love can be stronger if we respect each other's lens."

From there, conversations about the five competencies—accountability, respect, emotional intelligence, conflict resolution, and resilience—become shared work rather than competing evidence of who cares more.

Practical Moves for Educators and Systems

To move from scripted assurance to authentic partnership, schools can:

1. **Examine how caring language is used**
    - Notice when phrases like "we're a family" or "we love all our kids" show up.
    - Ask whether policies and practices match those claims.
2. **Train staff in culturally responsive, trauma-aware communication**
    - Explore how phrases land differently across cultures and histories.
    - Practice responses when families challenge educators' perceptions.

3. **Build structures that embody care**
    - Smaller caseloads or advisory systems where staff can build deeper relationships.
    - Time for home visits or community walks, especially in early grades.
    - Regular, positive contact with families that is not limited to crises.
4. **Co-create narratives about children**
    - Use meetings to jointly write "Student Strengths and Needs" summaries that include both family and educator perspectives.
    - Revisit these narratives over time, allowing them to evolve.

These moves do not eliminate tension, but they make it more likely that when someone says, "I care about your child," the words will ring true.

Conclusion: Love That Stays at the Table

At its best, education is an act of shared love: families, educators, and communities pooling their energy to help young people become who they are meant to be. At its worst, "love" is invoked as a soft cover for hard practices that exclude, shame, or sort children.

The clash between "I love your son" and "You don't even know him" is a reminder that language alone cannot carry the weight of trust. For love to be credible in schools, it has to show up in:

- How we speak *and* how we listen.

- How we hold boundaries *and* protect dignity.
- How we own our mistakes *and* repair when harm is done.

If preserving sandcastles means helping children build solid inner foundations, then adults have to be honest about the foundations of our relationships with each other. Authentic care is not afraid of being questioned. It does not collapse when a parent says, "You don't know him." It leans in, asks to know more, and keeps showing up in ways that match the words.

In the chapters that follow, we turn back to the sand itself: the policy, funding, and structural conditions that make it easier or harder for this kind of honest, shared love to thrive in schools and communities. The goal is not to find perfect phrases, but to build environments where words like "care" and "love" are backed by daily practices that children can feel in their bones.

References

Darling-Hammond, L. (2010). *The flat world and education: How America's commitment to equity will determine our future*. Teachers College Press.

Hargreaves, A. (1998). The emotional practice of teaching. *Teaching and Teacher Education, 14*(8), 835–854.

Hoover-Dempsey, K. V., & Sandler, H. M. (1997). Why do parents become involved in their children's education? *Review of Educational Research, 67*(1), 3–42.

Ishimaru, A. M. (2019). *Just schools: Building equitable collaborations with families and communities*. Teachers College Press.

Ladson-Billings, G. (2009). *The dreamkeepers: Successful teachers of African American children* (2nd ed.). Jossey-Bass.

López, G. R. (2001). The value of hard work: Lessons on parent involvement from an (im)migrant household. *Harvard Educational Review, 71*(3), 416–437.

Mapp, K. L., & Kuttner, P. J. (2013). *Partners in education: A dual capacity-building framework for family–school partnerships*. SEDL.

Noddings, N. (2013). *Caring: A relational approach to ethics and moral education* (2nd ed.). University of California Press

Noguera, P. A. (2003). The trouble with Black boys: The role and influence of environmental and cultural factors on the academic performance of African American males. *Urban Education, 38*(4), 431–459.

Santoro, D. A. (2018). *Demoralized: Why teachers leave the profession they love and how they can stay*. Harvard Education Press.

Skiba, R. J., Arredondo, M. I., & Williams, N. T. (2014). More than a metaphor: The contribution of exclusionary discipline to a school-to-prison pipeline. *Equity & Excellence in Education, 47*(4), 546–564.

Tatum, B. D. (2017). *"Why are all the Black kids sitting together in the cafeteria?" And other conversations about race* (20th anniversary ed.). Basic Books.

Chapter 16

Practicing Co-Regulation

Adults First, Children Second

Why We Have to Start With Grown-Ups

It is tempting to start every conversation about social and emotional learning (SEL) with children: how to teach them calming strategies, conflict skills, or emotional vocabulary. The reality is simpler and harder: children learn regulation inside relationships, not worksheets (Shonkoff et al., 2012; Siegel, 2012).

A kindergarten student who melts down after lunch is not just responding to hunger, noise, or a difficult task. They are responding to the nervous systems around them: the calm or tension in the teacher's voice, the predictability of routines, and the unspoken pressure in the room. A teenager who "blows up" when corrected is reading not only the words, but the adult's micro-expressions, body posture, and history of responses.

Co-regulation is the process by which one nervous system helps another find its footing. It is the adult who stays grounded while a child is flooded, the parent who breathes slowly while their teenager rages, the teacher who softens tone and lowers volume when the class escalates. Over time, repeated co-regulated experiences help children build self-regulation; the brain wires itself through thousands of shared moments (Porges, 2011; Perry & Szalavitz, 2017).

If we want accountability, respect, conflict resolution, emotional intelligence, and resilience to stick, then adults have to be the first and most consistent practitioners of regulation. Otherwise we are asking children to do something we are not modeling.

What Co-Regulation Is (and Is Not)

Co-regulation is not:

- Letting everything go.

- Avoiding consequences.
- Ignoring harm.

Co-regulation is:

- Helping a child's body and brain come back into a window where thinking and learning are possible (Siegel, 2012; Shanker, 2016).
- Staying connected and predictable long enough for teaching, consequences, or repair to land.
- Using your own regulation as a tool rather than relying only on rules and volume.

Neuroscience gives us a simple picture:

- When a child is calm, the "thinking brain" (prefrontal cortex) can handle instruction, feedback, and choices.
- When a child is threatened, shamed, or overwhelmed, the "alarm systems" (amygdala and related networks) dominate. In this state, the brain prioritizes survival; fight, flight, freeze, fawn, not reflection or compliance (Immordino-Yang, 2016; Perry & Szalavitz, 2017).

Co-regulation is how we help a child move from alarm back into a state where they can hear us, own their choices, and try again. It is a practical prerequisite for every other competency we care about.

Adults as Emotional Thermostats

In many classrooms and homes, adults function as emotional thermostats. Their internal state sets the baseline for everyone else.

- A calm teacher can lower the temperature of a rowdy class.
- An anxious administrator can send a wave of tension through an entire building.
- A parent who stays regulated during a child's tantrum can shorten and soften the episode.

This does not mean adults must be perfectly serene. It means their nervous systems are contagious. If adults are chronically over-taxed, sleep-deprived, unsupported, or carrying unprocessed trauma, their ability to serve as stable thermostats drops (Hydon, Wong, Langley, Stein, & Kataoka, 2015; Jennings & Greenberg, 2009).

You can see this in everyday scenarios:

- A teacher walks into class already frustrated from a staff meeting. Small noises feel bigger. Mild misbehavior gets labeled as defiance. The teacher's clipped tone activates students' defenses, and behaviors escalate.
- A parent, after a long shift, confronts a child about missing assignments. Their voice is sharp before the conversation even starts. The child senses attack and responds with fight or flight.

In each case, the adult's state—understandable given the circumstances—shapes the child's. Co-regulation invites us to **notice and adjust** our own settings before we try to change anyone else's.

The Adult's "Pause Button"

At the heart of co-regulation is a simple, difficult skill: the pause.

The pause is the moment between stimulus and response when an adult:

1. Notices their own bodily cues (tight chest, clenched jaw, racing thoughts).
2. Recognizes that they are moving out of their own regulation window.
3. Chooses a small stabilizing action before speaking or acting.

That action might be:

- Taking a slow breath in and a longer exhale.
- Glancing briefly away to reset visual focus.
- Planting both feet and relaxing shoulders.
- Saying, "Give me a second, I want to respond well."

This is not about being robotic. It is about protecting the relationship and the learning environment from our most reactive selves. Adults who practice this regularly are more likely to respond with:

- Firm but non-shaming language.
- Curious questions instead of instant accusations.
- Clear limits without personal attacks.

Research on emotion regulation suggests that how we appraise and respond to emotional triggers shapes long-term mental health and relational patterns (Gross, 2015). The pause is where appraisal can change: from "This child is disrespecting me" to "This child is dysregulated; how do I hold them accountable without losing my own footing?"

Co-Regulation in the Classroom

In schools, co-regulation is often the difference between a routine redirect and a full-blown crisis. Consider three snapshots.

Scenario 1: The Pushed Chair

A student slams their chair back and mutters when corrected.

- **Reactive response**: "Excuse me? We do not act like that. Go to the office."
- **Co-regulating response**: Teacher takes a breath, steps closer but sideways (not face-to-face), lowers voice. "Hey, I see you're heated. Sit back down for a minute. We'll talk in a bit. Right now just focus on breathing and not making it worse."

Later, when both are calmer:

"What was going on for you in that moment? Here's what I saw. Here's the impact on others. Let's talk about a better way next time, and there will still be a consequence for what happened."

Regulation comes first, accountability second.

Scenario 2: The Spiraling Class

After lunch, the classroom energy spikes. Side conversations multiply, small conflicts erupt.

A co-regulating teacher might say:

"Pause. Everyone, check your bodies. Are you at a calm level where you can learn? I'm noticing a lot of buzzing energy. Let's take 30 seconds feet flat, eyes on one point, three slow breaths. We're going to reset and then get back into this."

This is not a "baby" strategy. It is a practical way to bring 30 nervous systems back into a workable range.

Scenario 3: The Quiet Withdrawal

A usually talkative student goes silent and withdrawn for days.

Co-regulation here looks like:

- A gentle check-in: "I've noticed you seem quieter. How are you doing?"
- Adjusting expectations for public participation while maintaining connection.
- Looping in support staff if needed, with care and consent when possible.

In each case, the adult's steady presence is the intervention. Curriculum, consequences, and plans matter, but they ride on the back of that presence (Osher, Cantor, Berg, Steyer, & Rose, 2020).

Co-Regulation at Home

Families practice co-regulation constantly, often without naming it. Bedtime battles, homework struggles, sibling fights, and teenage boundary-testing all hinge on whether adults can stay regulated enough to guide instead of explode.

A few patterns:

- **Bedtime meltdown**

  - Co-regulating parent: "You're tired and your body is fighting sleep. I'm not going to argue. Let's do our routine together. You can be mad and still brush your teeth."

- **Homework refusal**
  - Co-regulating parent: "You're frustrated and done with today. I get that. We're going to take a 10-minute break, then do two problems together. I'll sit with you so you're not doing it alone."

- **Teen lateness**
  - Co-regulating parent: Waits until everyone has slept before addressing it. "We're talking about last night. I was worried and upset. I want us to agree on what happens next time. There will be limits because it's my job to keep you safe, but I don't want this to turn into a screaming match we both regret."

Parents do not need therapy degrees to do this. They need:

- Permission to acknowledge their own stress.
- Simple scripts and routines that keep them from defaulting to threat or withdrawal.
- Support from schools and communities that do not shame them for being human.

When home and school both practice co-regulation, children experience consistency instead of whiplash. The messages align: big feelings are real; behavior still matters; adults will stay in the room and help you through.

Adults' Unfinished Work

Co-regulation asks adults to touch their own unfinished stories:

- How was anger handled in your family?
- Were you allowed to cry without ridicule?
- Did adults apologize when they overreacted?
- Did anyone help you name what you were feeling?

Many educators and caregivers grew up with messages like:

- "Stop crying or I'll give you something to cry about."
- "We don't talk about that."
- "Be tough."

Those lessons do not disappear when we step into classrooms or parenting roles. They show up when we are tired and pushed.

Recognizing this is not self-indulgent. It is honest. Adults who have never had co-regulation themselves are being asked to provide it daily. That is a heavy lift. Without acknowledging this gap, we risk turning co-regulation into another standard people feel they are failing to meet.

Professional learning and parent workshops that include space for adult reflection and skill-building—not just strategies for kids—are essential (Jennings & Greenberg, 2009; Jones et al., 2017).

Co-Regulation and the Five Lifelong Competencies

Co-regulation is not a separate add-on to the five competencies; it underlies all of them.

- **Accountability**
  Children can only own their actions meaningfully when they are calm enough to think. Co-regulation creates the conditions for "What happened?" and "What will you do to repair it?" to land instead of triggering more shame or defiance.

- **Respect**
  Respect is often taught as tone and words. Co-regulation adds body and timing. An adult who regulates first is more likely to correct in a way that protects dignity, even while being firm.

- **Conflict Resolution**
  In heated moments, logic alone rarely works. Co-regulated adults slow the pace, name emotions, and structure the conversation so that problem-solving can occur without everyone going back into fight or flight.

- **Emotional Intelligence**
  When adults narrate their own regulation process ("I'm getting frustrated; I'm going to take a breath so I can listen better"), they are teaching EI in real time.

- **Resilience**
  Experiencing co-regulation teaches children that hard moments are survivable, not permanent disasters. Over time, this builds internal models of "When things go wrong, I can feel big emotions, get support, and then act."

Without co-regulation, efforts to teach these competencies often become abstract. With it, each competency has a living context.

What Systems Can Do

It is not enough to tell individual adults to "regulate better" without changing conditions. Systems that take co-regulation seriously:

- **Protect planning and collaboration time**
  Educators need time to breathe, think, and coordinate responses. Constant motion erodes regulation.
- **Integrate adult SEL into professional development**
  Not just how to run a student curriculum, but how to notice and manage one's own triggers and stress (Jennings & Greenberg, 2009; Durlak, Weissberg, Dymnicki, Taylor, & Schellinger, 2011).
- **Create reflective supervision and coaching**
  Principals, department heads, and coaches can normalize conversations about emotional load instead of focusing solely on compliance and test data (Hydon et al., 2015).
- **Align discipline policies with brain science**
  Policies that emphasize exclusion and rapid removal without regulation or repair often make behavior worse over time (Skiba, Arredondo, & Williams, 2014). Co-regulation-informed policies prioritize safety, connection, and learning over purely punitive responses.
- **Extend support to families**
  Offering accessible workshops, simple tools, and non-judgmental spaces where caregivers can learn about co-regulation pays dividends across home and school.

These are not luxuries. They are foundational if we are serious about building something more stable than test scores on shifting sand.

Conclusion: Calm Is Contagious, So Is Chaos

Tides will keep coming. Children will keep having big feelings, hard days, and rough seasons. Adults will, too. We cannot design a school or family life where nobody ever snaps, slams a door, or says something they regret.

What we can do is change the default pattern.

Instead of:

- Child escalates → adult escalates → everyone feels ashamed → trust erodes.

We can move toward:

- Child escalates → adult notices, regulates, and holds the line → everyone comes back to reflect and repair.

Co-regulation is not about being perfect. It is about who moves first. When adults take responsibility for their own nervous systems, they create a powerful ripple effect. Classrooms feel safer. Homes feel steadier. Children learn, in their bodies, that accountability and compassion can coexist.

In the next chapter, we will look at how a shared language. those five competencies we keep returning to. can function as a bridge between home and school. Co-regulation is how we keep the water calm enough for that bridge to be built. The language of accountability, respect, conflict resolution, emotional intelligence, and resilience is how we walk across it together.

References

Brackett, M. A. (2019). *Permission to feel: Unlocking the power of emotions to help our kids, ourselves, and our society thrive*. Celadon Books.

Durlak, J. A., Weissberg, R. P., Dymnicki, A. B., Taylor, R. D., & Schellinger, K. B. (2011). The impact of enhancing students' social and emotional learning: A meta-analysis of school-based universal interventions. *Child Development, 82*(1), 405–432.

Gross, J. J. (2015). Emotion regulation: Current status and future prospects. *Psychological Inquiry, 26*(1), 1–26.

Hydon, S., Wong, M., Langley, A. K., Stein, B. D., & Kataoka, S. H. (2015). Preventing secondary traumatic stress in educators. *Child and Adolescent Psychiatric Clinics of North America, 24*(2), 319–333.

Immordino-Yang, M. H. (2016). *Emotions, learning, and the brain: Exploring the educational implications of affective neuroscience*. W. W. Norton.

Jennings, P. A., & Greenberg, M. T. (2009). The prosocial classroom: Teacher social and emotional competence in relation to student and classroom outcomes. *Review of Educational Research, 79*(1), 491–525.

Jones, S. M., Brush, K. E., Bailey, R., Brion-Meisels, G., McIntyre, J., Kahn, J., Nelson, B., & Stickle, L. (2017). *Navigating SEL from the inside out: Looking inside & across 25 leading SEL programs*. The Wallace Foundation.

Osher, D., Cantor, P., Berg, J., Steyer, L., & Rose, T. (2020). Drivers of human development: How relationships and context shape learning and development. *Applied Developmental Science, 24*(1), 6–36.

Perry, B. D., & Szalavitz, M. (2017). *The boy who was raised as a dog: And other stories from a child psychiatrist's notebook* (Rev. ed.). Basic Books.

Porges, S. W. (2011). *The polyvagal theory: Neurophysiological foundations of emotions, attachment, communication, and self-regulation.* W. W. Norton.

Shanker, S. (2016). *Self-reg: How to help your child (and you) break the stress cycle and successfully engage with life.* Penguin.

Shonkoff, J. P., Garner, A. S., & the Committee on Psychosocial Aspects of Child and Family Health, et al. (2012). The lifelong effects of early childhood adversity and toxic stress. *Pediatrics, 129*(1), e232–e246.

Siegel, D. J. (2012). *The whole-brain child: 12 revolutionary strategies to nurture your child's developing mind.* Delacorte Press.

Skiba, R. J., Arredondo, M. I., & Williams, N. T. (2014). More than a metaphor: The contribution of exclusionary discipline to a school-to-prison pipeline. *Equity & Excellence in Education, 47*(4), 546–564.

Chapter 17

A Common Language

Five Competencies as the Home–School Bridge

Why We Need a Shared Vocabulary

Throughout this book, we have returned to the idea that schools and families are often talking about the same child in different dialects. Educators use words like "noncompliant," "disruptive," "disengaged," or "emotionally disturbed." Parents use words like "tired," "bored," "disrespected," "acting out," or "shut down."

Both sides are trying to describe what they see. Both are often frustrated that the other "doesn't get it." The result is what you have seen in meetings for years:

- A teacher describes a pattern and feels dismissed.
- A parent hears a judgment on their parenting and shuts down or attacks.
- The child learns to perform different identities in each setting and hopes the two worlds do not collide.

Research on family–school partnerships is clear: when adults share a common, concrete framework for what they are trying to build in children, collaboration improves and conflict becomes more constructive (Mapp & Kuttner, 2013; Ishimaru, 2019). Vague calls for "better behavior" or "higher expectations" are not enough.

This chapter offers the five competencies—accountability, respect, emotional intelligence, conflict resolution, and resilience—as that shared framework. They are not new buzzwords. They are a way of naming what we are really trying to grow, TK through adulthood, across home, school, and community.

The Problem With Jargon and Labels

Before we build the bridge, it helps to name what we are trying to cross.

School systems, like any profession, develop their own jargon:

- "Tier 2 supports"
- "Oppositional behavior"
- "Unmotivated"
- "Executive functioning deficits"

These terms can be useful among professionals, but they often leave families feeling confused or subtly judged. A parent who hears, "Your child has poor executive functioning" may interpret that as, "My child is broken," even if the educator's intention was simply to describe planning and organization struggles.

On the other side, families bring their own language shaped by culture, faith, and history:

- "He's hard-headed like his uncle."
- "She's grown; she thinks she's grown."
- "He doesn't respect authority."
- "She's sensitive."

None of these phrases are neutral either. They carry stories about gender, race, and what "good children" do in a given community (Lareau, 2011; López, 2001).

Then there are the labels everyone uses under stress:

- "Lazy"

- "Manipulative"
- "Crazy"
- "Bad kid"

Labels feel efficient. They simplify complexity. They also lock people into roles and make growth harder. When a student is consistently called "disruptive," adults may unconsciously stop looking for the anxiety, skill gaps, or trauma underneath the behavior (Skiba, Arredondo, & Williams, 2014).

A shared competency language does not erase all of this, but it gives adults a different starting point:

- Instead of "bad attitude," we can say, "He is struggling with respect in moments of embarrassment."
- Instead of "always fighting," we can say, "She needs more coaching in conflict resolution under peer pressure."
- Instead of "hopeless," we can say, "Right now his resilience is low; he has not experienced many successful rebuilds after failure."

The words we choose shape the options we see.

Introducing the Five Competencies as a Bridge

Earlier chapters defined each of the five competencies in depth. Here, we focus on how they function as a bridge vocabulary between home and school.

The bridge works when:

- Everyone (students, families, educators, leaders) knows the basic definitions.

- Incidents are routinely framed in terms of one or more competencies.
- Adults use the language with each other, not just with children.

In simple terms:

- **Accountability** – Owning actions and their impact, making amends, and learning from mistakes.
- **Respect** – Recognizing the dignity of self and others in words, tone, and action.
- **Emotional Intelligence (EI)** – Noticing, naming, and managing one's own feelings; reading others' emotions and context.
- **Conflict Resolution** – Handling disagreements in ways that protect safety and relationships, even when consequences are needed.
- **Resilience** – Recovering and rebuilding after setbacks, criticism, loss, or change.

When adults can say to each other, "We are focusing on resilience here," or "This incident is mostly about accountability and respect," the conversation becomes clearer and less personal.

Framing Incidents Through the Competencies

To see how this works, consider a few common school scenarios and how the competencies can reframe them.

Scenario 1: Cheating on a Test

A seventh grader is caught copying answers from a peer's paper.

Default framing

- "He is dishonest."
- "This generation just wants the easy way out."

Competency framing

- **Accountability**: "He made a choice that violated expectations. We need him to own what he did, understand the impact on trust, and participate in a fair consequence."
- **Resilience**: "He may be afraid of failing or believes he cannot succeed honestly. We need to build his confidence that he can struggle through material and still come out okay."

A home–school conversation might sound like:

Teacher: "We're addressing a breach of accountability. He copied on the test. At school, we'll have him redo the assessment and talk about how to repair trust. At home, you might talk with him about how your family sees honesty and what you expect when things feel hard."

This moves the focus from character assassination to skill-building and values.

Scenario 2: Disrespectful Tone

A high school student rolls her eyes and mutters under her breath when redirected.

Default framing

- "She is disrespectful."

- "These kids have no manners."

Competency framing

- **Respect**: "Her words and tone crossed a line. We need to address how she shows disagreement or frustration while still honoring others' dignity."
- **Emotional Intelligence**: "She might not fully recognize how her facial expressions and tone affect others, especially adults with authority. She needs coaching to connect internal feelings with external signals."

Home–school bridge:

Parent: "We're working on respect at home too. We've noticed the same eye-rolling. We can both send the message: you can disagree, but not in ways that tear people down."

Again, the shared language points toward a specific skill and boundary, not a fixed identity.

Scenario 3: Fight in the Hallway

Two students get into a physical fight after one feels disrespected on social media.

Default framing

- "They are violent."
- "That family is always causing trouble."

Competency framing

- **Conflict Resolution**: "They handled a real conflict by escalating to physical harm. They need intensive teaching and practice in how to respond when they feel humiliated or threatened."

- **Emotional Intelligence**: "Recognizing the early signs of anger and shame is part of prevention."
- **Accountability**: "There still need to be clear consequences for physical aggression."

The conversation can become:

Administrator: "We're taking safety seriously, so there are consequences. At the same time, we want this to be a turning point for conflict resolution and emotional intelligence, not just a suspension that teaches nothing. Can we work together on what both accountability and learning look like here?"

Scenario 4: Chronic Avoidance of Work

An elementary student consistently puts their head down and refuses to start assignments.

Default framing

- "Lazy."
- "Unmotivated."

Competency framing

- **Resilience**: "Right now, their ability to tolerate frustration is low. When tasks feel hard, shutting down is their default."
- **Emotional Intelligence**: "They may not know how to name or share their discouragement."

With families:

Teacher: "We're seeing a resilience challenge. When he thinks work will be hard, he gives up quickly. At school, we are setting up small, winnable steps and praising effort. At home, if you notice similar patterns, it could help to name when he sticks with something and talk about times in your own life when you had to keep going."

Each scenario becomes an opportunity to apply the same vocabulary in both settings.

Age-Appropriate Expectations

A common worry is that using shared language will turn into **adult expectations pushed onto children too early**. The goal is not for a first grader to give a TED Talk on "emotional intelligence." It is to grow these competencies in developmentally appropriate ways (Osher et al., 2020; Elias et al., 1997).

For example:

- **Accountability**
    - TK–2: Saying, "I did it," helping fix a small mistake, practicing simple apologies.
    - 3–5: Explaining what happened, noticing impact on others, participating in restitution plans.
    - 6–8: Reflecting on patterns, accepting fair consequences, planning different choices.
    - 9–12: Understanding how choices affect long-term goals, peers, and younger students; engaging in restorative processes.

Similar developmental "snapshots" can be mapped for respect, EI, conflict resolution, and resilience. The shared language stays the same; the **examples and expectations shift with age**.

When schools share these snapshots with families, it helps caregivers understand what is realistic at each stage and how to support growth instead of expecting adult-level skills from very young children or excusing everything as "just a phase" in older youth.

Culture, Race, and Whose Language Counts

Any common language has to grapple with a hard question: **Whose version of respect, accountability, and conflict resolution gets to define the terms?**

Without careful attention, school-defined norms can override cultural practices in ways that are inequitable. For example:

- Direct eye contact with adults is considered respectful in some cultures and rude or confrontational in others.
- Volume, gesture, and overlapping speech can signal engagement in one community and "talking back" in another (Gay, 2018; Hammond, 2015).

If the five competencies are taught only from a dominant cultural lens, students from marginalized backgrounds may hear, "Your way of being is wrong," not "Here are skills we can all use to navigate shared spaces."

To avoid this, schools can:

- Co-create definitions with students and families, incorporating community examples.

- Explicitly discuss how respect and conflict look different across settings and cultures.
- Reflect on discipline data to see whether certain groups are more often labeled as "disrespectful" or "non-accountable" (Skiba et al., 2014).

The goal is not to erase differences, but to establish **shared baselines for safety and dignity** while honoring multiple ways of expressing them.

Making the Language Real in Daily Practice

A common vocabulary is only powerful if it shows up **in the small moments**, not just in posters or strategic plans. A few concrete practices:

1. **Family–School Agreements**
    - At the start of the year, co-develop a short "Five Competencies Agreement" that describes how home and school will support each one.
    - Example: "At school, we will give students chances to repair harm when they make mistakes. At home, we will reinforce that mistakes are normal but taking responsibility matters."
2. **Incident Forms and Emails**
    - Replace generic "behavior forms" with brief descriptions tied to competencies: "This incident involved respect and conflict resolution."
    - Include a short note to families about which competency will be taught or practiced as part of the response.

3. **Student Self-Reflection**
    - After conflicts or challenges, ask students: "Which competency was hardest for you here? What would it look like to grow in that area?"
    - Over time, students learn to talk about themselves with more precision: "I struggle with resilience in math," instead of "I'm just bad at math."
4. **Staff Meetings and PLCs**
    - Use the five competencies to frame discussion about patterns, not just individual students.
    - "We're seeing a building-wide challenge in conflict resolution during lunch. How are we modeling and teaching it across grades?"
5. **Report Cards and Conferences**
    - Include short narrative comments that reference competencies alongside academic grades.
    - Example: "This term, Elijah has grown in accountability; he now turns in missing work more consistently after reminders."

These moves do not require buying a new program. They require a decision: this is the language we will use together.

Avoiding "Weaponized Competencies"

Any framework can be misused. The five competencies are no exception. If adults are not careful, the language can become another way to shame rather than support.

Examples of "weaponizing" the language include:

- "You're not being resilient; stop crying."
- "If you really cared about accountability, you'd agree with this consequence."
- "Respect means doing what I say without question."

To guard against this, schools can:

- Emphasize that competencies are skills to be practiced, not moral labels.
- Encourage adults to apply the language to themselves ("I did not handle that conflict well; I need to work on my own emotional intelligence").
- Build in regular check-ins about how the language is being experienced by students and families.

The bridge should feel sturdy, not like another tool for blame.

Conclusion: One Set of Words, Many Hands on the Sandcastle

A sandcastle built by one person washes away quickly. A sandcastle built by many hands—using the same basic tools and plans—stands longer, and even when it falls, everyone knows how to rebuild.

The five competencies are those basic tools. They do not solve poverty, erase trauma, or fix underfunded systems. They do give us a way to talk about what we are really trying to pass on to children when report cards are forgotten and test scores are no longer on a wall.

When parents, grandparents, teachers, principals, coaches, and community members can say in their own words, "We're working on accountability," or "This is a resilience moment," they are doing more than sharing jargon. They are acknowledging that they are on the same team, even when they disagree about strategy.

In the next chapters, we will follow these competencies across the lifespan, from TK sand play to high school hallways to adult workplaces, to see how they evolve and what it means to preserve sandcastles at each stage. For now, the invitation is simple:

Pick up this shared language. Use it gently. Use it often. Let it help you see the child in front of you as more than today's behavior and yourself as more than today's frustration. That is how bridges are built: one honest conversation at a time, using words that everyone can carry.

References

Brackett, M. A. (2019). *Permission to feel: Unlocking the power of emotions to help our kids, ourselves, and our society thrive*. Celadon Books.

Darling-Hammond, L. (2010). *The flat world and education: How America's commitment to equity will determine our future*. Teachers College Press.

Elias, M. J., Zins, J. E., Weissberg, R. P., Frey, K. S., Greenberg, M. T., Haynes, N. M.,… Shriver, T. P. (1997). *Promoting social and emotional learning: Guidelines for educators*. ASCD.

Gay, G. (2018). *Culturally responsive teaching: Theory, research, and practice* (3rd ed.). Teachers College Press.

Hammond, Z. (2015). *Culturally responsive teaching and the brain: Promoting authentic engagement and rigor among culturally and linguistically diverse students*. Corwin.

Hoover-Dempsey, K. V., & Sandler, H. M. (1997). Why do parents become involved in their children's education? *Review of Educational Research, 67*(1), 3–42.

Ishimaru, A. M. (2019). *Just schools: Building equitable collaborations with families and communities*. Teachers College Press.

Lareau, A. (2011). *Unequal childhoods: Class, race, and family life* (2nd ed.). University of California Press.

López, G. R. (2001). The value of hard work: Lessons on parent involvement from an (im)migrant household. *Harvard Educational Review, 71*(3), 416–437.

Mapp, K. L., & Kuttner, P. J. (2013). *Partners in education: A dual capacity-building framework for family–school partnerships*. SEDL.

Osher, D., Cantor, P., Berg, J., Steyer, L., & Rose, T. (2020). Drivers of human development: How relationships and context shape learning and development. *Applied Developmental Science, 24*(1), 6–36.

Skiba, R. J., Arredondo, M. I., & Williams, N. T. (2014). More than a metaphor: The contribution of exclusionary discipline to a school-to-prison pipeline. *Equity & Excellence in Education, 47*(4), 546–564.

Chapter 18

TK and Elementary

Sand, Buckets, and First Foundations

The First Castle Walls: Why Early Years Matter So Much

If you stand on a beach long enough, you can tell which sandcastles were built by very young children. The walls are thick and close to the ground. The design is simple. Adults hover nearby, helping pack sand and redirecting waves with their hands.

TK and elementary years are like that. Children's emotional and cognitive "walls" are just beginning to form. Neuroscience tells us that early childhood is a period of rapid brain development in which experiences of safety, connection, and moderate challenge literally sculpt neural pathways (Shonkoff et al., 2012; Immordino-Yang, 2016).

In these years, the five competencies we have named throughout this book are not abstract ideas. They are concrete, observable habits:

- A four-year-old saying "my turn" instead of grabbing.
- A first grader confessing, "I broke it," and staying in the room.
- A third grader trying again on a writing assignment after crumpling the first draft.
- A fifth grader walking away from an argument on the playground and asking an adult for help.

Too often, school systems treat TK and elementary as preparatory stages for "real" academic work later. Standards are pushed down; worksheets replace play; behavior is framed primarily in terms of compliance. When that happens, we pour energy into narrow skills while neglecting the broad foundations that will support – or sabotage – learning for decades.

This chapter focuses on those first foundations: what the five competencies look like in TK–5, how the sandcastle metaphor operates in early grades, and how families and schools can work together to protect what children are building.

Developmental Reality Check: What Is Reasonable to Expect?

Before we talk strategy, we need a developmental reset. It is easy to ask a kindergartener to "use your words" as if they had the vocabulary and impulse control of a college student. They do not.

A few key points from child development research:

- **Self-regulation is still emerging.** Many children are working hard just to sit in a group, wait a short turn, and manage disappointment without a meltdown. Executive functions like inhibition, working memory, and cognitive flexibility grow gradually through childhood and adolescence (Blair & Raver, 2015).
- **Emotion language is limited but malleable.** Young children often default to "mad," "sad," or "happy" for a wide range of experiences. Expanding vocabulary through stories, charts, and co-regulation increases their capacity to notice and manage feelings (Denham et al., 2012; Brackett, 2019).
- **Peer relationships are practice grounds, not finished products.** Conflicts, alliances, and hurt feelings are normal and necessary contexts for learning social skills, not signs that something is "wrong" with a class.
- **Family and cultural norms shape early behavior.** How loudly a child speaks, how they show respect, and how

they respond to adults are learned in homes and communities before school; school norms are an additional, not original, layer (Gay, 2018; Hammond, 2015).

When expectations ignore these realities, adults interpret developmentally normal behavior as moral failure. A five-year-old's tantrum becomes "defiance." A second grader's lying becomes "manipulative." A fourth grader's tears become "overly sensitive."

Refining our expectations means asking, "What does this competency look like *for a child this age* – and what is the next step forward?" rather than, "Why is this six-year-old not acting like a small adult?"

Accountability in TK–5: "I Did It" and "I Can Fix It"

For young children, accountability is not about lengthy explanations or complex restorative conferences. It starts with two simple abilities:

1. Naming their role in what happened.
2. Participating in a concrete repair.

A TK student who knocks over a peer's blocks can:

- Practice saying, "I pushed it."
- Help rebuild or fetch a teacher-approved replacement.

A second grader who blurts out a hurtful comment can:

- Acknowledge, "I said that."

- Offer a short apology and sit with a consequence (such as moving seats or losing a privilege) while still being welcomed back into the group.

A fifth grader who cheats on a quiz can:

- Admit, "I looked at someone else's paper."
- Retake the assessment and accept a natural consequence while working on study skills.

Adults support accountability by:

- Describing behavior clearly without global labels: "You threw the pencil," not "You're bad."
- Avoiding cornering questions that encourage lying ("Did you do that?" while staring at obvious evidence).
- Framing repair as a chance to fix, not erase, what happened: "You can't undo it, but you *can* help clean up and make things better."

Research on moral development suggests that young children build conscience not by fear alone, but by repeated experiences of making amends while remaining in caring relationships (Thompson, 2014). Early accountability is practice in staying in the room when you are wrong.

Respect: Dignity in Little Bodies

Respect in early grades is often reduced to surface markers: "Use kind words," "Hands to self," "Be quiet when the teacher talks." These cues matter, but dignity runs deeper.

For TK–5 students, respect includes:

- **For self**: Being allowed to say "no" to unsafe touch, to take a short break when overwhelmed, to have feelings without ridicule.
- **For others**: Learning that other people's bodies, materials, and ideas are not extensions of your own.
- **For differences**: Noticing that classmates have different family structures, skin tones, languages, or abilities – and seeing those differences treated as normal and valuable.

Early schooling is full of respect lessons disguised as routines: waiting in line, passing materials, taking turns speaking, listening when someone shares. Classrooms that emphasize mutual respect rather than one-way obedience are more likely to build lasting internal standards (Noddings, 2013; Elias et al., 1997).

Adults signal respect when they:

- Use children's names correctly and learn preferred nicknames or pronunciations.
- Apologize when they make mistakes ("I snapped at you; that wasn't okay.").
- Avoid public shaming (e.g., behavior clip charts that single out one child all day).

When children see that their dignity matters even when they are in trouble, "respect" becomes something they experience, not just something demanded of them.

Emotional Intelligence: Naming the Waves

In TK and elementary years, emotional intelligence (EI) is largely about recognition and naming:

- "My stomach hurts when I'm worried."
- "I feel hot and tight when I'm mad."
- "I get silly when I'm nervous."

Classrooms can build EI through:

- **Daily feeling check-ins** (face charts, mood meters, quick "thumbs up/side/down").
- **Story discussions** that ask, "How do you think she felt? What might he have been thinking?"
- **Modeling by adults**, narrating their own regulation in simple ways: "I am feeling frustrated. I'm going to take two breaths so I don't yell."

Evidence from SEL programs suggests that teaching young children to identify and talk about emotions increases prosocial behavior and reduces aggression (Durlak et al., 2011; Jones et al., 2017; Denham et al., 2012).

Families play a parallel role when they:

- Use specific feeling words at home ("disappointed," "excited," "worried," "embarrassed") instead of only "good" or "bad."
- Ask simple reflective questions: "What was the best part and hardest part of your day?"
- Share their own feelings in appropriate ways so children see that adults have emotions too.

The goal is not to turn every moment into therapy. It is to give children a vocabulary for the waves inside them so they are less likely to express everything through behavior alone.

Conflict Resolution: From "Mine!" to "Let's Fix It"

Conflict in TK–5 is predictable and frequent. Toys, space, attention, turn-taking, rules of games, and perceived fairness all generate disagreements. Early conflict resolution focuses on structured practice, not spontaneous wisdom.

Adults can:

- Teach and rehearse simple scripts:
    - "Stop. I don't like that."
    - "Can I have a turn when you're done?"
    - "Let's ask the teacher to help."
- Use visual tools (e.g., problem-solving steps on a poster) and walk children through them in real situations.
- Separate children temporarily when needed but prioritize return and repair when everyone is calm.

For example, two second graders push each other in line. After safety is addressed and everyone is calmer, the teacher might guide:

1. "Each of you tell me what happened, one at a time."
2. "What did you feel?"
3. "What do you wish had happened instead?"
4. "What can you say or do now to make it better?"

At home, caregivers can mirror this process with siblings: hearing both sides, naming feelings, and insisting on respectful repair even if they impose separate consequences.

Repeated practice builds internal scripts that students will reuse, consciously or not, in middle school, high school, and adulthood (Elias et al., 1997; Osher et al., 2020).

Resilience: Tiny Rebuilds Every Day

Resilience in early childhood is not heroic. It is often small, ordinary, and easy to miss:

- Trying to tie a shoe again.
- Going back to a puzzle after getting stuck.
- Returning to class after a hard morning and still raising a hand.

Adults can strengthen resilience by paying attention to **how** effort and recovery are praised. Research suggests that focusing on process ("You kept trying," "You found another way") builds a growth mindset and persistence, while focusing solely on innate traits ("You're so smart") can increase fear of failure (Yeager & Dweck, 2012).

In TK–5 settings, resilience grows when:

- Mistakes are normalized ("Everyone messes up; what matters is what we do next.").
- Perfection is not the standard; revision and drafts are expected.
- Adults avoid rescuing children too quickly from manageable frustration.

At the same time, resilience is not "tough it out" in all situations. Some children are carrying loads at home – poverty, violence, instability – that require additional support, accommodations, and referrals. True resilience-building acknowledges context rather than blaming children for understandable struggles (Masten, 2014; Jensen, 2009).

The Role of Play, Routines, and Relationships

It can be tempting, under academic pressure, to view play and relational time as luxuries. The opposite is true. Play, predictable routines, and warm relationships are the **mechanisms** through which the five competencies develop in early years.

- **Play** allows children to experiment with roles, rules, and emotions in relatively low-stakes environments. Negotiating who is "it," coping with losing a game, or pretending to be a parent or teacher are all SEL laboratories (Perry & Szalavitz, 2017; Whitebread et al., 2012).
- **Routines** (morning meetings, transitions, closing circles) provide a sense of safety and predictability that frees up energy for learning. Routines are also repeated opportunities to practice greetings, listening, turn-taking, and regulation.
- **Relationships** with teachers, aides, and peers shape whether school feels like a safe base or a threatening arena. A single stable, caring adult relationship has been repeatedly linked to better outcomes for children facing adversity (Osher et al., 2020; Masten, 2014).

When policy or practice squeezes these elements out in favor of more seatwork and testing, we may raise short-term scores at the expense of long-term competence. The sandcastle looks sharper for a moment but crumbles more quickly when real waves hit.

Co-Regulation in Early Grades: Adults as Breakwaters

Younger children borrow adult nervous systems constantly. A TK teacher's face when a cup spills, a first-grade aide's tone when a child cries, a parent's response to a scribble on the wall – these are co-regulation moments.

In practice, co-regulation with young children looks like:

- **Proactive regulation**
    - Building in movement, songs, and sensory breaks before children are "too far gone."
    - Using visual schedules and countdowns for transitions to reduce surprise.
- **In-the-moment support**
    - Kneeling to eye level, speaking softly, and offering simple choices ("Do you want to sit next to me or at the calm table?") when a child is overwhelmed.
- **Repair after adult missteps**
    - Acknowledging when adults lose patience: "I yelled. That may have scared you. I'm sorry. I'm going to work on using a calmer voice next time."

These practices do not eliminate misbehavior or meltdowns, but they shorten and soften them, making it easier to return to accountability, respect, and learning. They also model for children what it looks like when a grown-up is frustrated and chooses not to harm them.

Home–School Habits That Protect Early Sandcastles

The early sandcastle is especially vulnerable to differences between home and school. Children can adapt to multiple sets of rules, but they do best when the **themes** are aligned. A few examples of protective habits:

- **Shared language for feelings and behavior**
    - If a classroom uses color zones ("blue" for sad, "yellow" for wiggly, "red" for mad), families can adopt similar language at home, or vice versa.
- **Consistent messages about accountability**
    - When a child gets in trouble at school, families can avoid both extremes of "the teacher is always right" and "the teacher is always wrong." Instead: "We're going to listen to what happened, you will tell your side, and then we will plan how you will fix it."
- **Sleep, nutrition, and routines**
    - Basic needs are SEL supports. Reasonable bedtimes, breakfast, and predictable morning routines significantly affect regulation and attention in class (Jensen, 2009).
- **Positive contact before crisis**
    - Teachers sending brief positive notes, photos, or messages home build trust that makes hard conversations easier later. Parents doing the same ("He loved math today!") reminds everyone what is working.

None of these require extra funding. They require intentionality and a shared belief that **how** we handle small daily moments is as important as any single big program.

Equity in Early Years: Whose Sand, Whose Buckets?

The TK–5 years are where inequities often first appear in visible ways. Some children arrive with extensive preschool exposure, enriched vocabulary, and familiarity with school-like routines. Others arrive from under-resourced neighborhoods, unstable housing, or culturally mismatched early care.

If schools interpret these differences as deficits in children or families, they are likely to:

- Overidentify certain groups for behavior referrals or special education.
- Lower expectations for academic challenge.
- Rely on exclusionary discipline when children struggle to adapt quickly (Skiba et al., 2014; Darling-Hammond, 2010).

An equity lens in early childhood means asking:

- Have all children had access to the same kinds of buckets and tools – quality early learning, health care, stable housing?
- Are we judging families for structural barriers (transportation, inflexible work hours, language access) as if they were moral failings?
- Are our classroom expectations culturally responsive, or simply reflections of middle-class, majority norms (Gay, 2018; Hammond, 2015)?

When we see early differences as starting points rather than verdicts, we can design supports that expand opportunity instead of blaming children for the sand they were handed.

Conclusion: First Foundations, Not Final Products

By the end of fifth grade, many adults talk about children as if their trajectories are already set: "she's a leader," "he's a problem," "they're not college material." The sandcastle metaphor invites a different view.

In TK and elementary years, children are still learning:

- How to be in their bodies and in groups.
- How to recognize and express what they feel.
- How to recover from embarrassment and failure.
- How to treat themselves and others as people with dignity.

These are first foundations, not final products. The five competencies are in early draft form, written in wet sand. They will be revised many times by family events, adolescence, media, friendships, and work.

Our task in these years is not to perfect children. It is to:

- Give them safe places to practice accountability, respect, emotional intelligence, conflict resolution, and resilience in age-appropriate ways.
- Protect them, as much as we can, from unnecessary shame and exclusion.
- Help their caregivers and educators see each other as partners in shaping the same core capacities.

If we do this work well, the sandcastles children build later – in middle school identities, high school choices, and adult relationships – will rest on firmer ground. In the next chapter, we follow those children into middle and high school, where storms grow stronger, social tides shift, and the work of preserving sandcastles becomes more complex but no less possible.

References

Blair, C., & Raver, C. C. (2015). School readiness and self-regulation: A developmental psychobiological approach. *Annual Review of Psychology, 66*, 711–731.

Brackett, M. A. (2019). *Permission to feel: Unlocking the power of emotions to help our kids, ourselves, and our society thrive*. Celadon Books.

Darling-Hammond, L. (2010). *The flat world and education: How America's commitment to equity will determine our future*. Teachers College Press.

Denham, S. A., Bassett, H. H., Thayer, S. K., Mincic, M., Sirotkin, Y. S., & Zinsser, K. (2012). Observing preschoolers' social–emotional behavior: Structure, foundations, and prediction of early school success. *Journal of Genetic Psychology, 173*(3), 246–278.

Durlak, J. A., Weissberg, R. P., Dymnicki, A. B., Taylor, R. D., & Schellinger, K. B. (2011). The impact of enhancing students' social and emotional learning: A meta-analysis of school-based universal interventions. *Child Development, 82*(1), 405–432.

Elias, M. J., Zins, J. E., Weissberg, R. P., Frey, K. S., Greenberg, M. T., Haynes, N. M., … Shriver, T. P. (1997). *Promoting social and emotional learning: Guidelines for educators*. ASCD.

Gay, G. (2018). *Culturally responsive teaching: Theory, research, and practice* (3rd ed.). Teachers College Press.

Hammond, Z. (2015). *Culturally responsive teaching and the brain: Promoting authentic engagement and rigor among culturally and linguistically diverse students*. Corwin.

Immordino-Yang, M. H. (2016). *Emotions, learning, and the brain: Exploring the educational implications of affective neuroscience.* W. W. Norton.

Jensen, E. (2009). *Teaching with poverty in mind: What being poor does to kids' brains and what schools can do about it.* ASCD.

Jones, S. M., Brush, K. E., Bailey, R., Brion-Meisels, G., McIntyre, J., Kahn, J., … Stickle, L. (2017). *Navigating SEL from the inside out: Looking inside & across 25 leading SEL programs.* The Wallace Foundation.

Lareau, A. (2011). *Unequal childhoods: Class, race, and family life* (2nd ed.). University of California Press.

Masten, A. S. (2014). *Ordinary magic: Resilience in development.* Guilford Press.

Noddings, N. (2013). *Caring: A relational approach to ethics and moral education* (2nd ed.). University of California Press.

Osher, D., Cantor, P., Berg, J., Steyer, L., & Rose, T. (2020). Drivers of human development: How relationships and context shape learning and development. *Applied Developmental Science, 24*(1), 6–36.

Perry, B. D., & Szalavitz, M. (2017). *The boy who was raised as a dog: And other stories from a child psychiatrist's notebook* (Rev. ed.). Basic Books.

Shonkoff, J. P., Garner, A. S., & Committee on Psychosocial Aspects of Child and Family Health, et al. (2012). The lifelong effects of early childhood adversity and toxic stress. *Pediatrics, 129*(1), e232–e246.

Skiba, R. J., Arredondo, M. I., & Williams, N. T. (2014). More than a metaphor: The contribution of exclusionary discipline to a school-to-prison pipeline. *Equity & Excellence in Education, 47*(4), 546–564.

Whitebread, D., Basilio, M., Kuvalja, M., & Verma, M. (2012). *The importance of play: A report on the value of children's play with a series of policy recommendations.* Toy Industries of Europe.

Yeager, D. S., & Dweck, C. S. (2012). Mindsets that promote resilience: When students believe that personal characteristics can be developed. *Educational Psychologist, 47*(4), 302–314*.

Chapter 19

Middle and High School

Cracks, Storms, and Identity

Adolescence at the Water's Edge

By middle school, the shoreline looks different. The sandcastles are bigger, more detailed, and more fragile in new ways. The children who once needed help just to share a shovel are now asking harder questions:

- Who am I?
- Who sees me?
- Where do I belong?
- What kind of future is even possible for someone like me?

Developmentally, adolescence is a period of intense brain reorganization and social reorientation. Decision-making systems, reward sensitivity, and emotional circuits are all under renovation at the same time (Steinberg, 2014). Young people are more sensitive to peer evaluation, more driven to seek novelty, and more likely to experience emotional highs and lows.

Schools often respond by adding more rules, more tests, and more pressure, as if force could stabilize a moving shoreline. Families respond in varied ways: some tighten control, some step back and hope their teenager "figures it out," others are simply overwhelmed by economic or personal stress.

The result is a familiar picture in many middle and high schools:

- Students who look "grown" physically but are still learning to regulate like younger children.
- Dramatic shifts in effort and mood from one week to the next.

- Conflicts that move quickly from hurt feelings to online drama to real safety concerns.
- Educators who feel caught between teaching content and triaging crises.

This chapter looks at how the five competencies show up in this stage as cracks, storms, and identity work, and what it means to protect sandcastles that students are now building more independently but not yet securely.

When Early Cracks Become Visible Fractures

The patterns that surface in adolescence rarely start there. They are earlier threads woven tighter:

- A third grader who avoided reading because of shame becomes a ninth grader skipping English class.
- A fifth grader who hit peers when embarrassed becomes an eighth grader threatening violence when disrespected.
- An anxious child becomes a teenager who self-medicates, self-harms, or simply disappears from school altogether.

Research on adolescent development shows that middle and high school are years when prior risk factors – poverty, trauma, discrimination, learning differences – and prior protective factors – strong relationships, regulation skills, supportive families – interact powerfully (Eccles & Roeser, 2011; Fergus & Zimmerman, 2005).

By this stage, students who have never experienced school as a place of safety or dignity may have already rewritten the script in their heads:

- "School is not for people like me."

- "Teachers don't really care; they just want me quiet."
- "If I show I care, I'll look weak."

At the same time, many adolescents who appear to be "doing fine" on the surface are quietly struggling. National data show increases in reported anxiety, depression, and suicidal ideation among adolescents, especially girls and LGBTQ+ youth (Centers for Disease Control and Prevention [CDC], 2023). Grades alone do not tell the whole story.

The cracks show up in:

- **Attendance**: chronic absenteeism framed as "apathy" rather than a sign of distress, disconnection, or competing responsibilities.
- **Behavior**: escalation from minor defiance to serious incidents when young people feel disrespected or cornered.
- **Engagement**: either perfectionistic overwork driven by fear of failure or disengagement driven by a sense that effort will not matter.

If adults see these fractures only as moral failure or "typical teenage attitude," they are likely to reach for punishments that harden defenses rather than strengthen foundations.

Identity, Belonging, and the Five Competencies

Adolescence is often described as a time of "identity formation," but that phrase can sound abstract. In school hallways, identity work looks like:

- Deciding which peer group to stand with at lunch.

- Testing different ways of dressing, speaking, or refusing.
- Asking, silently or loudly, "Where do people who look like me, love like me, or believe like me actually belong?"

Belonging is not a bonus; it is a basic condition for learning and mental health (Allen & Kern, 2017; Osher et al., 2020). When students feel they belong, they are more willing to take academic risks, seek help, and accept correction. When they feel that school is hostile or indifferent, accountability and respect feel like one-way demands from an unfair system.

The five competencies take on new layers in this context:

- **Accountability** now includes choices about honesty with peers and adults, digital footprints, and long-term consequences (for example, whether to join in harassment, share harmful content, or admit substance use).
- **Respect** involves complex questions about identity, consent, privacy, and boundaries in friendships and relationships.
- **Emotional intelligence** means reading subtle social cues, understanding sarcasm and humor, and navigating the emotional politics of friend groups, dating, and adult authority.
- **Conflict resolution** includes knowing when to walk away, when to stand up, and how to use formal systems (counselors, administrators, restorative processes) without losing face.

- **Resilience** is tested by academic failure, peer rejection, family disruption, and a 24/7 online world that rarely lets mistakes fade quietly.

When secondary schools treat these as "side issues" instead of central curriculum, they miss the leverage point where academics and life skills intersect. A high schooler's refusal to revise an essay is about writing, but it is also about resilience, accountability, and whether feedback feels like an attack on their fragile sense of self.

Peer Pressure, Social Media, and Public Sandcastles

In middle and high school, sandcastles are no longer private. They are built in public view, documented in photos, screenshots, and posts. A single misstep – a fight, a rumor, an embarrassing video – can follow a student across schools and platforms.

Peers become central in this stage, and peer norms can either support or undercut adult efforts. Research on peer influence suggests that adolescents are especially sensitive to how their actions will be seen by friends, particularly in emotionally charged situations (Steinberg, 2014; Prinstein & Giletta, 2016).

Social media amplifies both connection and risk:

- It can provide support networks and identity-affirming spaces.
- It can also intensify comparison, cyberbullying, and exposure to risky behaviors or harmful content (Odgers & Jensen, 2020).

The five competencies matter here as well:

- **Accountability**: owning what is posted or shared, recognizing harm, and making amends even when embarrassment is high.
- **Respect**: refusing to forward humiliating images or rumors; honoring others' privacy.
- **Emotional intelligence**: noticing when online engagement is making one's own mood worse; reading tone without assuming the worst.
- **Conflict resolution**: moving difficult conversations offline; seeking mediation rather than escalating online "wars."
- **Resilience**: recovering from public mistakes without withdrawing completely or retaliating.

Adults sometimes respond to these realities with blanket prohibitions or lectures that do not acknowledge the real social stakes for teens. A more effective approach combines clear boundaries ("We do not tolerate harassment or threats") with authentic dialogue about the social pressures students face and concrete support for healthier choices.

Family Stress, Adult Expectations, and the "Almost Adult" Trap

By middle and high school, many adults subtly shift their expectations:

- "You're old enough to know better."
- "You should be able to handle this by now."

- "You're practically grown."

At the same time, adolescents are still living in bodies and brains under construction. Executive functions – planning, impulse control, future thinking – continue to mature well into the mid-twenties (Steinberg, 2014).

This mismatch fuels frustration on all sides. Teachers and families see young people making high-stakes choices around sex, substances, friendships, and academics and feel alarmed. Adolescents feel both judged and abandoned: treated like adults when it is convenient, treated like children when they seek voice.

Layered on top of this are family stresses that often peak during these years:

- Parents and caregivers managing their own aging, work instability, or health issues.
- Multi-generational households negotiating culture, language, and expectations.
- Economic pressures that lead teenagers to take jobs, care for siblings, or contribute to the household in ways that conflict with school demands.

In this context, accountability and respect can become battlegrounds:

- A parent experiences a teen's push for autonomy as disrespect.
- A teen experiences a parent's limit-setting as control or lack of trust.
- Schools experience both as "non-compliance."

Secondary educators who recognize these dynamics can reframe their work: not as "fixing attitudes" but as helping young people and families renegotiate roles while keeping safety, dignity, and education intact (Eccles & Roeser, 2011; Noguera, 2003).

Discipline, Safety, and the Cost of Exclusion

Concerns about safety often rise in secondary schools: fights, threats, substance use, and, in some communities, gang involvement or weapons. These are real risks. They deserve serious responses.

Yet the tools schools use to respond matter. Exclusionary discipline – suspensions, expulsions, and frequent removals from class – has been linked to higher dropout rates, lower achievement, and increased involvement with the juvenile justice system, especially for Black, Latino, Native, and disabled students (Skiba, Arredondo, & Williams, 2014). Repeated suspensions can send a clear message:

"You do not belong here."

From a sandcastle perspective, exclusion may temporarily smooth the surface – fewer visible disruptions in a given classroom – while quietly washing away entire sections of a young person's foundation.

An approach grounded in the five competencies asks different questions:

- What accountability looks like in this case (not "no consequences," but consequences that teach rather than simply remove).
- How respect can be maintained for all parties, including those harmed.

- What emotional realities are driving the behavior (shame, fear, grief, status).
- Whether conflict resolution can occur in a structured process that includes restoration where possible.
- How resilience can be supported, so students can return without permanent labels that close off opportunities.

Restorative practices, trauma-informed approaches, and tiered supports are not magic solutions, but research suggests they can reduce suspensions and improve school climate when implemented with fidelity and equity in mind (Gregory, Clawson, Davis, & Gerewitz, 2016; Osher et al., 2020).

The key is that discipline becomes part of **curriculum**, not a separate system of punishment.

Classrooms as Labs for Adult Life

Middle and high school classes are more than content delivery sessions. They are daily laboratories where students test adult roles in low- to medium-stakes form. In any given week, a secondary student may practice:

- Disagreeing (or refusing to disagree) with authority.
- Collaborating with peers they did not choose.
- Meeting deadlines or facing the fallout of missing them.
- Receiving criticism in front of others.
- Advocating for themselves when something feels unfair.

Each of these moments can build or erode the five competencies:

- A teacher who treats a late assignment as a character flaw rather than a chance to work on accountability and planning may unintentionally feed shame rather than growth.
- A class discussion about a controversial topic can either teach respectful disagreement or model public humiliation.
- Group projects can either reinforce unequal labor (a few students do everything) or teach real conflict resolution and shared responsibility.

When educators see themselves as directors of these "labs" – intentionally designing for practice in accountability, respect, emotional intelligence, conflict resolution, and resilience alongside academic content – classrooms become more than preparation for tests. They become rehearsal spaces for adulthood.

What Schools and Families Can Do Together in Secondary Years

The question, as always, is what is realistic. Secondary schools are busy, under-resourced, and often driven by external metrics. Families are juggling work, caregiving, and their own worries. Within those constraints, several practices are both feasible and impactful:

Name the competencies out loud.
Teachers, counselors, and families can explicitly connect academic and behavioral feedback to the five competencies:

- "This is a resilience moment. The grade is not what you hoped, but it does not define you."

- "We are focusing on conflict resolution here – not on who won the argument, but on whether you handled it in a way you are proud of."

Protect at least one safe adult relationship.
Research consistently shows that having even one stable, caring adult at school is a powerful protective factor for adolescents (Masten, 2014; Osher et al., 2020). Schools can:

- Ensure every student is known well by at least one adult (advisory periods, mentoring programs, check-in lists).
- Encourage staff to adopt a "small group" of students to track and encourage over time.

Families can ask their teens, "Who at school really sees you?" and, when possible, build bridge relationships with those adults.

Use discipline as a doorway to conversation, not an endpoint.
When crises happen – fights, substance use, serious disrespect – schools can:

- Combine necessary consequences with structured reflection (written or conversational).
- Invite families into problem-solving about underlying causes and supports, not just signatures on a discipline form.
- Offer pathways back into community (restorative circles, service, peer mediation) instead of leaving students in limbo.

Address identity and belonging directly.
Secondary students are already talking about race, gender, sexuality, religion, and politics – often without adult guidance. Schools and families can:

- Create spaces for honest dialogue where students' lived experiences are taken seriously.
- Offer curriculum and activities that reflect multiple identities and histories (Tatum, 2017; Ladson-Billings, 2009).
- Actively monitor whether some groups of students are consistently overrepresented in discipline or underrepresented in advanced courses and leadership roles.

Help teens connect choices to futures they can actually imagine.
Abstract warnings about "your permanent record" rarely land. Instead, adults can:

- Talk concretely about how accountability, respect, and resilience show up in real jobs, relationships, and community roles.
- Bring in near-peer mentors – recent graduates, young adults – who can speak honestly about what they wish they had practiced in high school.

These steps do not erase the storms of adolescence. They give students better tools to navigate them.

Conclusion: Holding the Castle While They Redraw the Map

By the end of high school, many young people have decided whether school is a place that strengthened or weakened their sense of self. They have drawn conclusions, fair or not, about what adults expect from them and what they can expect from adults.

Our task in middle and high school is not to control every choice. It is to:

- Keep **accountability** tied to growth, not permanent condemnation.
- Keep **respect** mutual, even when teens are at their least charming.
- Keep **emotional intelligence** on the table as a skill to learn, not a personality trait only some people have.
- Keep **conflict resolution** within reach, even when emotions are high.
- Keep **resilience** grounded in real support, not slogans that tell young people to "be strong" while leaving them alone with their pain.

In these years, students are starting to build their own sandcastles, sometimes far from where adults would choose. The waves are stronger, the stakes are higher, and the shoreline is crowded with competing voices.

If schools and families can stay present – not perfect, but present – and keep returning to the same five competencies with honesty and humility, more adolescents will leave secondary school with something sturdier than a transcript: a growing capacity to build, rebuild, and protect what matters most in the next chapters of their lives.

In the following chapter, we follow those lives beyond the school gates, into college, work, and adulthood, where grades disappear but the sandcastle work continues in boardrooms, break rooms, living rooms, and hospitals.

References

Allen, K., & Kern, M. L. (2017). *School belonging in adolescents: Theory, research, and practice*. Springer.

Centers for Disease Control and Prevention. (2023). *Youth risk behavior survey data summary & trends report: 2011–2021*. U.S. Department of Health and Human Services.

Darling-Hammond, L. (2010). *The flat world and education: How America's commitment to equity will determine our future*. Teachers College Press.

Eccles, J. S., & Roeser, R. W. (2011). Schools as developmental contexts during adolescence. *Journal of Research on Adolescence, 21*(1), 225–241.

Fergus, S., & Zimmerman, M. A. (2005). Adolescent resilience: A framework for understanding healthy development in the face of risk. *Annual Review of Public Health, 26*, 399–419.

Gregory, A., Clawson, K., Davis, A., & Gerewitz, J. (2016). The promise of restorative practices to transform teacher-student relationships and achieve equity in school discipline. *Journal of Educational and Psychological Consultation, 26*(4), 325–353.

Ladson-Billings, G. (2009). *The dreamkeepers: Successful teachers of African American children* (2nd ed.). Jossey-Bass.

Masten, A. S. (2014). *Ordinary magic: Resilience in development.* Guilford Press.

Noguera, P. A. (2003). The trouble with Black boys: The role and influence of environmental and cultural factors on the academic performance of African American males. *Urban Education, 38*(4), 431–459.

Odgers, C. L., & Jensen, M. R. (2020). Annual research review: Adolescent mental health in the digital age: Facts, fears, and future directions. *Journal of Child Psychology and Psychiatry, 61*(3), 336–348.

Osher, D., Cantor, P., Berg, J., Steyer, L., & Rose, T. (2020). Drivers of human development: How relationships and context shape learning and development. *Applied Developmental Science, 24*(1), 6–36.

Prinstein, M. J., & Giletta, M. (2016). Peer relations and developmental psychopathology. In D. Cicchetti (Ed.), *Developmental psychopathology* (3rd ed., Vol. 1, pp. 527–579). Wiley.

Skiba, R. J., Arredondo, M. I., & Williams, N. T. (2014). More than a metaphor: The contribution of exclusionary discipline to a school-to-prison pipeline. *Equity & Excellence in Education, 47*(4), 546–564.

Steinberg, L. (2014). *Age of opportunity: Lessons from the new science of adolescence.* Eamon Dolan/Houghton Mifflin Harcourt.

Tatum, B. D. (2017). *"Why are all the Black kids sitting together in the cafeteria?" And other conversations about race* (20th anniversary ed.). Basic Books.

Chapter 20

College, Work, and Adulthood

When the Grades Are Gone, What's Left?

When the Report Cards Stop Coming

At some point, the grades stop.

No more progress reports mailed home. No more automated calls when you miss "period three." No more parent–teacher conferences to negotiate make-up work or vouch for your character.

What remains are:

- How you show up.
- How you handle pressure.
- How you treat people.
- How you recover when things go wrong.

In other words, what remains are the sandcastle tools.

Adults rarely talk about themselves in terms of GPA. They talk about whether they:

- Can be trusted with a deadline or a child.
- Know how to disagree with a boss without losing their job or their self-respect.
- Stay married or keep repeating the same relationship cycle.
- Manage money or live in constant crisis.
- Spiral when criticized or use feedback to grow.

Research on life outcomes backs this up: social and emotional skills – persistence, self-control, empathy, cooperation – are linked to employment, health, and reduced involvement with the justice system, even after controlling for cognitive ability (Heckman & Kautz, 2012; Jones, Greenberg, & Crowley, 2015).

College admissions offices and HR departments may still collect numbers. Life, however, grades on a different scale. That is the scale this chapter explores.

The Five Competencies in Adult Clothing

The five competencies do not disappear after high school. They put on new outfits.

- **Accountability** becomes:
  - Meeting work deadlines without constant reminders.
  - Admitting mistakes to supervisors, partners, or children and making real repair.
  - Following through on promises, from rent to rides.
- **Respect** becomes:
  - Navigating race, gender, age, and power dynamics in workplaces and communities.
  - Honoring others' boundaries and your own in relationships.
  - Treating people in "lower status" roles – custodians, clerks, students – with the same dignity as those with titles.

- **Emotional Intelligence (EI)** becomes:
    - Reading office politics without being swallowed by them.
    - Recognizing when you are bringing old wounds into present conflicts.
    - Understanding how your moods affect those you supervise, love, or serve (Goleman, 1998; Boyatzis, 2018).
- **Conflict Resolution** becomes:
    - Handling disagreements with co-workers, partners, neighbors, and service providers without escalating or stonewalling.
    - Using formal channels – HR, mediation, grievance procedures – when needed.
    - Knowing when to stay and work it out and when to leave an unsafe situation.
- **Resilience** becomes:
    - Losing a job, relationship, or opportunity and not collapsing permanently.
    - Continuing to learn new skills when technology or industries change.
    - Keeping a core sense of worth when external status rises and falls.

Employers, when surveyed, consistently point to these kinds of capacities – often grouped under "soft skills" or "noncognitive skills" – as critical for hiring and promotion (Deming, 2017; Robles, 2012). In reality, they are the five competencies renamed.

College as an Unmasked Sandcastle

College, for those who attend, is often the first environment where childhood patterns are exposed without daily adult scaffolding.

In K–12, many students are held up by:

- Compulsory attendance laws.
- Parents or guardians waking them up.
- Teachers who accept late work or chase missing assignments.
- Small communities where someone notices if they disappear.

On campus, the structure loosens:

- Classes may not take attendance.
- Professors may not chase missing assignments.
- No one calls home if you skip three weeks.
- Health, housing, and finances become more complicated.

Gaps in the five competencies show quickly:

- **Accountability**: Can you track deadlines, manage time, and seek help without a parent in the portal? Students with strong academic skills but weak self-management often struggle more than peers with moderate academic skills but stronger accountability habits (Duckworth & Gross, 2014).

- **Respect**: Learning to live with roommates, navigate cross-cultural differences, and follow community norms around noise, substance use, and shared spaces stress-tests respect.
- **Emotional Intelligence**: Without familiar support systems, feelings of loneliness, anxiety, and impostor syndrome can spike. Students with more EI are better able to recognize these emotions and seek support proactively (Conley, Durlak, & Dickson, 2013).
- **Conflict Resolution**: Roommate disputes, group projects, and romantic relationships all require new levels of negotiation.
- **Resilience**: First failing grade, first breakup, first serious financial or health scare – these are powerful waves.

Many universities now invest heavily in mental health services, peer mentoring, and first-year experience programs precisely because they recognize that academic preparation alone is not enough (Conley, 2015; Steele & Aronson, 1995). The sandcastle metaphor fits: college is less about constructing something brand new than about learning whether the foundations you brought can hold under new tides – and what to do when they crack.

Workplaces: Where "Soft Skills" Are Hard Currency

In the workplace, the five competencies become visible in performance reviews, promotions, and quiet side conversations about "who is ready" for more responsibility.

Studies of employer surveys across industries repeatedly show that so-called soft skills – communication, teamwork, adaptability, problem-solving – are as important as, and sometimes more important than, technical skills for long-term success (Deming, 2017; Robles, 2012). These map directly onto the five competencies:

- Communicating clearly and respectfully under pressure (respect, EI).
- Adapting to feedback, learning from mistakes (accountability, resilience).
- Collaborating across roles and cultures (conflict resolution, respect, EI).
- Managing one's own emotions when projects change or leadership shifts (EI, resilience).

At work, people who lack these competencies are often labeled with informal reputations:

- "Great with content, hard to work with."
- "Brilliant, but volatile."
- "Nice, but unreliable."

Those reputations, fair or not, shape access to opportunities. They also shape whether workplaces feel psychologically safe or not. Employees who experience ongoing disrespect, conflict avoidance, or explosive reactions from leaders report higher stress, lower engagement, and more burnout (Edmondson, 2019; Porath & Pearson, 2013).

From a sandcastle perspective, organizations themselves have cultures – shared sandcastles – that either support or erode individual competencies. A workplace that models and rewards accountability, respect, EI, conflict resolution, and resilience strengthens its people. One that rewards only output, competition, and compliance while ignoring these qualities undermines them.

Adult Relationships: Love, Parenting, and Community

Outside of formal schooling and employment, adult life is full of roles that depend on the five competencies.

In intimate relationships, accountability is:

- Owning hurtful words or actions without immediately deflecting.
- Following through on agreements about money, time, and care.

Respect is:

- Treating a partner as an equal even in conflict.
- Making room for different emotional styles and histories.

Emotional intelligence is:

- Recognizing when you are triggered by something bigger than the current disagreement.
- Listening beneath the words to the fear, shame, or longing underneath.

Conflict resolution is:

- Arguing in ways that stay away from contempt, stonewalling, and character assassination (Gottman & Silver, 2015).
- Knowing when to pause a fight and come back instead of pushing until someone explodes.

Resilience is:

- Rebuilding trust after mistakes.
- Staying at the table through life events – illness, job loss, grief – without shutting down or running.

In parenting or caregiving, the competencies multiply: adults are practicing them for themselves while trying to model and teach them to children. A parent who never experienced respectful accountability in childhood may struggle to correct a teenager without either collapsing into guilt or exploding into threats.

In community and civic life, the competencies show up in how adults:

- Engage in disagreement across political, racial, or religious lines.
- Contribute to or withdraw from collective efforts – neighborhood associations, school boards, faith communities, advocacy groups.
- Respond to societal stressors like economic downturns, pandemics, or local crises.

The same patterns from childhood reappear: some people avoid conflict; some escalate quickly; some hold accountability only in one direction (others) but resist self-examination.

Seen this way, the question for schools was never just "Can we get children into college?" It was always, "Are we giving future adults the tools they will need to sustain work, love, parenthood, and citizenship under real conditions?"

When the Foundations Are Weak: Adult Consequences

When the five competencies are underdeveloped or distorted, the costs in adulthood are real.

- Low accountability can show up as repeated job loss, unstable housing, fractured relationships, or involvement with the criminal justice system.
- Distorted respect can show up as tolerating abuse, enforcing rigid hierarchies, or dehumanizing those with less power.
- Limited emotional intelligence can show up as explosive anger, chronic shutdown, or difficulty understanding others' perspectives.
- Poor conflict resolution can show up as endless cycles of reunion and rupture, workplace feuds, or estranged families.
- Fragile resilience can show up as giving up quickly, numbing through substances or screens, or living in a constant state of quiet despair.

These outcomes are not simply individual failings. They are shaped by structural forces – racism, poverty, inaccessible healthcare, underfunded schools, punitive policies – that create chronic stress and limit access to supportive relationships and opportunities (Adler et al., 2016; Garbarino, 1995).

At the same time, adults with strong foundations in the five competencies are not invincible. They still grieve, lose, and struggle. The difference is in how they move through those experiences:

- They are more likely to seek help rather than isolate.
- They are more able to reflect on patterns and make different choices.
- They are more capable of both giving and receiving support.

In that sense, investing in social and emotional competencies in childhood is not just about school success. It is a form of preventive mental health and public health across the lifespan (Jones et al., 2015; Masten, 2014).

Adult Learning: It Is Not Too Late

The good news is that social and emotional competencies are not fixed at 18. Adults can and do learn new ways of being.

Studies on adult development and leadership suggest that with intentional practice, feedback, and supportive environments, people can grow in self-awareness, empathy, conflict skills, and resilience even in midlife and beyond (Kegan & Lahey, 2009; Boyatzis, 2018).

Practical pathways include:

- **Therapy and counseling**, which can help untangle early experiences and build new regulation and relationship patterns.
- **Coaching and professional development**, which can focus on emotional intelligence, communication, and leadership competencies in workplace contexts.
- **Peer support groups** (recovery programs, parenting circles, support groups) where people can practice

vulnerability, accountability, and conflict resolution in contained settings.

- **Continuing education and community college**, where adults can re-enter learning environments with new motivations and more agency.

Adult learners often bring lived experience that makes the five competencies feel urgent, not theoretical. A parent who has seen how their own unaddressed anger affects their child has strong motivation to learn co-regulation. Someone who has lost jobs due to conflict may be deeply ready to practice new ways of handling disagreement.

From a policy perspective, this means investments in adult education, mental health access, and worker training programs are not separate from K–12 reform; they are part of the same ecosystem of preserving sandcastles across generations (Adelman & Taylor, 2006; Mallett & Smith, 2022).

Systems, Structures, and Shared Responsibility

It is tempting to end a chapter like this with a call for individuals to "work on themselves." That matters. Personal responsibility is real. Adults cannot simply blame their childhood or current systems for every choice.

Yet, just as we argued for children, individual effort alone is not enough. Adults live inside structures that either:

- Reward accountability, respect, emotional intelligence, conflict resolution, and resilience, **or**
- Reward short-term gain, exploitation, avoidance, and aggression.

Workplaces that prioritize psychological safety, fair processes, and growth feedback make it easier for employees to practice the five competencies (Edmondson, 2019). Organizations that rely on fear, secrecy, and rigid hierarchies make it harder.

Public policy choices – around healthcare, housing, labor protections, childcare, criminal justice – also affect whether adults have the bandwidth to reflect, learn, and show up well for others. Chronic survival-mode living squeezes out the space for growth.

Preserving sandcastles in adulthood, then, requires:

- **Micro-level work**: individuals examining their patterns and practicing new skills.
- **Meso-level work**: workplaces, colleges, and community organizations designing cultures and supports that align with the five competencies.
- **Macro-level work**: policies that reduce structural violence and chronic stress so that emotional and relational work is even possible.

The same three levels were present in our grandfather's 1902 school. They are still present in 21st-century America. The difference now is that we have more research – and more urgency.

Conclusion: The Castle You Take With You

By the time someone is sitting at a kitchen table at 35, 50, or 70, sorting bills or memories, the framed diplomas on the wall matter less than the patterns in their days:

- Do people trust them?
- Can they be honest when they are wrong?

- Do they know how to apologize – and how to forgive?
- Can they stay present when others are hurting?
- Do they believe they can rebuild after loss?

Those are sandcastle questions.

The grades and test scores that dominated so much of their childhood and adolescence have turned to faint lines on a transcript. The five competencies, by contrast, are still in use every single day. They shape whether families fracture or hold, whether workplaces nurture or deplete, whether communities pull together or tear apart.

If we want a different story for the next generation of adults, we cannot keep pretending that social and emotional learning is an "extra" or that it ends at graduation. We have to treat accountability, respect, emotional intelligence, conflict resolution, and resilience as lifelong practices – started in TK, refined in adolescence, and continued consciously in adulthood.

In the chapters that follow, we zoom back out to systems and measures. We ask what it would mean to build schools, districts, and policies that explicitly support these competencies across the lifespan, and to redefine "success" in ways that honor the sandcastles people actually live inside once the grades are gone.

References

Adelman, H. S., & Taylor, L. (2006). *The school leader's guide to student learning supports: New directions for addressing barriers to learning.* Corwin Press.

Adler, N. E., Cutler, D. M., Fielding, J. E., Galea, S., Glymour, M., Koh, H., & Satcher, D. (2016). Addressing social determinants of health and health inequalities. *JAMA, 316*(16), 1641–1642.

Boyatzis, R. E. (2018). *Helping people change: Coaching with compassion for lifelong learning and growth.* Harvard Business Review Press.

Conley, C. S., Durlak, J. A., & Dickson, D. A. (2013). An evaluative review of outcome research on universal mental health promotion and prevention programs for higher education students. *Journal of American College Health, 61*(5), 286–301.

Conley, D. T. (2015). *A new era for educational assessment.* Students at the Center, Jobs for the Future.

Deming, D. J. (2017). The growing importance of social skills in the labor market. *Quarterly Journal of Economics, 132*(4), 1593–1640.

Duckworth, A. L., & Gross, J. J. (2014). Self-control and grit: Related but separable determinants of success. *Current Directions in Psychological Science, 23*(5), 319–325.

Edmondson, A. C. (2019). *The fearless organization: Creating psychological safety in the workplace for learning, innovation, and growth.* Wiley.

Garbarino, J. (1995). *Raising children in a socially toxic environment.* Jossey-Bass.

Goleman, D. (1998). *Working with emotional intelligence.* Bantam Books.

Gottman, J. M., & Silver, N. (2015). *The seven principles for making marriage work* (Rev. ed.). Harmony Books.

Heckman, J. J., & Kautz, T. (2012). Hard evidence on soft skills. *Labour Economics, 19*(4), 451–464.

Jones, D. E., Greenberg, M., & Crowley, M. (2015). Early social–emotional functioning and public health: The relationship between kindergarten social competence and future wellness. *American Journal of Public Health, 105*(11), 2283–2290.

Kegan, R., & Lahey, L. L. (2009). *Immunity to change: How to overcome it and unlock the potential in yourself and your organization.* Harvard Business Press.

Mallett, S., & Smith, J. (2022). *Relational safety and resilience in high-stress educational environments* (Unpublished manuscript).

Masten, A. S. (2014). *Ordinary magic: Resilience in development.* Guilford Press.

Odgers, C. L., & Jensen, M. R. (2020). Annual research review: Adolescent mental health in the digital age: Facts, fears, and future directions. *Journal of Child Psychology and Psychiatry, 61*(3), 336–348.

Porath, C. L., & Pearson, C. M. (2013). The price of incivility: Lack of respect hurts morale—and the bottom line. *Harvard Business Review, 91*(1–2), 114–121.

Robles, M. M. (2012). Executive perceptions of the top 10 soft skills needed in today's workplace. *Business Communication Quarterly, 75*(4), 453–465.

Steele, C. M., & Aronson, J. (1995). Stereotype threat and the intellectual test performance of African Americans. *Journal of Personality and Social Psychology, 69*(5), 797–811.

Chapter 21

On Stage, Not Under Attack

Teaching as Performance and Protection

.Why Teaching Feels So Personal

If you ask teachers why they entered education, very few say, "For the metrics." They talk about children, justice, community, and the teacher who changed *their* lives. Teaching, for many, is a vocation, not just a job (Hargreaves, 1998; Nias, 1996).

At the same time, U.S. culture often encourages people to define themselves through their work:

- "What do you do?" is usually the first question after learning someone's name.
- Being a "good teacher" is framed not only as technical competence, but as a measure of moral worth and care.
- Social narratives praise educators as heroes while simultaneously scrutinizing them through test scores, social media, and public debate.

When work is fused with identity, the stakes of everyday classroom life rise. A student rolling their eyes, refusing work, or saying, "I hate this class," does not just feel like feedback on a lesson; it feels like a judgment on who the teacher is. Over time, this can lead to:

- Chronic defensiveness ("They don't appreciate how much I do").
- Burnout and emotional exhaustion (Jennings & Greenberg, 2009).
- Difficulty setting boundaries with students and families.

In this context, the idea of teaching as *performance* is not about being fake. It is about reclaiming a healthy distinction between *you as a person* and *you as the professional character* who walks into the classroom each day.

Teaching as Performance: Front Stage and Back Stage

Sociologist Erving Goffman (1959) described everyday life as a kind of theater. We present ourselves differently "front stage" (in public roles) than "back stage" (in private). All of us shift how we speak, stand, and emote depending on context: at work, with family, with friends.

For educators, the classroom is a literal front stage:

- There is a physical stage, the room, the board, the routines.
- There is an audience, students, sometimes families, administrators, and observers.
- There is a script, lesson plans, norms, and school policies.
- There is improvisation, responses to questions, misbehavior, humor, and unexpected events.

Thinking in these terms can be liberating:

"When I walk into the classroom, I am stepping into a role—'Ms. Rivera, the 4th-grade teacher'—that is *part of me* but not the whole of me. I can act as that character with intention, even when my private self is tired, worried, or hurt."

This does not mean the role is fake. Skilled actors draw on real emotions and values. The role is a *channel*: a consistent way of speaking, reacting, and holding boundaries that serves the students and protects the person playing it.

Goffman also described role distance, the capacity to be engaged in a role while also knowing, internally, that you are more than that role (Goffman, 1959). For teachers, role distance is the internal statement:

"This student is lashing out at my *teacher role* right now. They are not attacking my entire worth as a human being."

That small distance can prevent shame, overreaction, and the sense of being personally under siege.

Emotional Labor and the "Teacher Costume"

Arlie Hochschild (1983) introduced the concept of emotional labor: the management of feeling to create a publicly observable facial and bodily display that produces a desired emotional state in others. Nurses, flight attendants, social workers, and teachers all perform emotional labor.

Teachers routinely:

- Stay calm when they are angry.
- Show enthusiasm when they are exhausted.
- Offer warmth when they feel numb.

This is not hypocrisy; it is part of the work. But without awareness and boundaries, emotional labor can become internalized as "I must *always* feel this way," which is impossible and leads to burnout (Hochschild, 1983; Hargreaves, 1998).

The actor metaphor helps by treating some aspects of emotional labor as part of a professional costume:

- **Voice**: a calm, assertive tone that signals safety and structure even when the teacher feels rattled.

- **Body**: open posture, steady movement, intentional positioning in the room.
- **Language**: phrases that embody the five competencies ("I'm holding you accountable *and* I still respect you").

Like a costume, the teacher persona is something the educator can put on and take off:

- Before class, they "step into character"—reviewing their role, intentions, and boundaries.
- After class, they "step out of character"—allowing themselves to feel their own emotions, vent to colleagues, or debrief privately.

This does not mean becoming robotic. It means not demanding that their *private* emotional life always match their *professional* display. Surface and deep emotions can differ without the educator being dishonest (Hochschild, 1983; Schutz & Zembylas, 2009).

Healthy Distance: When Students' Behavior Isn't About You

Students bring their own storms to school:

- Family stress, poverty, or instability.
- Trauma, grief, or ongoing community violence.
- Neurodevelopmental differences that affect impulse control or emotional regulation.
- Social dynamics—bullying, shame, crushes, peer pressure—that feel overwhelming.

When a student explodes, withdraws, or tests limits, it is rarely about the teacher's inherent worth. It is usually about:

- The student's inner state.
- The gap between what is being asked and what they can handle at that moment.
- The meaning they attach to adults and authority based on past experiences.

The actor lens supports a helpful internal script:

"Right now my *character*—'Mr. Lopez, the math teacher'—is getting the brunt of this student's frustration with life, school, and maybe themselves. My job is to play my role well: stay grounded, hold the boundary, protect the group, and leave space for repair later. I don't have to *like* how this feels, but I also don't have to treat it as a verdict on me."

This distance:

- Reduces the urge to retaliate ("You don't talk to *me* like that").
- Makes it easier to implement co-regulation and consistent consequences.
- Protects the teacher's long-term sense of self.

Over time, students also benefit. They experience an adult who can stay in role—calm, accountable, respectful—even when provoked. That is powerful modeling for their own future roles as workers, partners, and parents (Jennings & Greenberg, 2009; Osher, Cantor, Berg, Steyer, & Rose, 2020).

Practical Ways to Use the Actor Frame

The actor metaphor becomes useful when it shapes daily practice, not just theory. Below are concrete strategies educators can use.

Pre-Show: Entering the Role

Before class or a difficult meeting, teachers can adopt short "pre-show" rituals:

- **Costume cue**: putting on a lanyard, jacket, or specific shoes becomes a physical reminder: "I am stepping into my professional character now."
- **Breath and intention**: one minute of slow breathing while repeating, "I will be firm, fair, and kind. I am not here to win; I am here to teach."
- **Role reminder**: writing a brief cue on a sticky note: "Calm voice. Short sentences. Separate behavior from person."

These small rituals help the body and brain shift from private mode (parent, partner, individual) into professional mode.

On Stage: Staying in Character During Storms

When a student or class situation becomes heated, the teacher can silently invoke the actor frame:

- "What would my *best professional self* do in this scene?"
- "How would a wise, steady mentor character respond?"
- "What does this moment need from the character I play, not from my raw emotions?"

This might translate to:

- Lowering voice instead of raising it.
- Standing still instead of pacing.
- Using rehearsed phrases instead of reacting impulsively:

- "I'm not okay with how you're speaking to me. We'll talk about it later. For now, you need to move to the back table."
- "You're allowed to be upset. You are not allowed to curse at people in this room."

Because the teacher is acting from a role, not from pure reactivity, they are more able to uphold the five competencies *in themselves*: accountability for their own tone, respect for the student's dignity, and resilience in returning to the lesson.

Backstage: Stepping Out of Role

After the "show"—end of class, the day, or a hard meeting—teachers need a backstage space where the performance can drop. This can include:

- **Private emotional release**: venting to a trusted colleague, journaling, crying, or laughing about the day.
- **Critical reflection without self-attack**: "Where did my character handle it well? Where did I step out of character and react from old wounds?"
- **Deliberate transition home**: a small ritual (short walk, music, prayer, deep breathing in the car) signaling, "I am now leaving my staff room character and re-entering my family role."

These practices align with research on teacher well-being, which emphasizes emotion regulation, boundary-setting, and supportive collegial relationships as buffers against burnout and secondary trauma (Hydon, Wong, Langley, Stein, & Kataoka, 2015; Jennings & Greenberg, 2009).

Authenticity vs. Acting: Is This Just "Faking It"?

A reasonable concern is that the actor metaphor might encourage inauthenticity—smiles masking resentment, "professionalism" masking real pain. There is a difference between deceptive acting and professional role-taking.

Unhealthy acting looks like:

- Pretending to like students while secretly despising them.
- Putting on cheerfulness that contradicts deeply held values ("Everything is fine" in unjust conditions).
- Using the role to avoid any vulnerability or honesty.

Healthy role-taking looks like:

- Aligning the character with genuine values (care, fairness, high expectations).
- Expressing a *portion* of one's emotional life that serves the students and the task.
- Choosing *how much* to disclose and *when*, in ways that are ethical and boundaried (Schutz & Zembylas, 2009).

Brené Brown (2012) notes that vulnerability in professional life does not mean oversharing everything; it means being honest about limits and uncertainty in service of connection and learning. A teacher might say:

- "I'm feeling frustrated too, but I'm still here and we're going to get through this."
- "I don't know the answer yet; let's figure it out together."

These are authentic statements made *within* the role. The actor metaphor simply reminds us that we are choosing which parts of our full self to bring forward in a given scene.

How the Actor Frame Supports the Five Competencies

The stage metaphor is not separate from this book's core framework; it strengthens it.

- **Accountability**
  - Teachers can examine, "Did my *character* act in line with my professional standards today?" rather than collapsing into global self-blame ("I'm a terrible teacher").
  - Students see adults owning missteps ("I raised my voice; that wasn't how I want my character to act") and modeling repair.
- **Respect**
  - A strong teacher persona can maintain respect for students even when they are rude or resistant, by holding onto the principle: "My role is to treat you with dignity even when you are not showing me the same."
  - The actor frame prevents teachers from retaliating out of personal hurt.
- **Emotional Intelligence**
  - Taking a role perspective builds **meta-awareness**: educators can observe, in real time, their own feelings and choose whether and how to express them.

  - This self-observation is a core component of emotional intelligence (Goleman, 1998).

- **Conflict Resolution**
  - In conflict, teachers can consciously choose dialogue scripts—curiosity, boundary-setting, options—rather than default to fight, flight, or freeze.
  - The role gives a repertoire of practiced responses that turn conflict into teachable moments.

- **Resilience**
  - When rough days are framed as "hard performances" rather than total personal failures, it is easier to return the next day.
  - The character can grow: teachers can revise the role over time, adding new lines, boundaries, and responses based on reflection.

In short, the actor frame makes it more likely that educators can live the very competencies they are trying to teach.

Parenting, Community, and Multiple Stages

This chapter has focused on classroom teachers, but the metaphor applies across roles:

- **Administrators** shift between being instructional leaders, crisis managers, and public representatives of the school.
- **Parents and caregivers** juggle work roles, family roles, and community roles; seeing each as a distinct character

can help prevent complete identity collapse when one area is in crisis.

- **Support staff**—bus drivers, paraprofessionals, office staff—also perform crucial emotional labor and can benefit from similar framing and support (Hargreaves, 1998; Osher et al., 2020).

Recognizing these multiple stages reinforces a broader theme of the book: none of us is only one thing. The five competencies are practiced in overlapping performances across a lifetime. Seeing them as role skills—not fixed traits—opens up more room for learning and change.

Conclusion: Teaching Without Losing Yourself

Our grandfather, opening a school for Black children in 1902, was not just "being himself"; he was stepping into a role that combined educator, advocate, and protector under hostile conditions. He needed a strong professional character to stand at the front of that room and say, with his body as much as his words, "You matter. Your mind matters. This sandcastle is worth building."

Educators today inhabit different but still demanding stages. Students arrive carrying 21st-century burdens. Policies and politics swirl. Social media watches. Amid all this, teachers need ways to care deeply *without* disappearing into the role or taking every wave as a personal indictment.

Viewing teaching as performance offers one such way:

- It gives permission to step in and out of the role.

- It honors the craft involved in choosing tone, posture, and language.

- It protects the private self while allowing the professional self to be generous, steady, and brave.

Most importantly, it helps educators remember:

"I am more than what happens in period three. I am more than this week's data. I am playing this role for children and families, and I can keep refining the character without sacrificing my humanity."

In that space—between self and role—there is room for growth, healing, and longevity in the work. There is room to preserve not only students' sandcastles, but the educator's own.

References

Bellah, R. N., Madsen, R., Sullivan, W. M., Swidler, A., & Tipton, S. M. (1985). *Habits of the heart: Individualism and commitment in American life*. University of California Press.

Brown, B. (2012). *Daring greatly: How the courage to be vulnerable transforms the way we live, love, parent, and lead.* Gotham Books.

Goffman, E. (1959). *The presentation of self in everyday life*. Anchor Books.

Goleman, D. (1998). *Working with emotional intelligence*. Bantam Books.

Hargreaves, A. (1998). The emotional practice of teaching. *Teaching and Teacher Education, 14*(8), 835–854.

Hochschild, A. R. (1983). *The managed heart: Commercialization of human feeling*. University of California Press.

Hydon, S., Wong, M., Langley, A. K., Stein, B. D., & Kataoka, S. H. (2015). Preventing secondary traumatic stress in educators. *Child and Adolescent Psychiatric Clinics of North America, 24*(2), 319–333.

Jennings, P. A., & Greenberg, M. T. (2009). The prosocial classroom: Teacher social and emotional competence in relation to student and classroom outcomes. *Review of Educational Research, 79*(1), 491–525.

Nias, J. (1996). Thinking about feeling: The emotions in teaching. *Cambridge Journal of Education, 26*(3), 293–306.

Osher, D., Cantor, P., Berg, J., Steyer, L., & Rose, T. (2020). Drivers of human development: How relationships and context shape learning and development. *Applied Developmental Science, 24*(1), 6–36.

Schutz, P. A., & Zembylas, M. (2009). *Advances in teacher emotion research: The impact on teachers' lives*. Springer.

Chapter 22

Redefining Success

Measures, Systems, and the Sandcastles We Choose to See

The Problem of the Visible and the Invisible

Education systems tend to focus on what is easiest to count:

- Test scores.
- Graduation rates.
- Attendance percentages.
- Discipline incidents.

These numbers matter. They can reveal patterns of access, opportunity, and disparity. They can signal when schools are seriously under-serving students, especially those historically marginalized (Darling-Hammond, 2010; Ladson-Billings, 2009).

But numbers also distort attention. What is easiest to measure is not always what is most important. The five competencies we have traced across this book—accountability, respect, emotional intelligence, conflict resolution, and resilience—rarely appear on spreadsheet dashboards. Yet, as we saw in the previous chapter, they are central to how people live, work, and relate long after their last report card (Heckman & Kautz, 2012; Jones, Greenberg, & Crowley, 2015).

The sandcastle metaphor helps:

- **Visible sand**: test scores, course completion, graduation.
- **Invisible sand**: capacity to navigate conflict without violence, to apologize and repair, to keep trying when life is hard, to treat others with dignity across difference.

Systems that focus only on visible sand may congratulate themselves for clean data while missing that entire sections of the human foundation are crumbling.

This chapter is about that gap: how we might redefine success and re-design measures so they better align with what children, families, and communities actually need.

How Metrics Shape Behavior

It is often said in management circles, "What gets measured gets managed." In schools, the deeper truth might be, "What gets measured gets *pressured*" (Bryk, Sebring, Allensworth, Luppescu, & Easton, 2010).

When state accountability systems:

- Tie funding, public ranking, and public perception primarily to standardized test performance,
- Compare districts and schools based on narrow indices,
- And publish lists of "failing" schools without context,

they send a clear message:

"Your primary job is to raise these numbers."

This pressure can lead to:

- Narrowing curriculum.
- Teaching to the test.
- Reducing time for art, physical education, and social-emotional learning.
- Avoiding students perceived as "risky" for scores (tracking, exclusion, subtle discouragement).

In some cases, schools serving students with the greatest needs face the harshest judgments and least supportive conditions, intensifying rather than reducing inequity (Darling-Hammond, 2010; Noguera, 2003).

At the classroom level, teachers feel the tension between what they know students need—relationships, regulation, co-created norms—and what systems reward. Many educators can tell you about days when they index their value to a few test outcomes rather than the quieter evidence of growth in their students' lives.

Metrics do not merely describe reality; they participate in constructing it.

Re-centering the Five Competencies in System Goals

If we take seriously that accountability, respect, emotional intelligence, conflict resolution, and resilience are core educational outcomes, they cannot live only in mission statements and posters. They must be woven into goals, measures, and decision-making.

This does not mean inventing a standardized "resilience test." It means asking at each level—classroom, school, district, state:

- **Accountability**
    - Do our policies hold *adults* and *systems* accountable for providing equitable learning environments, not just students for complying?
    - How do we measure whether commitments to support, staffing, safety, and inclusion are being kept?

- **Respect**
  - How do we know whether students and families experience school as a place where they are heard and treated with dignity?
  - Are we tracking patterns of exclusion, microaggressions, or disparate treatment by race, disability, language, or gender identity?
- **Emotional Intelligence**
  - Are we offering students structured opportunities to practice emotional awareness, perspective-taking, and regulation?
  - Do staff have access to professional learning that builds their own emotional competence, not just their content knowledge (Jennings & Greenberg, 2009)?
- **Conflict Resolution**
  - When conflicts arise—between students, between adults, or across school–family lines—do we have processes that prioritize safety, repair, and long-term skills rather than only punishment?
  - Are we gathering data on the use and outcomes of restorative practices, mediation, and student–family conferences?
- **Resilience**
  - How do we support students and staff through collective and individual shocks (community

violence, pandemics, economic crises, personal loss)?

- Are there indicators that we are building the capacity to recover and adapt, not just survive?

When these questions are part of planning, monitoring, and improvement cycles, the five competencies move from "nice language" to actual system priorities (Osher, Cantor, Berg, Steyer, & Rose, 2020; Durlak, Weissberg, Dymnicki, Taylor, & Schellinger, 2011).

Mixed-Methods Data: Numbers, Stories, and Voices

Redefining success does not mean discarding quantitative data. It means placing numbers alongside stories and voices.

Balanced systems use mixed methods:

1. **Quantitative indicators**
    - Academic growth over time, not just proficiency snapshots.
    - Attendance and chronic absenteeism, disaggregated by student group.
    - Discipline patterns by race, disability, gender, and school.
    - Course-taking patterns (who gets access to advanced courses, arts, career pathways).
2. **Qualitative inputs**
    - Student, family, and staff surveys about belonging, safety, support, and high expectations (Bryk et al., 2010; Allen & Kern, 2017).

- Focus groups and listening sessions with underrepresented communities.
- Classroom observations that attend to relational climate, not only instructional pacing.
- Narratives and case studies of students' trajectories, including long-term outcomes.

3. **Contextual information**
   - Community-level data on poverty, housing, health, and environmental stressors.
   - Historical patterns of investment or neglect in particular neighborhoods or schools.

In our grandfather's 1902 school, measures were simple: Could children read? Could they write? Did they return each year? But there was also a clear contextual understanding: rural segregation, limited resources, and overt racism. Today, data systems are more complex, yet often less connected to context.

A district truly committed to preserving sandcastles will not compare a school in a heavily resourced community to a school in a community facing concentrated disadvantage without nuance. Instead, it will ask:

"Given the context, what growth and strengths do we see? What supports are missing? Where are we failing to live up to our commitments?"

This approach requires humility and a willingness to admit that numbers alone cannot tell us whether we are honoring the full humanity of students and families.

Using Data for Learning, Not Just Judgment

The same dataset can serve different purposes depending on mindset.

- In a compliance frame, data are used primarily to identify "good" and "bad" schools, justify rewards and sanctions, and protect institutions.
- In a learning frame, data are used to surface patterns, generate questions, and guide improvement with shared responsibility (Bryk et al., 2010; Fullan, 2016).

For example, a district sees that suspension rates for Black students are triple those for white students. In a compliance frame, the response might be:

- "We need to lower suspension numbers or we'll face criticism."

This can lead to superficial solutions:

- Renaming consequences without changing underlying practices.
- Pressuring principals not to report certain incidents.

In a learning frame, the same data prompt deeper inquiry:

- "What behaviors are being disciplined, and how consistently across groups?"
- "How are teachers interpreting and responding to student actions?"
- "What training, support, and policy changes are needed to reduce harm and bias?"

The goal becomes **changing experiences**, not just numbers.

Similarly, if a school sees low scores in reading growth, leaders might ask:

- "How are we supporting teachers with knowledge, time, and materials?"
- "Are there patterns by grade, subgroup, or instructional approach?"
- "What are students telling us about their reading experiences?"

Data become conversation starters, not weapons.

Measuring What Matters Without Doing Harm

There are real risks in trying to measure social and emotional competencies at the student level:

- Over-simplifying complex human capacities into checklists or single scores.
- Misusing data to label students as "low resilience" or "poor emotional intelligence."
- Ignoring cultural, linguistic, and contextual differences in how emotions and relationships are expressed (Halle & Darling-Churchill, 2016).

Because of these concerns, many experts recommend focusing measurement on **conditions and practices** rather than assigning SEL "scores" to individual children (Osher et al., 2020; Durlak et al., 2011).

Examples include:

- Observing whether classrooms use consistent routines for co-regulation and conflict resolution.
- Surveying students about whether they feel they have at least one adult at school who knows them well.
- Tracking the availability and use of counseling, mentoring, and restorative practices.
- Assessing whether staff receive ongoing training in trauma-informed, culturally responsive pedagogy.

In other words, measure the soil and weather, not just the plant.

When individual-level SEL assessments are used, they should:

- Be voluntary, with clear communication about purpose.
- Inform instruction and support, not high-stakes decisions.
- Be interpreted cautiously and complemented with qualitative understanding.

The objective is to improve environments so that competencies can grow, not to sort children into new categories.

Equity: Who Benefits, Who Is Blamed?

Redefining success also means asking hard equity questions about our measurement systems:

- Who is most likely to be labeled "failing" under current accountability structures?
- Whose strengths are invisible because they do not fit into existing metrics?

- Whose voices shape the design of measures and consequence systems?

Historically, standardized tests and rigid accountability regimes have often penalized schools serving low-income communities and students of color, while ignoring structural inequities in funding, segregation, and opportunity-to-learn (Darling-Hammond, 2010; Ladson-Billings, 2006).

An equity-centered approach to measurement would:

- Include equity itself as a key outcome: reductions in opportunity gaps, discipline disparities, and tracking by race and class.
- Disaggregate all data by student group and examine patterns regularly with stakeholders.
- Use data to argue for increased resources and support where needs are greatest, rather than punishment of those schools.
- Incorporate measures of culturally responsive teaching, representation in curriculum, and inclusive decision-making (Gay, 2018; Hammond, 2015).

In practical terms, that might look like a district dashboard where:

- Academic growth and graduation rates are shown alongside climate survey results, restorative practice use, and staff diversity metrics.
- Each school's data are paired with a narrative developed with local staff and families explaining context, strengths, and challenges.

- Improvement plans are co-created with those most affected, not imposed from afar.

The sandcastle is then seen as a shared construction, not a product for which only teachers and students are blamed.

Supporting Educators Within New Measures

Any shift in measures and accountability must consider teachers' realities. If systems simply add more metrics without removing old pressures or providing support, educators experience "initiative fatigue" and cynicism (Fullan, 2016).

To align with the five competencies, systems can:

- **Streamline measures** around a small set of core indicators that reflect both academic and human outcomes.
- **Engage educators** in designing and refining tools; teachers are more likely to trust and use data they helped create.
- **Protect time** for collaborative inquiry into data—grade-level teams, cross-role groups, school–family data walks.
- **Model accountability with respect**: when results are not where hoped, leaders own system-level decisions and conditions instead of blaming individual teachers.
- **Invest in adult SEL and well-being**, acknowledging that teachers cannot nurture competencies in students if they are chronically depleted (Jennings & Greenberg, 2009; Hydon, Wong, Langley, Stein, & Kataoka, 2015).

In our grandfather's day, there were few formal measures, but community expectations and mutual accountability were strong: elders watched, families talked, and the teacher's role was publicly honored. Modern systems can learn from that relational accountability even as they use more sophisticated tools.

Beyond the Schoolhouse: Community Indicators of Preserved Sandcastles

If we widen the lens further, we might ask:

"How would we know, at a community level, that our sandcastles are holding?"

Potential indicators include:

- Decreases in youth involvement with the justice system.
- Increases in high-quality early childhood enrollment and completion.
- Higher rates of postsecondary persistence, not just entry.
- Lower rates of youth homelessness and disconnection from school and work.
- Greater participation of families and young people in local decision-making (school boards, advisory councils, civic organizations).

These are not the sole responsibility of schools, but schools contribute significantly to them. Data-sharing partnerships between districts, municipalities, health systems, and community organizations can help track broader outcomes and align efforts (Adelman & Taylor, 2006; Mapp & Kuttner, 2013).

When we see improved community indicators, we are glimpsing preserved sandcastles at scale: more adults able to work, care, and contribute because their early foundations were honored.

Conclusion: Choosing the Sand We Count

Our grandfather's 1902 school did not exist so children could score well on a test that would never come. It existed so they could:

- Read contracts before signing.
- Challenge injustice with informed voices.
- Pray, vote, farm, work, parent, and lead with a sense of worth in a world designed to deny it.

Those were the sandcastles he was trying to preserve.

Today, we have more tools, more data, more research. But we face the same core question:

What are we really trying to build—and how will we know if we are succeeding?

If we choose to count only what is most visible and easiest to quantify, we will keep mistaking tall but fragile structures for true success. If we choose to attend to the deeper foundations—the five competencies expressed in relationships, communities, and adult lives—we will design measures that are humbler, more complex, and more honest.

Redefining success does not happen with a single new dashboard or mandate. It happens when:

- A school staff meeting spends as much time on student voice and climate as on test prep.
- A district chooses to publicly report and address discipline disparities.

- A state includes measures of school climate, access to arts, and advanced coursework in its accountability system.
- Families and students help define what "a good education" means in their context, and their definitions shape policy.

In those shifts, we begin to count different sand. We start to see, in clearer relief, the real work of education: helping human beings carry with them the tools they need to build, lose, and rebuild what they love—without losing themselves in the process.

References

Adelman, H. S., & Taylor, L. (2006). *The school leader's guide to student learning supports: New directions for addressing barriers to learning.* Corwin Press.

Allen, K., & Kern, M. L. (2017). *School belonging in adolescents: Theory, research, and practice.* Springer.

Bryk, A. S., Sebring, P. B., Allensworth, E., Luppescu, S., & Easton, J. Q. (2010). *Organizing schools for improvement: Lessons from Chicago.* University of Chicago Press.

Darling-Hammond, L. (2010). *The flat world and education: How America's commitment to equity will determine our future.* Teachers College Press.

Durlak, J. A., Weissberg, R. P., Dymnicki, A. B., Taylor, R. D., & Schellinger, K. B. (2011). The impact of enhancing students' social and emotional learning: A meta-analysis of school-based universal interventions. *Child Development, 82*(1), 405–432.

Fullan, M. (2016). *The new meaning of educational change* (5th ed.). Teachers College Press.

Gay, G. (2018). *Culturally responsive teaching: Theory, research, and practice* (3rd ed.). Teachers College Press.

Halle, T. G., & Darling-Churchill, K. E. (2016). Review of measures of social and emotional development. *Journal of Applied Developmental Psychology, 45*, 8–18.

Hammond, Z. (2015). *Culturally responsive teaching and the brain: Promoting authentic engagement and rigor among culturally and linguistically diverse students.* Corwin.

Heckman, J. J., & Kautz, T. (2012). Hard evidence on soft skills. *Labour Economics, 19*(4), 451–464.

Hydon, S., Wong, M., Langley, A. K., Stein, B. D., & Kataoka, S. H. (2015). Preventing secondary traumatic stress in educators. *Child and Adolescent Psychiatric Clinics of North America, 24*(2), 319–333.

Jennings, P. A., & Greenberg, M. T. (2009). The prosocial classroom: Teacher social and emotional competence in relation to student and classroom outcomes. *Review of Educational Research, 79*(1), 491–525.

Jones, D. E., Greenberg, M., & Crowley, M. (2015). Early social–emotional functioning and public health: The relationship between kindergarten social competence and future wellness. *American Journal of Public Health, 105*(11), 2283–2290.

Ladson-Billings, G. (2006). From the achievement gap to the education debt: Understanding achievement in U.S. schools. *Educational Researcher, 35*(7), 3–12.

Ladson-Billings, G. (2009). *The dreamkeepers: Successful teachers of African American children* (2nd ed.). Jossey-Bass.

Mapp, K. L., & Kuttner, P. J. (2013). *Partners in education: A dual capacity-building framework for family–school partnerships*. SEDL.

Noguera, P. A. (2003). The trouble with Black boys: The role and influence of environmental and cultural factors on the academic performance of African American males. *Urban Education, 38*(4), 431–459.

Osher, D., Cantor, P., Berg, J., Steyer, L., & Rose, T. (2020). Drivers of human development: How relationships and context shape learning and development. *Applied Developmental Science, 24*(1), 6–36.

Chapter 23

Preserving Sandcastles

A Hopeful Conclusion

Back at the Water's Edge

Throughout this book, we have stood on the same imaginary beach. We watched a four-year-old pack wet sand into thick, clumsy walls. We watched a seventh grader build a more elaborate structure, constantly looking over their shoulder to see who was watching. We watched adults walk up and down the shore with a mix of pride, worry, exhaustion, and regret.

We also watched the tide.

Sometimes the waves were small: a bad morning, a misunderstanding with a teacher, a pop quiz. Sometimes they were enormous: eviction notices, community gun violence, immigration threats, death in the family, pandemics. None of those waves asked for permission to hit. None of them paused to ask whether the child had mastered long division.

The central claim of this book has been simple and relentless:

If we ignore emotional foundations, the sandcastles of academic skills, credentials, and career pathways will not hold.

We used different language along the way – regulation, attachment, emotional intelligence, resilience, cultural context, family–school partnership – but the core argument remained. We are not just preparing children to pass tests. We are preparing them to live.

In this conclusion, we step back one last time and ask three final questions:

1. What are we really trying to preserve?
2. Who is responsible for protecting these sandcastles?

3. What does hope look like in practice, not just in slogans?

What We Are Really Trying to Build

Early in the book, we named five competencies as the real "learning outcomes" of a life:

- **Accountability** – the ability to own choices, make amends, and still see oneself as worthy of love and growth.
- **Respect** – for self and others, rooted in dignity, boundaries, and an understanding of power.
- **Emotional intelligence** – the capacity to notice, name, and navigate feelings in oneself and others.
- **Conflict resolution** – the skill of staying at the table when things are hard, using words and processes instead of violence or withdrawal.
- **Resilience** – the ability to suffer losses, face setbacks, and rebuild without losing the sense that life is still worth investing in.

Every chapter has been an attempt to show how those five competencies:

- Begin in TK and elementary school in tiny, concrete acts.
- Are tested and stretched in middle and high school.
- Follow people into college, work, parenting, and community life.
- Are affected, for better or worse, by systems that either support or sabotage development (Masten, 2014; Osher, Cantor, Berg, Steyer, & Rose, 2020).

Academics still matter. Reading, writing, mathematics, science, and the arts are tools children need to move in the world. But without the five competencies, those tools can be misused, distorted, or abandoned under stress. A brilliant engineer without accountability can build systems that harm. A gifted writer without respect can weaponize language. A highly trained professional without resilience can collapse under the weight of normal life.

When we say we want students to be "college and career ready," we are really saying:

- We want them to be able to navigate complex institutions without losing themselves.
- We want them to handle criticism, uncertainty, and conflict without breaking others or breaking apart.
- We want them to build relationships that can survive disagreement, stress, and change.

Those are sandcastle skills. They cannot be crammed in a single workshop or advisory period. They must be woven into how families, schools, and communities treat children every day (Durlak, Weissberg, Dymnicki, Taylor, & Schellinger, 2011; Jones, Greenberg, & Crowley, 2015).

Who Is Responsible? Everyone at the Beach

One of the most painful dynamics we explored is the mutual blame between families and schools:

- Parents and caregivers who feel judged, unheard, or dismissed by schools.

- Educators who feel disrespected, undermined, or abandoned by families.
- Children caught in the middle, absorbing the message that the adults closest to them are at war.

Our family's story – 23 educators across generations, beginning with a grandfather who opened a Negro school in 1902 – reminds us that this divide is not inevitable. In that one-room schoolhouse, there was no illusion that the teacher alone could save children; families walked their children to class knowing they were defying segregation together.

In modern systems, roles are more fragmented. There are administrators, specialists, counselors, case managers, and outside agencies. But the principle remains:

No single adult, profession, or institution can preserve sandcastles alone.

Responsibility is shared:

- **Families and caregivers** bring knowledge of the child's history, culture, strengths, and pain. They provide love and connection that no school can replace.
- **Educators and school staff** provide structure, learning opportunities, and daily co-regulation in a setting where children spend a large portion of their waking hours.
- **Leaders and policymakers** control resources, rules, and narratives that can either support frontline work or make it nearly impossible.

- **Community organizations, faith institutions, and employers** create the broader environment in which families live and youth transition into adulthood.

Bronfenbrenner's ecological model of development described these layers decades ago: children grow within nested systems – family, school, community, culture – that interact continuously (Bronfenbrenner, 1979). When we insist that one layer do all the work, we guarantee disappointment.

The more productive question is not, "Whose job is this?" but, "Given our role, what is our part of the work, and how can we align it with others?"

The Tide Is Real: Naming Harm Without Losing Hope

We have not sugar-coated the waves.

We have named:

- Structural racism and economic inequality that load some children's sand with rocks from birth (Darling-Hammond, 2010; Ladson-Billings, 2006).
- Punitive discipline systems that wash away children's connection to school, especially for Black, Latino, Native, and disabled youth (Skiba, Arredondo, & Williams, 2014).
- Underfunded schools, overworked staff, and the emotional labor educators perform without enough support (Hargreaves, 1998; Jennings & Greenberg, 2009).
- Family stress, trauma, and mental health struggles that are often invisible in official records but very visible in children's behavior.

Naming these realities is not pessimism; it is honesty. Hope built on denial cannot hold.

At the same time, we have seen ordinary magic – the phrase Masten (2014) uses to describe resilience – in small, daily acts:

- A parent who shows up to a meeting even after years of feeling judged.
- A teacher who apologizes to a student and starts again.
- A principal who looks at discipline data and admits, "We have a bias problem; we need to change how we operate."
- A bus driver who greets each student by name and notices when someone is off.

These moments do not make headlines. They do not show up on state dashboards. But they are the actual mechanisms by which sandcastles are preserved.

Hope, then, is not a mood. It is a practice:

- The practice of telling the truth about waves.
- The practice of building anyway, together.

Letters from the Beach

To close, it is helpful to speak directly to the people who have shown up on these pages.

A Letter to Educators

You stand on the sand every day, often with wet feet and no break between waves. You are expected to deliver curriculum, manage behaviors, respond to crises, enter data, and somehow embody grace under pressure. There are days when you go home feeling like every castle collapsed, and it was all your fault.

Please remember:

- You are playing a role in a very difficult play. You matter, but you are not all-powerful.
- Your job is to hold space and structure for growth, not to fix every wave or heal every wound.
- When you practice your own regulation, boundaries, and repair, you are teaching even more powerfully than when you deliver a perfect lesson (Jennings & Greenberg, 2009).

You are not the sand. You are not the tide. You are a builder, a protector, and sometimes a witness. That is sacred work. You deserve systems, colleagues, and leaders who treat it that way.

A Letter to Families and Caregivers

You have carried children through nights that nobody at school has seen. You have read letters that made your stomach drop, juggled work shifts to attend meetings, and walked into school buildings that did not always feel friendly.

Please remember:

- You are your child's first and longest-lasting teacher. Even when you feel overwhelmed, your presence, routines, and words shape their foundations (Mapp & Kuttner, 2013).
- You have the right to ask questions, push back respectfully, and expect to be treated with dignity.
- Educators are also humans with their own histories, stressors, and limitations. Many of them entered the

profession because they care deeply and are trying to make impossible choices inside flawed systems.

You and the school are not on opposite sides. The real fight is against anything that tells your child they do not matter.

A Letter to Young People

If you are somewhere along the TK–adult continuum and happen to read this, know this:

- You are **not** your grades, your worst day, or the labels adults have used about you.
- Your sandcastle is still being built, no matter how old you are.
- When you own your choices, respect yourself and others, learn to name your feelings, stay in hard conversations, and get back up after trouble, you are doing the real work of education.

You will meet adults who see your potential and some who do not. You will attend schools that feel like community and some that do not. You are allowed to be angry about what has harmed you and still decide to build something different.

Your sandcastle matters more than you know.

From 1902 to Now: A Family Story in a Larger Story

Our grandfather's 1902 school was, in many ways, a small structure on a hostile shore. Jim Crow laws, economic exploitation, and racial terror were the waves. Books were scarce. Desks were simple. Yet families sent their children, and he kept the doors open, because education was a form of resistance and hope.

In that room, he was not talking about "social and emotional learning." He was living it:

- Accountability, as students were expected to contribute to the community.
- Respect, as Black children were addressed by name and taught to carry themselves with dignity.
- Emotional intelligence, as he navigated fear, pride, and humiliation in a racist society.
- Conflict resolution, as he handled disputes among students and with authorities.
- Resilience, as he kept going despite limited resources and real danger.

Our family's 23 educators are part of that legacy, but the story is not about one family. Every community has its own version: elders who built schools under trees, parents who organized for bilingual programs, teachers who risked their jobs to stand with students.

By telling this story alongside research and frameworks, we are saying:

The work you do today – in classrooms, living rooms, boardrooms, and council chambers – is part of a long line of people who refused to let children's sandcastles wash away without a fight.

Next Steps: Three Levels of Commitment

As we leave the beach, it helps to name concrete commitments at three levels:

Personal

- Identify one of the five competencies you want to strengthen in yourself this year.
- Practice one small daily ritual that supports your regulation (breathing, walking, reflection, prayer, journaling).
- Choose one relationship – child, student, colleague – where you will commit to more curiosity and less assumption.

Organizational

- In your school, department, or organization, name explicitly how accountability, respect, emotional intelligence, conflict resolution, and resilience show up in your work.
- Review data and stories through this lens: Where are we living these values? Where are we not?
- Protect time for adults to learn, practice, and debrief together; emotional competence is a team sport (Bryk, Sebring, Allensworth, Luppescu, & Easton, 2010).

Policy and Community

- Advocate for accountability systems that include climate, belonging, and equity indicators, not just test scores (Darling-Hammond, 2010).

- Support investments in mental health, early childhood, and family engagement as core educational strategies, not side programs.
- Join or build coalitions where families, educators, and community members can co-design solutions instead of talking past each other (Mapp & Kuttner, 2013; Osher et al., 2020).

These are not exhaustive lists. They are starting points, consistent with the idea that preserving sandcastles is both intimate and political work.

Final View of the Shore

If you stand at the water's edge at the end of a long day, you will see ruins and beauty side by side. Some castles will be intact. Others will be half-erased. Children will have gone home, leaving behind only small traces of their effort.

The temptation is to see only what collapsed. But if you look closely, you will notice something else:

- Children and adults talking about what they will do differently tomorrow.
- New plans sketched in the sand with fingers and sticks.
- People sharing buckets, tools, and techniques.

That is the work this book has tried to honor and strengthen.

We cannot stop every wave. We can stop pretending that sandcastles stand on grades alone. We can stop blaming each other for patterns that were set in motion long before any of us arrived. We can decide, together, that what we are really trying to preserve are human beings who know how to build, rebuild, and protect what matters most.

And we can keep coming back to the shore.

References

Bronfenbrenner, U. (1979). *The ecology of human development: Experiments by nature and design*. Harvard University Press.

Bryk, A. S., Sebring, P. B., Allensworth, E., Luppescu, S., & Easton, J. Q. (2010). *Organizing schools for improvement: Lessons from Chicago*. University of Chicago Press.

Darling-Hammond, L. (2010). *The flat world and education: How America's commitment to equity will determine our future*. Teachers College Press.

Durlak, J. A., Weissberg, R. P., Dymnicki, A. B , Taylor, R. D., & Schellinger, K. B. (2011). The impact of enhancing students' social and emotional learning: A meta-analysis of school-based universal interventions. *Child Development, 82*(1), 405–432.

Hargreaves, A. (1998). The emotional practice of teaching. *Teaching and Teacher Education, 14*(8), 835–854.

Heckman, J. J., & Kautz, T. (2012). Hard evidence on soft skills. *Labour Economics, 19*(4), 451–464.

Jennings, P. A., & Greenberg, M. T. (2009). The prosocial classroom: Teacher social and emotional competence in relation to student and classroom outcomes. *Review of Educational Research, 79*(1), 491–525.

Jones, D. E., Greenberg, M., & Crowley, M. (2015). Early social–emotional functioning and public health: The relationship between kindergarten social competence and future wellness. *American Journal of Public Health, 105*(11), 2283–2290.

Ladson-Billings, G. (2006). From the achievement gap to the education debt: Understanding achievement in U.S. schools. *Educational Researcher, 35*(7), 3–12.

Mapp, K. L., & Kuttner, P. J. (2013). *Partners in education: A dual capacity-building framework for family–school partnerships*. SEDL.

Masten, A. S. (2014). *Ordinary magic: Resilience in development*. Guilford Press.

Osher, D., Cantor, P., Berg, J., Steyer, L., & Rose, T. (2020). Drivers of human development: How relationships and context shape learning and development. *Applied Developmental Science, 24*(1), 6–36.

Skiba, R. J., Arredondo, M. I., & Williams, N. T. (2014). More than a metaphor: The contribution of exclusionary discipline to a school-to-prison pipeline. *Equity & Excellence in Education, 47*(4), 546–564.

Conclusion – Teaching on the Stage Without Losing Yourself

Throughout this book, we have explored the emotional, relational, and professional demands of teaching in a way that does not reduce educators to either heroes or martyrs. We have tried to hold two truths at once: teaching is deeply personal, and yet it cannot be allowed to consume or define the whole person.

One of the central metaphors we introduced is the idea of teaching as "being on a stage." This is not about being fake or pretending to be someone you are not. It is about recognizing that the classroom is a professional performance space, with expectations, boundaries, and roles. When you step into that space, you bring skill, preparation, and emotional presence. When you step off, your worth is not measured by how perfectly every scene went that day.

This distinction matters, especially in the United States, where people often tie identity and self-worth to job performance. Educators are particularly vulnerable to this pattern, because the work is relational, emotionally charged, and constantly judged by others. When a student lashes out, refuses to work, or disengages, it is easy to interpret that behavior as a personal attack. Over time, that interpretation erodes self-confidence and increases burnout (Jennings & Greenberg, 2009; Skaalvik & Skaalvik, 2017).

Seeing yourself as an actor or character in a professional role can offer a healthy form of distance. In sociological terms, Erving Goffman described social life as a series of performances, where individuals manage impressions depending on the "stage" they are on (Goffman, 1959). For educators, this perspective can be freeing. It invites questions such as:

- Who is my "teacher self" on stage?
- What does that character sound like, look like, and prioritize?
- How does that character respond to conflict, disrespect, or withdrawal from students?

When teachers consciously develop this professional character, they are better able to respond intentionally rather than react emotionally. The goal is not to be robotic; it is to have a stable, practiced way of showing up, even when emotions run high (Schon, 1983).

At the same time, we have emphasized that emotional authenticity still matters. Students can tell when adults are pretending to care or going through the motions. Research on teacher-student relationships consistently shows that warmth, respect, and genuine interest in students' lives are key predictors of engagement and outcomes (Cornelius-White, 2007; Roorda et al., 2011). The "teacher on stage" metaphor should not erase your humanity. Instead, it gives you a frame for expressing that humanity in a way that is boundaried, professional, and sustainable.

Another major theme in this book is that teaching does not happen in a vacuum. Educators are working within systems shaped by inequity, trauma, policy, and history. For many students, especially those from historically marginalized communities, school is a place where past harms and current stressors collide. Trauma-informed and culturally responsive practices are not optional add-ons; they are core to creating classrooms where students feel safe enough to learn (Brunzell, Waters, & Stokes, 2015; Hammond, 2015).

Yet we also know that you cannot pour from an empty cup. The "stage" metaphor applies to students too. Many of them are performing roles of toughness, apathy, humor, or rebellion as ways to protect themselves or make sense of their worlds. When educators understand these performances as survival strategies rather than personal insults, they are more likely to respond with curiosity instead of punishment. This shift is at the heart of de-escalation, restorative approaches, and relationship-centered teaching.

In addition, we have tried to name the cost of constantly absorbing stress without support. The emotional labor of education is real. It includes managing your own reactions, holding students' pain, navigating conflict with families, meeting administrative expectations, and trying to stay current on new practices and regulations. Unaddressed, that labor can lead to compassion fatigue, secondary trauma, and burnout (Figley, 1995; Jennings, 2015).

Our argument throughout these chapters is not that educators simply need to "try harder" or "care more." Instead, we suggest that educators need:

- Practical tools grounded in research, not trends.
- Permission to see teaching as a role they *play well*, not an identity that swallows everything else.
- Structures for reflection, coaching, and peer support.
- Leaders who understand that adult wellness is a precondition for student success.

We have also been honest that this work is unfinished. No single book can capture the full complexity of teaching, particularly across special education, general education, and diverse school settings. What we hope we have offered is a framework for thinking differently: about students' behavior, about our own responses, about professional identity, and about the long arc of educational justice that stretches from a small Negro school in 1902 to today's classrooms.

As you close this book, our invitation is simple:

1. Keep reflecting. Notice when you begin to take student behavior personally and ask what your "on-stage" professional self would do.
2. Keep learning. Return to the research, revisit the tools, and adapt them to your context.
3. Keep protecting your humanity. Your value does not begin and end with test scores, classroom observations, or daily behavior charts.
4. Keep remembering that you are part of a story larger than any one school year.

Teaching is both fragile and powerful. It is fragile because it depends on relationships that can easily be strained by stress, misunderstanding, and fear. It is powerful because, when grounded in reflection, boundaries, and care, it can alter the trajectory of a child's life.

Our family has seen that power across generations. We hope that, in some small way, the ideas in these pages help you stand on your own stage with more clarity, confidence, and compassion – for your students, and for yourself.

References

Brunzell, T., Waters, L., & Stokes, H. (2015). Teaching with strengths-based practice: Developing student wellbeing and resilience in schools. *International Journal of Child, Youth and Family Studies, 6*(2), 197–207.

Cornelius-White, J. (2007). Learner-centered teacher-student relationships are effective: A meta-analysis. *Review of Educational Research, 77*(1), 113–143.

Figley, C. R. (1995). *Compassion fatigue: Coping with secondary traumatic stress disorder in those who treat the traumatized*. Brunner/Mazel.

Goffman, E. (1959). *The presentation of self in everyday life*. Anchor Books.

Hammond, Z. (2015). *Culturally responsive teaching and the brain: Promoting authentic engagement and rigor among culturally and linguistically diverse students*. Corwin.

Jennings, P. A. (2015). Early childhood teachers' well-being, mindfulness, and self-compassion in relation to classroom quality and attitudes towards challenging students. *Mindfulness, 6*(4), 732–743.

Jennings, P. A., & Greenberg, M. T. (2009). The prosocial classroom: Teacher social and emotional competence in relation to student and classroom outcomes. *Review of Educational Research, 79*(1), 491–525.

Roorda, D. L., Koomen, H. M. Y., Spilt, J. L., & Oort, F. J. (2011). The influence of affective teacher–student relationships on students' school engagement and achievement: A meta-analytic approach. *Review of Educational Research, 81*(4), 493–529.

Schon, D. A. (1983). *The reflective practitioner: How professionals think in action*. Basic Books.

Skaalvik, E. M., & Skaalvik, S. (2017). Dimensions of teacher burnout: Relations with potential stressors at school. *Social Psychology of Education, 20*(4), 775–790.*

Appendix A

Tools and Protocols: Quick Reference

This appendix gathers practical routines, scripts, and protocols that support the five core competencies discussed throughout the book: accountability, respect, emotional intelligence, conflict resolution, and resilience.

It is meant to be copied, posted, and adapted. Think of it as the "backstage" notebook for educators, leaders, and families who want concrete moves they can reach for under pressure.

A1. Micro-Practices for Adult Regulation

These are short, repeatable practices adults can use before, during, or after stressful interactions with students, families, or colleagues. They are designed to be simple enough to use in a hallway or Zoom call, not only in a quiet office.

4–4–4 Breath Reset

Use this when you feel your heart rate rising or your thoughts speeding up.

1. Inhale gently through your nose for a slow count of 4.
2. Hold your breath for a count of 4.
3. Exhale through your mouth for a count of 4.
4. Repeat 3–5 times while keeping your eyes open if you are in front of students.

Silent cue to yourself:

"I can slow down my body even if the situation is fast."

Feet-and-Seat Grounding

Use this when you feel unsteady, spacey, or like you are "leaving" the moment.

1. Notice your feet pressing into the floor; if helpful, wiggle your toes.
2. Notice the weight of your body in the chair (or your stance if you are standing).
3. Gently press your hands together or rest them flat on a solid surface.
4. Silently name three things you can see in the room.

Silent phrase:

"My feet are on the floor. My body is here. I can ride this moment."

Name and Aim

Use this when you are irritated and tempted to react quickly.

1. **Name**: Identify your current emotion clearly.
   - "Right now I feel… frustrated / anxious / embarrassed / angry."
2. **Aim**: State your intention for how you want to show up.
   - "My goal is… to stay respectful / to listen / to set a clear boundary."

You can do this silently or quietly out loud with older students (which also models emotional literacy).

A2. Student Co-Regulation Routines

These practices help students check in with themselves and the group, while allowing adults to scan the room for patterns of distress.

60-Second Check-In

Use at the start of class, after transitions, or following a difficult event.

1. Prompt:
    - "On a scale from 1 to 5…
      1 = not okay at all,
      3 = in the middle,
      5 = feeling solid… where are you right now?"
2. Students can respond with:
    - Fingers (1–5), sticky notes, or digital poll.
3. Follow-up:
    - "If you're 1 or 2 and want to talk, I'll check in with you later or you can leave me a note."

This turns "behavior" into data about emotional state and helps you decide when to adjust expectations or provide extra support.

Pause–Breathe–Return

Use when the class is escalating or energy is scattered.

1. Say: "We're going to pause for 30 seconds to reset."
2. Invite heads down or eyes on one fixed point.
3. Lead 3 slow breaths (or use a brief timed visual on the board).

4. Say: "Okay, we're coming back now. Here's our next step…"

This is most effective when it is a known routine, not a punishment.

Problem-Solving Circle Prompts

Use in small groups or advisory when there has been low-level conflict, tension, or miscommunication.

Ask each person, in turn:

1. "What happened from your point of view?"
2. "What were you feeling at the time?"
3. "Who was affected, and how?"
4. "What needs to happen now to make things as right as possible?"

Keep the circle short (10–20 minutes). The goal is repair, not courtroom-style cross-examination.

A3. Scripts for Difficult Conversations

These are starting points, not exact lines. Adjust language for age, culture, and context. The aim is to combine **clarity** and **respect** under stress.

When a Parent or Caregiver Arrives Upset

Common opener: "You're always picking on my child."

Goal: De-escalate, show respect, and move toward shared problem-solving.

- "I can hear how frustrated and protective you are. Your child is important to us, and I want to understand what you're seeing."
- "Can you tell me what happened from your perspective first?"
- "Let me share what we saw on our end, and then we can talk about what support and accountability might look like together."
- "I may not get every word right today, but my goal is that we both leave feeling heard and clearer about next steps."

When a Colleague Makes a Personal Remark in a Meeting

Common situation: a comment that feels dismissive, embarrassing, or targeted.

Goal: Set a boundary while preserving the working relationship if possible.

In the moment (if appropriate):

- "I want to stay focused on the idea, not personal comments. Let's come back to the proposal."

Later, one-on-one:

- "In today's meeting, when you said ____, I felt undermined. I'd like us to be able to disagree about ideas without going personal."
- "Going forward, if you have concerns about my work, can we talk about them directly rather than in front of the group?"

When a Student Says, "I Hate This Class / I Hate You"

Goal: Avoid personalizing, hold boundaries, keep the relationship open.

- "You're really upset right now. You don't have to like this class, and you don't have to like me. You do have to follow the expectations in this room."
- "We're not going to solve this while everyone's watching. Right now, your choices are [two clear options]. We can talk more one-on-one later."
- "I'm here for your learning, even when you're mad at me. Let's figure out what's underneath this when you're calmer."

A4. Meeting Protocols

These protocols can be used in IEP meetings, student support meetings, team meetings, and family–school conferences. They are especially helpful when emotions run high or there is a history of mistrust.

10–10–10 Meeting Structure (30 Minutes)

Use when time is limited but you want to honor both emotion and action.

1. **First 10 minutes – Check-in and purpose**
    - Each person briefly shares:
        - Name and role.
        - One word about how they are coming into the meeting (e.g., hopeful, tired, worried).

   - Facilitator states the purpose in plain language:
     - "We are here to understand what is happening for [student], and to agree on concrete supports and next steps."

2. **Second 10 minutes – Focused discussion**
   - Guiding questions (choose one or two):
     - "What are we most worried about right now?"
     - "Where do we see [student] doing well?"
     - "What's getting in the way of learning or behavior?"
   - Keep contributions concise; redirect side issues to a "parking lot" list.
3. **Final 10 minutes – Agreements and next steps**
   - For each person or role:
     - "What will you do?"
     - "By when?"
   - Confirm how progress will be checked and when the group will touch base again.

Document agreements before the meeting ends and share them in writing.

Listen–Speak–Reflect for Conflict

Use when two parties (staff–staff, staff–family, or student–student) are stuck in back-and-forth argument.

1. **Person A speaks** for up to 3 minutes while Person B listens without interrupting.
2. **Person B reflects back:**
    - o "What I heard you say is…" (no rebuttal, just summary).
3. **Switch roles.**
4. Only after both have been heard do you move to problem-solving:
    - o "Given what we've heard, what's one step each of you is willing to take?"

This simple structure slows the pace, reduces misinterpretation, and models accountable listening.

A5. Using This Appendix Well

A quick-reference appendix is only useful if it becomes part of daily practice, not a forgotten list at the back of the book. A few suggestions:

- Pick one micro-practice for adult regulation and use it daily for two weeks.
- Choose one student routine and make it a class norm instead of a one-time activity.
- Practice one script with a colleague in a role-play before you need it in real life.
- Use the 10–10–10 structure for the next meeting that often runs off-track, and debrief with the group afterward.

Over time, these small moves add up. They help adults stay in role without burning out, and they give children repeated experiences of accountability, respect, emotional intelligence, conflict resolution, and resilience in action.

Appendix B

Discussion, Reflection, and Training Guides

This appendix is designed to help you turn the ideas in this book into real conversations and practice. You can use these guides for:

- Staff professional learning
- Cross-role meetings (teachers, paraprofessionals, office staff, bus drivers)
- Book study groups
- Family and community workshops
- Personal reflection

Adapt timing and language for your setting. Treat these as starting points, not scripts carved in stone.

B1. Using the Book for a 60–90 Minute Staff Session

Purpose:
Introduce the "sandcastle" idea and the five core competencies, and connect them to your school's daily reality.

Suggested time: 75 minutes

Part 1 – Opening and framing (10 minutes)

Prompt for the facilitator to share:

- One or two sentences about why this book was chosen.
- A brief reminder of the five competencies:
    - Accountability
    - Respect

- Emotional intelligence
- Conflict resolution
- Resilience

Opening question (pair share):

"Think of one adult who helped preserve *your* sandcastle when you were young. What did they actually *do* that stayed with you?"

Have a few volunteers share with the whole group.

Part 2 – Mini input: The sandcastle lens (10 minutes)

Short talk or slides:

- Academic outcomes are important, but they sit on an emotional and relational base (Durlak, Weissberg, Dymnicki, Taylor, & Schellinger, 2011; Masten, 2014).
- The five competencies show up:
  - In TK as sharing, waiting, and naming feelings.
  - In secondary grades as identity, belonging, and conflict.
  - In adulthood as work, parenting, and community life.

Prompt:

"When we look at our school through this lens, what are we building *well* already? Where do you see cracks?"

Capture a few answers on chart paper.

Part 3 – Small-group discussion (30 minutes)

Group people by grade span, role, or mixed teams. Give each group this set of questions:

1. **Daily reality question**
    - "Where do you already see students practicing accountability, respect, emotional intelligence, conflict resolution, or resilience in your setting? Name real examples."
2. **Tension question**
    - "Where do our current rules, schedules, or pressures make it hard to support these competencies?"
3. **Adult lens question**
    - "Which of the five competencies is hardest for *us* as adults to model under stress? What gets in the way?"

Each group writes down:

- 2 existing strengths
- 2 specific barriers
- 1 small change they would like to try

Part 4 – Harvest and next step (25 minutes)

Whole group:

- Each group shares their one small change idea (for example, "We want to build a 60 second check-in at the start of science," or "We want a consistent script for hallway conflicts").

- Facilitator clusters ideas:
  - Things teachers can do on their own
  - Things that need grade or department coordination
  - Things that require leadership or policy change

Close with:

"Choose one action from today that you personally will try in the next two weeks. Write it somewhere you will see it."

You can collect optional copies of these commitments to revisit later.

B2. Half-Day Training Plan: Adults as Co-Regulators

Purpose:
Deepen the idea that adult nervous systems and emotional habits drive school climate and student experience.

Suggested time: 3 hours (can be split into two sessions)

Segment 1 – The adult nervous system (45 minutes)

Short input:

- Why adult regulation matters for student outcomes (Jennings & Greenberg, 2009; Hydon, Wong, Langley, Stein, & Kataoka, 2015).
- Basic idea of co-regulation: students borrow our nervous systems in hard moments.

Reflection in writing:

"When I am under stress at school, my most common pattern is: fight, flight, freeze, or please. How do students likely experience me in those moments?"

Share in pairs. No one reads aloud what they are not ready to share.

Practice:

- Introduce one or two micro-practices from Appendix A (4–4–4 breathing, feet and seat grounding).
- Let people practice them standing, sitting, eyes open, eyes down.

Segment 2 – Role, performance, and protection (60 minutes)

Prompt:

- Revisit the "teaching as performance" chapter: front stage, back stage, role distance (Goffman, 1959; Hochschild, 1983).

Small-group activity:

1. In groups of 3–4, ask:
    - "What is your *professional character* at work? If they had a name and three traits, what would they be?"
    - "What does that character do on a hard day that your private self might not be able to do?"
2. Each person writes a brief character card:
    - Name of their teacher or staff persona
    - Three core traits

    - One line they want this character to say often (for example, "I will hold the line and hold your dignity").

3. Invite volunteers to share.

Debrief:

- How does thinking in terms of a role help you not take student behavior personally?
- Where is the line between acting that protects you and acting that hides real problems?

Segment 3 – Practice in scenarios (60 minutes)

Give each group 2–3 short scenarios (adapt to your setting):

- A student shouts "You're racist! I hate this class!" in front of peers.
- A parent storms in and says "You people never listen to us."
- A colleague makes a joking remark in a meeting that lands as disrespectful.

For each scenario, groups answer:

1. "What is my first private reaction likely to be?"
2. "What would my professional character say or do instead?"
3. "Which of the five competencies am I trying to embody in that response?"

Groups can role-play briefly, but only if it feels safe. The focus is not performance quality; it is noticing choices.

Segment 4 – Agreements and supports (30 minutes)

Whole group:

- "What do we need from leadership, schedules, or each other to support us in showing up this way?"
- "What is one realistic change we can make in the next month?"

Record and share back a summary with timelines and point people.

B3. Book Study Guide

Below are sample questions you can use for a multi-session book group. Adjust pacing based on how quickly your group reads.

Session 1 – Introduction and early chapters (Grandfather's story, TK and elementary)

- "What emotions came up for you in the opening story about the 1902 school?"
- "Where do you see your own childhood experiences reflected or not reflected in the early chapters?"
- "Which of the five competencies shows up most clearly in TK and early elementary stories? Which feels underdeveloped in your setting?"

Personal action prompt:

"Name one thing you could do in your current role to better protect early sandcastles."

Session 2 – Middle and high school, identity, and belonging

- "What resonated with you in the chapter on adolescence and identity?"
- "Where do you see school practices helping or hurting students' sense of belonging?"
- "How does your school currently respond to 'public' mistakes (fights, social media incidents)? What would a response that builds accountability and resilience look like instead?"

Session 3 – Adults, work, and teaching as performance

- "How did the chapters on college, work, and adulthood change the way you think about your role with students now?"
- "What stood out to you about teaching as performance or being 'on stage'?"
- "Where do you wish you had been taught one of these five competencies earlier in your own life?"

Session 4 – Systems, measures, and equity

- "Which current data or metrics in your system feel most disconnected from the real work you do?"
- "What would a more honest definition of success look like at your school?"
- "What is one measure or data conversation you would like to see added or changed?"

Session 5 – Conclusion and next steps

- "If our school or district truly put sandcastles at the center, what might look different in five years?"

- "Which group in our community (students, families, staff, a specific subgroup) is most at risk of having their sandcastles washed away? What might it mean to focus on them first?"
- "What personal commitment are you willing to carry out of this book, and how will you hold yourself accountable?"

Invite the group to write short letters to themselves about their commitment and revisit them later.

B4. Family and Community Discussion Guide

Purpose:
Use the book's language in family and community spaces without jargon.

Suggested format: 60–90 minute circle

Part 1 – Welcome and story (15 minutes)

Opening question:

"When you think about your child or a young person you care about, what is one 'sandcastle' you hope they carry into adulthood? It can be a skill, a value, or a way of being."

Invite brief shares.

Short explanation of the metaphor in plain language:

- "In this group, when we say sandcastle, we mean the inner things that help a child stand in life: being honest, respecting themselves and others, handling feelings, working through conflict, and getting back up after hard times."

Part 2 – Family realities (30 minutes)

Whole group or small groups:

- "What makes it hard to protect kids' sandcastles in our community right now?"
- "Where do you already see your child's school helping?"
- "Where have you or your child felt unseen, unheard, or disrespected?"

Record themes without names. The goal is to surface patterns, not blame individuals.

Part 3 – Shared responsibilities (30 minutes)

Guiding questions:

- "What is the part families can play in building accountability, respect, emotional intelligence, conflict resolution, and resilience at home?"
- "What is the part schools must play that families cannot do alone?"
- "If we were going to work together better, what would that look like in simple, concrete terms?"

Close by identifying:

- One thing families want from schools
- One thing schools can commit to changing in communication or practice
- One ongoing way to keep talking (family advisory, smaller circles, regular check-ins)

B5. Individual Reflection and Journaling Prompts

These prompts are for personal use. They can also be used as optional homework in PD, coaching, or leadership development.

- "Which of the five competencies feels strongest in my life right now? Which feels most fragile? What three experiences shaped those strengths and fragilities?"
- "Write about one student or young person whose sandcastle haunts you, either because you saw it crumble or you are afraid it might. What was in your control? What was not? What do you wish you had known or done then?"
- "Describe a time a colleague or family member helped preserve *your* sandcastle as an adult. What did they do that you might imitate for someone else?"
- "Where do I currently confuse my role with my worth? How might the 'actor on the stage' idea help me hold a healthier distance without becoming cold?"
- "If I looked back from 10 years in the future, what would I hope my impact had been on the young people and adults I work with now?"

Encourage people to keep these private unless they choose to share.

Appendix C

Implementation Planner and Sample Templates

This appendix turns the book's ideas into concrete planning tools you can adapt for your site, district, or program. Use them as working drafts. Change language, add sections, or merge them with templates you already use.

C1. Schoolwide Implementation Roadmap

You can use this as a one-page plan for a year or multi-year rollout. The idea is to keep the work focused and realistic.

Phase 1 – Listening and Framing (Months 1–3)

Goals

- Build shared understanding of the five competencies.
- Hear from staff, students, and families about current strengths and pain points.

Key actions

- Hold at least one staff session using Appendix B, Section B1.
- Run brief listening activities with students (surveys, circles, or classroom discussions).
- Hold one family/community conversation using questions from Appendix B, Section B4.

Artifacts

- Summary of themes (2–3 pages):
    - What people say is working.

  - Where sandcastles are crumbling.
  - Priority concerns across groups.

Phase 2 – Focus and Pilot (Months 3–9)

Goals

- Choose **one or two** focus areas for the year.
- Pilot specific routines or protocols in a limited number of classrooms/teams.

Key actions

- Decide focus area(s), for example:
  - Adult regulation and co-regulation.
  - Reducing exclusionary discipline and strengthening conflict resolution.
  - Belonging and respect for a specific student group.
- Select 3–5 tools from Appendix A to pilot (for example, 60-second check-in, pause–breathe–return, 10–10–10 meetings).
- Identify pilot teams (by grade, department, or role).
- Set a simple data plan (what you will look at before and after: climate surveys, referrals, attendance, etc.).

Artifacts

- One-page focus document:
  - "This year our school is focusing on ______ and ______. Here is what that means in practice."

- Pilot schedule (who is trying what, when, and how feedback will be collected).

Phase 3 – Reflect, Adjust, and Scale (Months 9–12+)

Goals

- Learn from the pilots.
- Decide what to keep, modify, or drop.
- Plan expansion or deeper work for next year.

Key actions

- Gather feedback from staff, students, and families on the pilot practices.
- Review simple outcome data (for example, discipline incidents in pilot vs. non-pilot classrooms, self-reported stress levels, student perception of respect and belonging).
- Celebrate small wins publicly.
- Decide:
    - Which practices become schoolwide.
    - What support is needed (time, training, leadership actions).
    - What the next focus will be.

Artifacts

- Short "learning brief" for your community (2–4 pages or a slide deck) summarizing:
    - What you tried

- o What you learned
- o What changes you're making next

This cycle can repeat each year, moving from starting small to embedding practices at scale (Bryk, Sebring, Allensworth, Luppescu, & Easton, 2010).

C2. Student Support Plan Template (One Page)

Use this for individual students when you want to keep the focus on both **support** and **accountability**. It can be attached to IEPs, 504 plans, MTSS plans, or used informally.

Student Support Plan – "Sandcastle Snapshot"

Student name:
Grade:
Date created:
Review date:

1. What we're worried about

- Brief description of the main concerns (behaviors, attendance, academic struggles).

2. Student strengths (sandcastle assets)

- At school (for example, good with younger students, artistic, funny, persistent).
- At home/community (for example, helps care for siblings, works, involved in faith or sports).

3. Current stressors / context

- Recent changes or ongoing pressures (family, health, housing, peers, identity, etc.).

4. Supports the student will receive
Check or list what applies:

- Trusted adult check-in:
    - Who:
    - How often:
- Academic support (tutoring, small-group instruction, study skills help):
- Mental health/behavioral support (counselor, social worker, outside clinician):
- Schedule or environment adjustments (seating, break passes, quiet space):
- Peer support (mentor, buddy, club, group):

5. Clear expectations and accountability

- Specific behaviors we are working on (up to 3):
  1.
  2.
  3.
- What success looks like in each (concrete, observable):
    - "Arrives to first period by ____ four days per week."
    - "Uses agreed-upon signal to request a break instead of walking out."

6. Crisis / escalation plan

- Early warning signs for this student:

- Adults' first steps when they see these signs (co-regulation, space, specific phrases):
- Who is called if the situation escalates:

7. Student voice

- "When I'm upset at school, what helps me most is…"
- "Something adults often misunderstand about me is…"

8. Agreements

- Student will…
- School staff will…
- Family will…

Signatures (optional but recommended)
Student:
Family member/caregiver:
Staff:

This format keeps the student's humanity at the center and aligns directly with the five competencies.

C3. Reflection Forms (Student and Adult)

C3a. Student Reflection Form (After an Incident)

Keep it short. The goal is understanding and learning, not a written confession.

Student Reflection – "What Happened and What's Next"

Name:
Date:
Staff present:

1. **What happened?**
   - Tell the story in your own words.
2. **What were you feeling at the time?**
   - (You can circle more than one or write your own.)
   - Angry / Embarrassed / Disrespected / Sad / Confused / Scared / Bored / Other:
3. **Who was affected and how?**
   - Students:
   - Adults:
   - You:
4. **Looking back, what could you have done differently (even if others were also wrong)?**
5. **What do you need to do now to make things as right as possible?**
   - (Examples: apology, repair, conversation, agreement about future behavior.)
6. **What do you need from adults to help you do better next time?**

This can be used as part of restorative conversations or reintegration meetings (Gregory, Clawson, Davis, & Gerewitz, 2016).

C3b. Adult Reflection Form (After a Hard Moment)

This is for private or coaching use, not evaluation. It helps adults build accountability and resilience.

Adult Reflection – "Staying in Role Under Stress"

Name:
Date:
Role:

1. **Briefly describe the situation.**
2. **What did you feel in the moment (honestly)?**
    - Angry / Helpless / Embarrassed / Defensive / Afraid / Numb / Other:
3. **What did you do or say?**
4. **If you look at this through the five competencies, where were you strongest? Where did you struggle?**
    - Accountability:
    - Respect:
    - Emotional intelligence:
    - Conflict resolution:
    - Resilience:
5. **What, if anything, do you want to repair (with a student, family, or colleague)? How will you do it?**
6. **What did this moment teach you about your own triggers or "role"?**
7. **Next time I'm in a similar situation, I want my professional character to…**

This supports adult growth without turning every misstep into formal discipline (Jennings & Greenberg, 2009).

C4. Data Reflection Protocol (Team Use)

Use this in leadership teams, grade-level teams, or school–family advisory groups.

Data Reflection – "What Are We Really Seeing?"

Step 1 – Describe (10–15 minutes)
Bring 2–4 pieces of data, for example:

- Discipline data by student group.
- Attendance patterns.
- Climate survey results.
- Academic growth data.

Questions:

- "What do we notice, just at face value?"
- "What surprises us?"
- "What confirms what we already suspected?"

No explanations yet. Just noticing.

Step 2 – Interpret (15–20 minutes)

Questions:

- "What might be underneath these patterns?"
- "Where could our own practices or systems be contributing?"
- "Where do we need more information or perspective (for example, student or family voices)?"

Encourage people to distinguish between **facts** ("suspension rate for group X is double") and **stories** ("maybe they don't care").

Step 3 – Connect to the five competencies (15–20 minutes)

For each major pattern, ask:

- "How is accountability showing up here—for students, staff, systems?"
- "Where might respect be strong or lacking in these interactions?"
- "What might these numbers say about emotional safety and conflict resolution?"
- "What does resilience look like at the individual and school level in this area?"

Step 4 – Decide on one concrete next step (10–15 minutes)

Criteria:

- Small enough to try within 6–8 weeks.
- Aligned with the five competencies.
- Clear owner and timeline.

Examples:

- "Pilot a restorative conference protocol for level-2 behavior incidents in 7th grade."
- "Add two student focus groups about belonging before changing advisory schedule."
- "Provide one after-school session on de-escalation scripts for staff who request it."

This kind of structured inquiry keeps data from becoming tools of blame and moves them toward improvement (Eryk et al., 2010).

C5. Adapting Templates to Your Context

Every school, program, and community has its own language, culture, and constraints. As you adapt these templates, consider:

- **Language:** Replace jargon with words families and staff actually use. Translate documents where needed.
- **Length:** Shorten or expand. Some settings need half-page tools; others can handle longer forms.
- **Access:** Make sure templates are easy to find and share (shared drive, binder, LMS, etc.).
- **Feedback:** After a few uses, ask, "What's helpful here? What feels like busywork?" and adjust.

The test of a good template is simple:

"Does this help us preserve sandcastles better than what we were doing before?"

If the answer is yes—even in small ways—you are moving in the right direction.

References

Bryk, A. S., Sebring, P. B., Allensworth, E., Luppescu, S., & Easton, J. Q. (2010). *Organizing schools for improvement: Lessons from Chicago.* University of Chicago Press.

Durlak, J. A., Weissberg, R. P., Dymnicki, A. B., Taylor, R. D., & Schellinger, K. B. (2011). The impact of enhancing students' social and emotional learning: A meta-analysis of school-based universal interventions. *Child Development, 82*(1), 405–432.

Gregory, A., Clawson, K., Davis, A., & Gerewitz, J. (2016). The promise of restorative practices to transform teacher-student relationships and achieve equity in school discipline. *Journal of Educational and Psychological Consultation, 26*(4), 325–353.

Hydon, S., Wong, M., Langley, A. K., Stein, B. D., & Kataoka, S. H. (2015). Preventing secondary traumatic stress in educators. *Child and Adolescent Psychiatric Clinics of North America, 24*(2), 319–333.

Jennings, P. A., & Greenberg, M. T. (2009). The prosocial classroom: Teacher social and emotional competence in relation to student and classroom outcomes. *Review of Educational Research, 79*(1), 491–525.

Masten, A. S. (2014). *Ordinary magic: Resilience in development.* Guilford Press.

Appendix D

Recommended Readings and Resources

This appendix offers a curated list of books, articles, and frameworks for readers who want to go deeper. It is not exhaustive. Instead, it highlights works that strongly informed the ideas in this book and that are practical for educators, families, and leaders.

You can use this appendix to:

- Build a school or district professional library.
- Choose texts for staff book studies or graduate courses.
- Offer families and community partners credible resources instead of random internet lists.

D1. Social and Emotional Learning (SEL) and Child Development

Core SEL and whole-child frameworks

- Durlak, J. A., Weissberg, R. P., Dymnicki, A. B., Taylor, R. D., & Schellinger, K. B. (2011). The impact of enhancing students' social and emotional learning: A meta-analysis of school-based universal interventions. *Child Development, 82*(1), 405–432.
- Jones, D. E., Greenberg, M., & Crowley, M. (2015). Early social–emotional functioning and public health: The relationship between kindergarten social competence and future wellness. *American Journal of Public Health, 105*(11), 2283–2290.

- Osher, D., Cantor, P., Berg, J., Steyer, L., & Rose, T. (2020). Drivers of human development: How relationships and context shape learning and development. *Applied Developmental Science, 24*(1), 6–36.

These works provide the research backbone for treating SEL as foundational, not extra. They show clear links between early social–emotional skills and long-term academic, occupational, and health outcomes.

Developmental and resilience perspectives

- Masten, A. S. (2014). *Ordinary magic: Resilience in development.* Guilford Press.
- Bronfenbrenner, U. (1979). *The ecology of human development: Experiments by nature and design.* Harvard University Press.

Masten offers a powerful framing of resilience as "ordinary magic," emerging from everyday relationships and supports. Bronfenbrenner's ecological model underlies the multi-layered "beach" metaphor used throughout this book.

D2. Teacher Emotions, Burnout, and Adult SEL

Teacher emotional life and practice

- Hargreaves, A. (1998). The emotional practice of teaching. *Teaching and Teacher Education, 14*(8), 835–854.
- Schutz, P. A., & Zembylas, M. (Eds.). (2009). *Advances in teacher emotion research: The impact on teachers' lives.* Springer.

These works explore the emotional complexity of teaching and validate what many educators feel but rarely see acknowledged in policy.

Adult SEL and classroom climate

- Jennings, P. A., & Greenberg, M. T. (2009). The prosocial classroom: Teacher social and emotional competence in relation to student and classroom outcomes. *Review of Educational Research, 79*(1), 491–525.
- Hydon, S., Wong, M., Langley, A. K., Stein, B. D., & Kataoka, S. H. (2015). Preventing secondary traumatic stress in educators. *Child and Adolescent Psychiatric Clinics of North America, 24*(2), 319–333.

These articles ground the idea that adults are co-regulators. They show how teacher well-being and emotional competence affect students' behavior, engagement, and achievement.

Performance, roles, and emotional labor

- Goffman, E. (1959). *The presentation of self in everyday life*. Anchor Books.
- Hochschild, A. R. (1983). *The managed heart: Commercialization of human feeling*. University of California Press.

Goffman and Hochschild are classic sociological texts that inform the "on stage" chapter: front stage/backstage, role distance, and emotional labor.

D3. Trauma, Adversity, and Healing-Centered Schools

Trauma-informed education

- Blitz, L. V., Anderson, E. M., & Saastamoinen, M. (2016). Assessing perceptions of culture and trauma in an elementary school: Informing a model for culturally responsive trauma-informed schools. *Urban Review, 48*(4), 520–542.

- Cole, S. F., Eisner, A., Gregory, M., & Ristuccia, J. (2013). *Helping traumatized children learn, Volume 2: Creating and advocating for trauma-sensitive schools.* Massachusetts Advocates for Children.

These works support the idea that behavior is often communication about nervous systems and stress, not simply "choices."

Adverse childhood experiences (ACEs) and resilience

- Felitti, V. J., Anda, R. F., Nordenberg, D., et al. (1998). Relationship of childhood abuse and household dysfunction to many of the leading causes of death in adults. *American Journal of Preventive Medicine, 14*(4), 245–258.
- Bethell, C., Newacheck, P., Hawes, E., & Halfon, N. (2014). Adverse childhood experiences: Assessing the impact on health and school engagement and the mitigating role of resilience. *Health Affairs, 33*(12), 2106–2115.

These studies connect early adversity to lifelong outcomes, reinforcing the argument that schools are part of a broader health and social safety net.

Healing-centered approaches

- Ginwright, S. (2018). The future of healing: Shifting from trauma informed care to healing centered engagement. *Medium.*

- Bath, H. (2008). The three pillars of trauma-informed care. *Reclaiming Children and Youth, 17*(3), 17–21.

Ginwright's "healing-centered engagement" is a key underpinning for moving from a deficit lens ("what's wrong with you?") to a strengths and justice lens.

D4. Equity, Culture, and Culturally Responsive Teaching

Equity and education debt

- Ladson-Billings, G. (2006). From the achievement gap to the education debt: Understanding achievement in U.S. schools. *Educational Researcher, 35*(7), 3–12.
- Darling-Hammond, L. (2010). *The flat world and education: How America's commitment to equity will determine our future.* Teachers College Press.

These works frame disparities not as individual failures, but as the result of systemic underinvestment and inequity.

Culturally responsive pedagogy

- Gay, G. (2018). *Culturally responsive teaching: Theory, research, and practice* (3rd ed.). Teachers College Press.
- Hammond, Z. (2015). *Culturally responsive teaching and the brain: Promoting authentic engagement and rigor among culturally and linguistically diverse students.* Corwin.

These books provide practical and theoretical guidance for teaching in ways that honor students' cultures and identities while maintaining high expectations.

Discipline, race, and the school-to-prison pipeline

- Skiba, R. J., Arredondo, M. I., & Williams, N. T. (2014). More than a metaphor: The contribution of exclusionary discipline to a school-to-prison pipeline. *Equity & Excellence in Education, 47*(4), 546–564.
- Gregory, A., Clawson, K., Davis, A., & Gerewitz, J. (2016). The promise of restorative practices to transform teacher-student relationships and achieve equity in school discipline. *Journal of Educational and Psychological Consultation, 26*(4), 325–353.

These studies support the book's argument that discipline systems often erode sandcastles for specific groups of students unless they are redesigned with equity and restoration at the center.

D5. Family–School Partnerships and Community

Family engagement frameworks

- Mapp, K. L., & Kuttner, P. J. (2013). *Partners in education: A dual capacity-building framework for family–school partnerships.* SEDL.
- Ishimaru, A. M. (2014). Rewriting the rules of engagement: Elaborating a model of district–community collaboration. *Harvard Educational Review, 84*(2), 188–216.

These works move beyond "parent involvement" as attendance at events and toward shared leadership and capacity-building on both sides.

Community schools and wraparound supports

- Adelman, H. S., & Taylor, L. (2006). *The school leader's guide to student learning supports.* Corwin Press.

- Maier, A., Daniel, J., Oakes, J., & Lam, L. (2017). *Community schools as an effective school improvement strategy: A review of the evidence*. Learning Policy Institute.

These texts reinforce the idea that schools need integrated supports—mental health, family services, community partners—to preserve sandcastles in high-stress contexts.

D6. Systems, Improvement, and Risk Thinking

School improvement and system change

- Bryk, A. S., Sebring, P. B., Allensworth, E., Luppescu, S., & Easton, J. Q. (2010). *Organizing schools for improvement: Lessons from Chicago*. University of Chicago Press.
- Bryk, A. S., Gomez, L. M., Grunow, A., & LeMahieu, P. G. (2015). *Learning to improve: How America's schools can get better at getting better*. Harvard Education Press.
- Fullan, M. (2016). *The new meaning of educational change* (5th ed.). Teachers College Press.

These books provide practical frameworks for cycles of inquiry, improvement, and change at the school and district level, aligning with the book's implementation appendix.

Risk, systems, and safety culture (for leaders and cross-sector readers)

- Reason, J. (1997). *Managing the risks of organizational accidents*. Ashgate.
- Dekker, S. (2014). *Safety differently: Human factors for a new era*. CRC Press.

These texts come from safety and risk management but are useful for educators and policymakers thinking about how systems fail or succeed in protecting people.

D7. Practical Books for Educators and Families

Classroom practice and behavior

- Noddings, N. (2013). *Caring: A relational approach to ethics and moral education* (2nd ed.). University of California Press.
- Greene, R. W. (2014). *Lost at school: Why our kids with behavioral challenges are falling through the cracks and how we can help them.* Scribner.

Communication and conflict

- Rosenberg, M. B. (2003). *Nonviolent communication: A language of life* (2nd ed.). PuddleDancer Press.
- Johnson, D. W., & Johnson, R. T. (2009). *Energizing learning: The instructional power of conflict.* Interaction Book Company.

These are practical texts that educators, parents, and community leaders can read together to build a shared language for accountability, respect, and repair.

How to Use This Appendix

You do not need to read everything here to act on the ideas in this book. A few simple ways to start:

- Pick one book or article from each category that speaks to your current challenges.
- Build a small professional learning group around one text, using the discussion guides in Appendix B.

- Choose 2–3 resources to recommend to new staff as part of onboarding.
- Share accessible pieces (for example, family engagement or trauma-informed school guides) with parent leadership groups and community partners.

The goal is not to become an expert in every subfield. The goal is to keep learning in community, so that you, your colleagues, and your families have solid research under your feet as you stand at the water's edge and keep preserving sandcastles.

About the Authors

This book was written by a multigenerational family of educators whose collective experience spans more than a century. Together, the 23 contributors have served as classroom teachers, special education specialists, school psychologists, counselors, principals, paraeducators, professors, coaches, and district leaders. We represent urban, suburban, and rural schools across early childhood, K–12, and higher education.

Our family story in education begins in 1902, when our grandfather opened a Negro school at a time when access to literacy for Black children was both limited and dangerous. That act of defiance against segregation and systemic exclusion has shaped how we understand teaching: as both a profession and a social responsibility. Each generation since has added its own chapter, adapting to new policies, student populations, and challenges, while still holding to the belief that education can transform lives.

Collectively, our work has centered on:

- Supporting students with special education needs and complex behavioral and emotional profiles.
- Implementing trauma-informed and culturally responsive practices in classrooms and schools.
- Coaching educators in classroom management, de-escalation, and social and emotional learning.
- Leading schools and programs that serve historically marginalized communities.

Although our paths have been different, we share a commitment to honest reflection about what it really means to be an educator in the United States today. We have all felt the tension between caring deeply and feeling exhausted, between wanting to help every student and knowing we cannot do it alone. This book is our attempt to name those realities, share what we have learned, and offer practical ways forward.

We also see ourselves as students. Throughout these chapters, you will notice that we return to key themes: the importance of self-reflection, the need for boundaries, the power of viewing teaching as a role or "character" on a stage, and the value of separating our core identity from daily classroom turbulence. These ideas were not invented in isolation; they emerged from mistakes, rethinking, and dialogue with colleagues, students, and families.

Our hope is that, whatever your role in education, you can see parts of your own story in ours and find language, tools, and encouragement that support your growth.

www.ingramcontent.com/pod-product-compliance
Lightning Source LLC
LaVergne TN
LVHW010629110826
845149LV00014B/2813
9781967055234